Children, Families, and Substance Abuse

Children, Families, and Substance Abuse

Challenges for Changing Educational and Social Outcomes

by

G. Harold Smith, Ed.S.
Executive Director
Services for Exceptional Children
Fulton County Schools
Atlanta, Georgia

Claire D. Coles, Ph.D.
Director
Clinical and Developmental Research
Human Genetics Laboratory
Georgia Mental Health Institute
Associate Professor of Psychology
Department of Psychiatry
Emory University School of Medicine
Director
Psychological Services
Marcus Center at Emory University
Atlanta, Georgia

Marie Kanne Poulsen, Ph.D.
Clinical Associate Professor of Pediatrics
University of Southern California
School of Medicine
Director of Education
Center for Child Development and
Developmental Disorders
USC/University Affiliated Program
Childrens Hospital Los Angeles
Los Angeles, California

and

Carol K. Cole, M.A.
Project Leader
Los Angeles Unified School District
Division of Special Education
Infant/Preschool Program
Los Angeles, California

·P·A·U·L·H·
BROOKES
PUBLISHING CO.

Baltimore • London • Toronto • Sydney

Paul H. Brookes Publishing Co.
Post Office Box 10624
Baltimore, Maryland 21285-0624

Typeset by Maple-Vail Composition Services, Binghamton, New York.
Manufactured in the United States of America by
The Maple Press Company, York, Pennsylvania.

The names appearing in the case studies in this book have been
changed to protect the right of privacy of the individuals.

Library of Congress Cataloging-in-Publication Data

Children, families, and substance abuse : challenges for changing
    educational and social outcomes / G. Harold Smith ... [et al.].
        p.   cm.
    Includes bibliographical references and index.
    ISBN 1-55766-175-8
    1. Children of prenatal alcohol abuse—Education—United States.
2. Children of prenatal alcohol abuse—United States—Social
conditions.   3. Children of prenatal substance abuse—Education—
United States.   4. Children of prenatal substance abuse—United
States—Social conditions.   I. Smith, G. Harold.
    LC4806.4.C45   1995
    371.91—dc20   95-6406
                                                           CIP

British Library Cataloguing-in-Publication data are available from the
British Library.

Contents

About the Authors

G. Harold Smith, Ed.S., is Executive Director, Services for Exceptional Children, Fulton County Schools, Fulton County Board of Education, 554 Parkway Drive, Atlanta, Georgia 30354.

Mr. Smith has provided extensive support to school districts in various consultative roles and staff development activities to help teachers and administrators understand the educational needs of children affected by substance abuse and strategies for working effectively with them and their families.

Claire D. Coles, Ph.D., is Director of Clinical and Developmental Research, Human Genetics Laboratory, Georgia Mental Health Institute, 1256 Briarcliff Road, N.E., Atlanta, Georgia 30306.

Dr. Coles is also Associate Professor of Psychology, Department of Psychiatry, Emory University School of Medicine, and Director of Psychological Services for the Marcus Center at Emory University, which provides services to families and children with developmental disabilities. Dr. Coles is recognized as an expert at the national level in addiction and teratogenic research literature. Of particular importance have been her contributions to the development of programs for children and families affected by prenatal drug exposure, treatment, and rehabilitation program services.

Marie Kanne Poulsen, Ph.D., is Clinical Associate Professor of Pediatrics, University of Southern California, University Affiliated Program, Childrens Hospital Los Angeles, 4650 Sunset Boulevard, Los Angeles, California 90027.

Dr. Poulsen is also the Prevention and Early Intervention Program Director for the University of Southern California, University Affiliated Program at Childrens Hospital Los Angeles, and the Director of the

Region IX Infant Mental Health Leadership Training Project. She is recognized for her significant contributions in the development of effective family-centered policies, programs, and services for infants, young children, and families affected by alcohol and other drug use. She contributes extensively to the literature on policy and program development, child care, Head Start, and early intervention issues.

Carol K. Cole, M.A., is Project Leader, Los Angeles Unified School District, Division of Special Education, Infant and Preschool Program, G-369, 450 North Grand, Los Angeles, California 90012.

Ms. Cole has worked with young children at risk and their families for more than 25 years. She taught at the Sophia T. Salvin Special Education Center in Los Angeles in one of the first public school pilot programs in the country for children prenatally exposed to drugs. She has served as an expert witness to both California and United States legislative committees and has written numerous articles and presented workshops nationwide on educational issues involving children exposed to substance abuse. At the time of publication, Ms. Cole is Project Leader for *Project Relationship:* Special Education at Children's Centers, funded through the U.S. Department of Education, Office of Special Education and Rehabilitative Services, and administered by Los Angeles Unified School District.

Foreword

"By the year 2000, all children in America will start school ready to learn."

Thus begins the U.S. Department of Education's National Education Goals (National Education Association, 1993), this country's commitment to educating all its children. The first goal, building on the critical role of parents as the child's first teacher, targets children with disabilities who are also disadvantaged and ensures that they will have access to high quality and developmentally appropriate preschool programs that will help them prepare for school. Nutrition and health care are recognized as important antecedents to learning, as the first goal pledges that "all children will . . . arrive at school with healthy minds and bodies" (National Education Association, 1993).

Nothing interferes more with the realization of the National Education Goals, however, than the growing number of children affected by prenatal exposure to alcohol and other drugs and the health and psychosocial risk factors that invariably accompany that exposure. During the critical early years of life, children growing up enmeshed in a world of substance abuse, violence, and social chaos are not going to be provided with the support and positive opportunities that will enable them to develop the attitudes, skills, and behaviors essential for arriving at school "ready to learn."

The early research into the impact of prenatal substance exposure tells us that this exposure indeed does have a role in placing children at educational risk. But the most recent research also tells us that by the age of 3 years, the environment in which the child is being raised plays just as large a role in determining developmental outcome as does the fact that the child was prenatally exposed to alcohol or other drugs. Children's cognitive, behavioral, and educational development are dynamic processes, involving both social and biological issues, and, regardless of socioeconomic status, the social environment of many addicted women is one of chaos and flux. These difficulties are magnified in the woman living in poverty, for she frequently lacks the social and economic supports that could help ameliorate some of the biological impact of the alcohol or other drugs to which the child was exposed. Thus, it never can become clear as to what a specific etiology may be for a particular problem a child is demonstrating.

In turn, schools across the country are caught unprepared by the numbers of children needing special services due to any of a number of environmental risk factors. There are many reports from all over the country describing substance-exposed children, but most of these reports are misleading because of the difficulty of identifying psychosocial issues in the long history of the family, identifying patterns of prenatal alcohol or other drug exposure, and, finally, accounting for the environment in which the child is being raised. The fact is, parents affected by substance abuse and a multitude of other risk factors will not have the necessary skills to guide their children's healthy development. In addition, the negative legacy of the family, oftentimes stretching across multiple generations, leaves the mother with no model for parenting and no social or family support. These are all issues that come together to produce children who have developmental or behavior problems that disrupt the learning process and the classroom. They are children in need, and the school often is the one, and only, place upon which many of them can rely.

But the teacher will not become involved with a child affected by substance exposure until many years after the prenatal exposure. The diagnosis of maternal substance abuse may or may not have been made during the pregnancy. The classroom teacher thus is caught in a quandary, attempting to work with a family whose very functioning is proscribed by addiction, all the while with only limited access to knowledge of the whole picture. The role of the teacher then comes down to a responsibility of identifying, as early as possible, children at risk and children with behavior, developmental, or learning problems, no matter what the etiology, so that timely initiation of interventions can be instituted. This is the way a teacher can enhance the child's ultimate medical, developmental, and behavioral outcome. It is not the responsibility of the teacher to specifically identify which children were prenatally exposed, but to identify any children who need help.

In addition, the teacher often must serve as the advocate for the family and the child. The hysteria of the public media that has accompanied the recognition of large numbers of children exposed to substance abuse has resulted in increasingly punitive measures being taken against mothers and families. In turn, the pendulum recently has begun to swing in the opposite direction, with reports in the press that the problems purported to be displayed by infants exposed to cocaine are a "myth." The truth lies somewhere in between. Children exposed to alcohol and other drugs prenatally are not doomed to failure in the school system, but neither are they free from risk. It takes the skills and perceptions of a concerned and well-trained teacher to identify children in need and to provide and guide their learning process. No book can help the teacher specifically identify a child with prenatal exposure, nor should a teacher be concerned with obtaining a specific drug history. But with a better knowledge base and an understanding of the multiple issues affecting a child in the classroom, the teacher can place the child's possible prenatal exposure into the context of the child's current environment and educational progress.

Prenatal drug exposure is not a new problem, and it will continue to be with us as we enter the next century. Our job is to see that every child is given the chance to reach his or her full potential and to participate in society as a productive adult. It is hoped that this book will help you accomplish that task.

Ira J. Chasnoff, M.D.
President
National Association for
Perinatal Addiction Research and Education
Chicago, Illinois

REFERENCE

National Education Association. (1993). *Goals 2000: Mobilizing for action. The national education goals.* Washington, DC: Author.

Preface

This book was conceived at a time when a great deal of attention was being paid to effects that drugs and alcohol have on children and their families, effects sometimes confirmed and often suspected. Horrific accounts of the impact that a family's abuse of drugs and alcohol has on children were presented on the front pages of newspapers in every community and on the covers of national news magazines. Even the professional literature was not immune from the developing myths about the effects of prenatal drug exposure, especially crack cocaine, on children.

Some of this information was and continues to be correct; namely, drug abuse has the potential for very serious adverse effects on children and their development. However, much of the information that was provided led to the creation of very harmful conclusions and the development of very hostile and antagonistic public policies, especially for women who abused drugs and alcohol and for their children. The following are some examples:

- While emphasizing the potential danger for unborn children that may result from a pregnant woman's use of crack cocaine, the known danger of prenatal alcohol exposure and the multiple causal factors that contribute to poor birth outcomes and long-term developmental needs were ignored.
- The belief that drug addiction and dysfunctional families are limited to lower-income minority families resulted in a perception that higher-income majority communities were immune from alcoholism, drug addiction, and vulnerable children.
- Children who were identified as being prenatally exposed to crack cocaine were perceived and often treated as "lost children," "children without hope," or "children who cannot play, do not smile, and are without consciences." This belief totally ignored the value

and impact that early intervention programs can have in creating positive outcomes for these children and their families.

- The "win the war on drugs" belief, which was stated at the highest governmental levels, implied that all of the factors that contribute to and are associated with drug use—poverty, dysfunctional families, lack of basic housing, crime, unemployment, exposure to violence, and lack of education—will somehow go away.

- The prosecution and imprisonment of women who tested positive for crack cocaine and other drugs upon the birth of their children did damage and created tremendous barriers between these women and the agencies responsible for providing treatment and social services to them and their children.

Whether and how often these beliefs and responses were a result of public policy, rather than political expediency, is certainly a debatable issue.

Research is not consistent on the outcomes of maternal use of drugs and alcohol during pregnancy. Lack of consistent information on the result of single and multiple drug usage and the level of dosage on fetal outcomes has led to inconsistent responses from public agencies. Likewise, the resiliency of children, with its varying outcomes for children whose families use drugs and alcohol in the postnatal environment, presents sometimes conflicting results; at the same time it underscores the great potential for affecting positive outcomes for children and their families.

Practitioners are becoming increasingly aware that many of the cognitive and emotional behavior problems ascribed to prenatal exposure may be more related to environmental factors in the child's home and community. Lack of prenatal care, increased risk of sexually transmitted diseases resulting from prostitution and sexual abuse of children and their caregivers, physical abuse, violence in the home and community, and inadequate health care all contribute to the potential for long-term developmental issues. Many of these children also are affected by the drug abuse–related death or imprisonment of their primary caregiver, which increases the possibility of the children entering the foster care system with its unique issues and problems.

This book was written as a result of the authors' concern that factual and timely information is needed to help service providers understand the potential effects of prenatal exposure and the effects that the abuse of drugs and alcohol by a child's family will have on his or her development, to emphasize the value of comprehensive and appropriate intervention strategies to promote positive child outcomes, and to support the development of comprehensive and collaborative community responses.

Children and their families who are affected by the misuse of drugs and alcohol present a broad constellation of social, medical, educational, and treatment issues. If these children and their families are to be successful in their communities, it will be essential that a collaborative comprehensive community effort address all of the elements of a vulnerable family's needs and that appropriate resources be provided. Interagency collaboration will be required to help families become more self-sufficient, to support children's success in school and community.

It is the authors' wish that this publication provide practitioners, service providers, public policy makers, and legislators with information and insight into vulnerable families and their children. Such knowledge and sensitivity are necessary to support the development of effective support systems for children and their families. A broad approach to program planning and collaborative delivery of services is required to address the constellation of needs evidenced by vulnerable families affected by drugs and alcohol.

Some chapters contain actual case studies with the identity of individual children and families protected. The authors' purpose in presenting these stories is not to shock, although admittedly some are almost unbelievable in their tragedy, but to demonstrate the broad range of issues and needs that must be addressed for effective program services. The failure of the existing system of services evidenced in these stories is not intended to indict, but rather to present evidence of where additional resources are required if children and their families are to be less vulnerable for failure.

This book is organized into three major sections. Section I provides background information about the characteristics and needs of children whose families abuse drugs and alcohol with implications for the development of programs and services. This section contains three chapters. In Chapter 1, the literature is reviewed to identify the most current knowledge about the effects of prenatal and environmental exposure to drugs and alcohol on children and youth. A number of myths and misperceptions are addressed that have, to date, influenced many of the responses by community agencies to these youngsters. Recommendations are presented for effective multidisciplinary program services based on research findings and experience.

Chapter 2 then discusses the process of use, misuse, abuse, and addiction to drugs and alcohol as well as critical issues for treatment and rehabilitation. The impact of addiction on the family and the child also is brought to the reader's attention. A review of clinical and research literature also is provided.

In the third chapter many issues for families with multiple needs are identified and critical issues to guide effective working relationships with families are presented. Alternatives for responding to these problem areas are presented with two very striking case histories that emphasize the complexity of issues presented by children and their families.

The three chapters in Section II address developmental and educational needs of infants, preschool and school-age children, and youth, while making recommendations for intervention strategies and program organization. Chapter 4 supports the proposition that infants and young children have the capacity to overcome biological and psychosocial hurdles if they are reared in a climate of mutual respect, meaningful relationships, and opportunities for self-mastery. The need to focus on resiliency through supporting infants, parents, and families is of paramount importance in the development of early intervention programs.

The development of classroom interventions for young children at risk is addressed in Chapter 5. The author's experience as a classroom teacher in an educational program for vulnerable children has enabled her to identify critical classroom and instructional factors for success for children of preschool and early school age.

The needs of school-age children who are affected by drug and alcohol abuse are discussed in Chapter 6. A variety of factors are identified that must be considered with regard to school and classroom organization for school-age children and youth, including adolescents. Recommendations are provided for instructional strategies, classroom and school organization, supporting staff, and developing effective school and family relationships.

Section III then emphasizes that effective programs must be organized to address multiple needs of children and their families. Usually, this is easier said than done. Issues for multiple agency cooperation and examples of successful programs are provided.

Chapter 7 addresses the removal of children from their biological parents and how this presents significant issues for healthy child development and for service delivery systems. Although out-of-home placement can be a positive alternative, a persuasive case that the inherent issues of separation and loss always place the child in a vulnerable situation is presented. Social and emotional care plans are needed for all children who experience the loss of their primary family.

Collaborative service delivery systems will be required if communities are to successfully marshall required resources. In Chapter 8, the issues and priorities that must be addressed if agencies are to successfully combine resources for vulnerable families and their children are discussed. Strategies for building effective interagency service models, including community planning councils, are presented.

Chapter 9 then describes selected exemplary programs throughout the United States that provide services to children and their families. In the opinion of the authors, these programs have identified and are responding to critical issues for children and families and offer effective models of services for replication support.

This book was written for classroom teachers, school administrators, and community service providers from social service agencies, early childhood programs, mental health programs, and treatment and rehabilitation programs that are responsible for services to children and families affected by substance abuse. Of primary concern are agencies that will be more effective when services are delivered with a complete understanding of the needs of children and families as well as when services are provided in collaboration with, and an understanding of, other agencies' roles and responsibilities.

Acknowledgments

Children and their families who are vulnerable for failure because of their family's misuse of drugs and/or alcohol offer tremendous challenge and, at the same time, great opportunity to those of us who work with them. It is critical that service providers be knowledgeable about the realities of their lives and have a better understanding of how our communities must respond if they, and we, are to realize a higher quality of life. Regardless of our income or professional standing, we are all affected by drug use, by violence in our communities and homes, by broken and dysfunctional homes, and especially by children who have not been given the opportunity to dream and to be given a hope of realizing those dreams.

Four individuals from different professional and personal experiences have worked for many months in preparing this book. In the process of comparing ideas, reaching consensus on content, and helping one another understand the unique value of each of our individual professional affiliations, we have benefited greatly from each other's knowledge of, experience with, and philosophies regarding children who are affected by their families' misuse of drugs and alcohol. Sometimes this growth has been wonderful. At other times it may have been somewhat painful as we have collectively examined—and reexamined—our expectations and perceptions of families in need and their children.

As lead writer, it has been my privilege to work with three very talented, knowledgeable, and terrific individuals in developing this book. To Claire, Marie, and Carol: Thank you for your contributions to this work. I sincerely appreciate each of you for your friendship and your continuing personal and professional support of me.

On behalf of Dr. Claire D. Coles, I acknowledge the contributions of Jeff Silverstein in the development of various tables and figures and Connie Russell for research support.

Sarah Cheney, Acquisitions Editor, at Paul H. Brookes Publishing Co., has given great support to this project from its inception. She has guided, prodded, encouraged, advised, challenged, and applauded all at the right times. Sarah is a very special person who deserves significant credit for this project coming to completion. Other staff members at Brookes Publishing, especially Kristine DeRuchie and Ken Foye, who supported our efforts are recognized with appreciation.

G. Harold Smith

Introduction

Society has been aware for hundreds of years that the use of drugs and alcohol by a pregnant woman may have very serious effects on the developing fetus. In the Book of Leviticus in the Old Testament of the Bible, the prophet cautions against pregnant women drinking wine. It was not until the late 1960s that various clinicians made the connection between the use of alcohol by pregnant women and the effect that this may have for fetal physical and cognitive outcomes (Jones, Smith, Ulleland, & Streissguth, 1973; Lemoine, Haronsseau, Borteyru, & Menuet, 1968).

Maternal abuse of heroin, nicotine, and other drugs also may interfere with fetal development and/or create high risk for premature births and low birth weights. It is important to be aware that poor birth outcomes, especially prematurity and low birth weight, may result from a variety of factors including, but not limited to, substance abuse. The synergistic effects of drug use combined with environmental and/or biological issues increases the risk for poor outcomes (Kleinfeld, 1991; Poulsen, 1992; Regan, Ehrlich, & Finnegan, 1987).

Risk factors for pregnant women who use drugs and their babies represent a constellation of issues, including lack of prenatal care, inadequate prenatal nutrition, exposure to violence and trauma, sexually transmitted diseases, lack of adequate housing, inadequate education, and inadequate parenting models, which will affect how the mother–child bond will develop following birth. It is the combination of these issues that must be addressed as our communities confront the challenge presented by families and their children.

Although a great deal of attention has been paid to the effects of crack cocaine on the fetus, research is very inconclusive on the specific effects of this particular drug. Leading researchers have begun to draw important conclusions that if there is damage to the fetal brain as a result of prenatal drug exposure, it may be limited to fairly specific areas of the brain. Cognitive and neurobehavioral functions that are at high risk for prenatal damage appear to focus on the child's ability to control environmental stimuli and attending behaviors rather than on decreased cognitive functioning (Chasnoff, Griffith, Frier, & Murray, 1992).

The exposure of children to the environmental misuse of substances during childhood is known to have significant potential for very serious long-term consequences. These may include social and emotional effects, relationships with others, and adaptive behavioral issues. An increased risk for physical and sexual abuse, abandonment, and loss of caregivers as a result of imprisonment or death are additional risk factors for the child.

Along with an increasing awareness of the risk factors for children, research is beginning to emphasize the resiliency of infants and children as it relates to the importance of early intervention. In Chapter 4, the factors that assist young children in overcoming these negative issues are reviewed. Resilience of children may explain, in part, why some children are affected by clinical or environmental drug abuse issues while other children in identical or similar settings are not affected.

Early intervention is addressed in the classroom and school. But before attention can be focused, teachers and school personnel must be aware of a child's needs.

Success in school is contingent upon a variety of factors. Schools typically assume that students 1) have achieved developmental skills based on normative data from the general population, 2) have had experiences in their family and community that have prepared them for learning, 3) have support from their family to participate in and succeed in school, and 4) have intact neurobehavioral processes necessary for learning.

Students are expected to be capable of chronological age–appropriate social responses in peer and adult relationships, to have sufficient self-esteem that will allow them to experience some failure without undue consequences to their positive self-concept and confidence in undertaking new tasks, and to be able to operate at an appropriate level of independence for adaptive skills and self-directed activities (Smith, 1993). Children who have been exposed prenatally and/or who are growing up in a home in which drug abuse is evident should not be assumed to have achieved these important milestones nor should they be assumed capable of chronological age–appropriate responses. Because of these issues, these children are extremely vulnerable for failure at school and in their communities.

During the 1960s, there was considerable support of political interventions for social solutions. At that time, a variety of government-sponsored programs were initiated. As part of an initiative to eliminate the "cycle of poverty" that was responsible for "social retardation," a number of programs were begun. The most widely known is Head Start, which was founded in 1965 and continues to be supported despite considerable controversy about its effectiveness in various areas (Zigler & Styfco, 1993).

In the next decade, the U.S. population became less interested in eradicating poverty and other social inequities as the basis for resolving the country's social problems. The focus turned instead to helping children with developmental disabilities.

In 1975, the U.S. Congress enacted PL 94-142, the Education for All Handicapped Children Act. This law established the right of children with disabilities to be provided a free, appropriate public education. PL 94-142 mandated the development of individualized education programs (IEPs), which set forth a plan of services based on nonbiased assessment. Regulations required the involvement of parents in the process of assessment and development of appropriate interventions. This law also included a provision that education services to children with disabilities must be carried out in as typical a setting as possible (i.e., in the least restrictive environment). PL 94-142 was the forerunner for the development of an extensive program of special education services for children, beginning at birth, in all states.

Although they were encouraged, services for children from birth to school age were not required by PL 94-142 (Smith, 1993). In 1986 and 1990, Congress passed PL 99-457, the Education of the Handicapped Act Amendments, and PL 101-476, the Individuals with Disabilities Education Act (IDEA), respectively. PL 99-457 was a major step forward for young children because it mandated services for infants with special needs and their families. In 1991, the Act was again amended (PL 102-119, the Individuals with Disabilities Education Act Amendments), further strengthening birth to 3 services and recognizing two new categories of disability for service delivery under the law, autism and traumatic brain injury.

Under IDEA, service requirements are distinguished for 1) infants and toddlers (birth–3 years), 2) preschoolers (3–5 years), and 3) school-age children and youth (6–21 years). Regulations for implementing PL 102-119 require that every participating state create an interagency coordinating council (ICC) and that the governor of each state designate a *lead agency* to coordinate the service system for each of the age groups below school age. Some states have designated an agency for the birth to age 3 group and another agency for children age 3 to school age. In some instances, this has resulted in fragmentation where there has not been close coordination among state agencies, particularly when these agencies perceive significantly different missions for their designated populations. Lead agencies may be divisions within the state's department of education or department of health. Lead agencies also may be designated through the state's department of mental health or through another human services agency. The level and scope of services to young children with developmental delays or disabilities can vary widely in different parts of the United States as a result of the flexibility in states' provision of services.

A critical provision of IDEA that affects children, particularly those who are vulnerable for failure because of their family's misuse of drugs, requires that service planning be based on assessments of the child's and the family's resources and needs (Beckwith & Amaro, 1986; Goodman, 1994). This regulation is designed to ensure the inclusion of the family's perspective in the treatment of the child. Additionally, planning for services to infants and toddlers age birth to 3 years must identify resources that may be required by the family to support the child's optimal development.

Plans for transition of children and their families between agencies responsible for services must be included in the child's individualized family service plan (IFSP) or individualized education program beginning at age 3. These programs may be called different names in different states (e.g., individualized service plan [ISP]). Regulations require that each child's program include a statement of current status, appropriate outcome goals and objectives for development, and a commitment of services to achieve these outcomes. Parental consent and involvement in the development of these programs are required.

Funding for services to children and youth with disabilities comes from a combination of federal, state, and local education agency sources. Federal funding through the U.S. Congress has never been sufficient to cover the full cost of these programs. State and local school districts provide substantial funding support to meet requirements for services imposed by the federal legislation.

A goal of the writers of PL 99-457 was to facilitate the collaboration of different service providers, specifically the medical and educational disciplines. Service providers who work with children and their families often have different philosophies toward services that are required and appropriate strategies for delivery programs. These differences can lead to the fragmentation of services and even conflict between agencies and the families they are mandated to serve. To support a more effective delivery of comprehensive services and the transition of children and their families to service agencies, PL 99-457 and subsequently PL 102-119 mandated the development of ICCs, and stipulated that parents be included as members to represent service consumers. In addition to the state-level ICCs, communities have also created local interagency councils that include the child and family service providers in a community.

As noted in Chapter 9, the ICC model has evidenced varying degrees of implementation and success in bringing about collaborative service models. Key issues affecting interagency collaboration are 1) ownership of the process by cooperating agencies, particularly at the local community level; 2) political issues that affect agencies; 3) the ability and willingness of agencies, both private and public, to make changes in service delivery priorities and strategies; and 4) the establishment of realistic goals for transagency collaboration at varying administrative staff levels (Swan & Morgan, 1992).

Under the federal regulations, states may serve children who are at developmental risk as a result of defined environmental or biological conditions that may place the child at risk for developmental vulnerabilities. The two most common criteria are the family's economic status and parental substance abuse.

Children who are affected by substance misuse can be served in special education programs if they meet diagnosis eligibility and eligibility under one or more of the service categories that have been established by PL 99-457/PL 102-119 or state-initiated legislation or regulations defining maternal suspected or confirmed substance abuse as a risk to the fetus. Some states have developed criteria that permit documentation of maternal use of drugs or alcohol during pregnancy. Other states permit placement if the child evidences a significant developmental delay in one or more of the developmental areas. Others require diagnosis of a disability according to the federal and state placement criteria.

Specific areas of disability, which support a child's eligibility for special education services, are included in the broad definitions and categories set forth in IDEA. Although the federal regulations present definitions of each area of disability, states vary in specific criteria that establish eligibility for services. Differences in criteria for services between states may result in a student being eligible for special education services in one state and not being eligible in another. For example, a student in one state may be diagnosed as having a learning disability and be eligible for special education services. However, if that same student moved to another state, he or she may be found to be ineligible because of different criteria used to diagnose a learning disability.

In summary, children whose families misuse drugs and alcohol are affected by a range of biological and environmental factors. Service providers require an understanding of issues that affect these children and their families, which may or may not lie within their field(s) of expertise. For example, classroom teachers who work with children who are at risk because of drug and alcohol issues in their families must understand the complexity of drug addiction and how it may affect parenting and the potential outcomes of neonatal drug exposure. Synergistic outcomes of social needs of the family will determine the characteristics and needs of children for appropriate educational planning.

G. Harold Smith and Claire D. Coles

REFERENCES

Beckwith, L., & Amaro, H. (1986). Personal and social differences faced by females and males entering alcoholism treatment. *Journal of Studies on Alcohol, 45*, 135–145.

Chasnoff, I.J., Griffith, D.R., Frier, C., & Murray, J. (1992). Cocaine/polydrug use in pregnancy: Two-year follow-up. *Pediatrics, 89*(2), 284–289.

Education for All Handicapped Children Act of 1975, PL 94-142. (August 23, 1977). Title 20, U.S.C. 1401 et seq: *U.S. Statutes at Large, 89*, 773–796.

Education of the Handicapped Act Amendments of 1986, PL 99-457. (October 8, 1986). Title 20, U.S.C. 1400 et seq: *U.S. Statutes at Large, 100*, 1145–1177.

Goodman, J.F. (1994). Perspective: "Empowerment" versus "Best Interests": Client–professional relationships. *Infants and Young Children, 6*, 6–10.

Individuals with Disabilities Education Act Amendments of 1991, PL 102-119. (October 7, 1991). Title 20, U.S.C. 1400 et seq: *U.S. Statutes at Large, 105*, 587–608.

Individuals with Disabilities Education Act of 1990 (IDEA), PL 101-476. (October 30, 1990). Title 20, U.S.C. 1400 et seq: *U.S. Statutes at Large, 104*, 1103–1151.

Jones, K.L., Smith, D.W., Ulleland, C.H., & Streissguth, A.P. (1973). Pattern of malformation in offspring of chronic alcoholic mothers. *Lancet, 9*, 1267–1271.

Kleinfeld, J. (1991). *Fetal alcohol syndrome in Alaska: What the schools can do.* Anchorage: Alaska Department of Education.

Lemoine, P., Haronsseau, H., Borteyru, J.P., & Menuet, J.C. (1968). Les enfants de parents alcooliques: Anomalies observées a oriosis de 127 cas. *Ouest Med, 25,* 477–482.

Poulsen, M.K. (1992). *Perinatal substance abuse—What's best for the children?* Sacramento: Child Development Program Advisory Committee, State of California.

Regan, D.O., Ehrlich, S.M., & Finnegan, L.P. (1987). Infants of drug addicts: At risk for child abuse, neglect, and placement in foster care. *Neurotoxicology and Teratology, 9,* 315–319.

Smith, G.H. (1993). Intervention strategies for children vulnerable for school failure due to exposure to drugs and alcohol. *International Journal of the Addictions, 28*(13), 1435–1470.

Swan, W.W., & Morgan, J.L. (1993). *Collaborating for comprehensive services for young children and their families: The local interagency coordinating council.* Baltimore: Paul H. Brookes Publishing Co.

Zigler, E., & Styfco, S.J. (1993). Using research and theory to justify and inform Head Start expansion. *Society for Research in Child Development, Social Policy Report, 7*(2), 1–21.

For the Reader
Terms and Vocabulary

Because the media and general public use certain terms loosely when referring to drug addiction, the authors of this book have provided explanations of terms that are used frequently in the following chapters. They believe clarification of the terms is important to fully understand the relationship among children, families, and substance abuse.

SUBSTANCES AND DRUGS

The terms *substances* and *drugs* are used interchangeably by the authors of this volume. For the purposes of this book the term *substance* is understood to include drugs and alcohol. When the discussion is specific to the effects of alcohol (e.g., fetal alcohol syndrome), then *alcohol* is used specifically. Otherwise, when the term *drug* is used, it should be understood to mean all drugs, including alcohol.

A *teratogenic substance* is any drug—legal or illegal—that has negative effects on the developing fetus. Research on the teratogenic effects of prenatal drug and alcohol exposure is complicated by the fact that women who use drugs rarely limit themselves to one drug. Typically, people who are addicted use a variety of drugs. Polydrug use may have a synergistic effect that increases the risk of damage to the baby and may compound the potential addictive influence of the individual drugs.

USE, MISUSE, ABUSE, AND ADDICTION

It is easy to get confused about drugs and their effects. In American culture, use of certain psychoactive drugs is customary and socially correct. The use of other drugs, which appear to be no more physically or psychologically deleterious (Brecher & Editors of Consumer Reports, 1972), is illegal and can result in lengthy prison terms. It is clear from much research that excessive use of most drugs has negative consequences. However, in conformity to cultural values, the negative effects of some drugs (e.g., alcohol and nicotine) tend to be underestimated, and the ill effects of unfamiliar drugs (e.g., marijuana and cocaine) tend to be overestimated.

Similarly, as a culture, the United States often ignores any potential negative side effects of prescription drugs that are used for their beneficial qualities. Because people often have emotional, rather than logical, reactions to drug and alcohol use, it is easy to become confused about what is the "right" amount of use, what is abuse, and what is addiction. Although we often speak of recreational use of drugs in contrast to abusive or addictive use, many people find this concept difficult to understand when they think about cocaine and marijuana. However, if we use the more familiar drug, alcohol, as an example, we find it somewhat easier to make this discrimination. Nevertheless, these distinctions remain confusing, and guidelines have been developed to help in understanding these concepts (see below).

Use

The *use* of drugs, including alcohol, by an individual represents a continuum ranging from no experiences, through experimentation and recreational use, to addiction and dependence. It is within this context that the pervasive use of various drugs within our community becomes apparent. Drugs can have very positive benefits to the user; however, when a particular drug or combination of drugs is used for other than intended purposes, the effects can be very dangerous.

Experience Very few individuals in our society have had no experience with drugs—legal or illegal. A cup of coffee in the morning to "get one's motor running," pain killers to make dental work more bearable, and aspirin to relieve a tension headache are examples of how drugs are used in every household. At this level, drug use remains relatively harmless and may in fact be very beneficial to the individual.

In rare cases, drug use at this level may have negative outcomes for the developing fetus. The extent to which a particular drug will be harmful is due to a variety of issues, including individual maternal and fetal responses to the chemical(s). The use of thalidomide in the 1960s to assist pregnant women in overcoming morning sickness and nausea is an example of a drug that was prescribed for very beneficial reasons. Unfortunately, this drug was later found to have very damaging outcomes for fetal development.

Experimentation Most individuals have at some time or other experimented with drugs. Nicotine and alcohol, and perhaps marijuana, are the most common drugs of choice for initial use. At this point the individual is most likely responding to peer pressure or is curious about what happens when a particular drug is used. This first experience may be so distasteful that any further use is discouraged. For example, the first time that an individual inhales cigarette smoke may set off violent gagging and even nausea.

In terms of danger to a child, this level of use is most likely relatively harmless, depending on the particular drug that is being tried and its effect on the pregnant woman and the developing fetus. For example, if crack cocaine is the drug of choice for experimentation during pregnancy, spontaneous abortion may result.

Recreational or Situational Specific Use Frequently, drug use, especially by young people, is restricted to social settings or activities. When the use of a drug is coupled with pleasant experiences, a classical conditioning situation is presented:

$$\frac{Friends\ and}{Good\ Food} + \frac{Cigarettes\ and}{After\text{-}Dinner\ Drinks} = \frac{Good}{Times!}$$

The relationship between drug use and perceived necessity of the drug in the particular setting or activity places the individual at increased risk for frequent drug use in expanding social contexts.

Binging, a period of uncontrolled self-indulgence, is sometimes associated with recreational use. Binging presents significant risk for negative outcomes for fetal development. For example, if use of a drug results in increased blood pressure for the pregnant woman, the drug will have the same effect on the immature neurological and metabolic systems of the fetus. Although a drug might have a relatively mild effect on the mother's brain, it potentially may have very damaging outcomes (e.g., strokes, hemorrhages) for the fetal brain.

Misuse

Misuse of drugs may be defined as the level of drug intake that is not appropriate to one's social expectations or obligations, family responsibilities, or employment. The individual who feels he or she must have a few drinks before going to a party with his or her boss to relax and be able to have fun and then continues to drink during the party may end up very intoxicated, with consequences that could include being fired.

Another and perhaps more common example of the misuse of drugs is the individual who at the end of each day—every day—returns home and immediately has a drink. Although this may not present a danger of job loss (unless work that has to be done at home is not completed or is completed incorrectly), the individual is vulnerable for consequences to the family and involvement with his or her children. This level of drinking may be described as compulsive and can lead to more frequent use of drugs for longer periods of time.

Abuse

Substance *abuse,* in contrast to addiction, is defined as a maladaptive pattern of psychoactive substance use that involves continuing to use the substance despite having knowledge of a persistent or recurrent social, occupational, psychological, or physical problem that is caused or made worse as a result of use (American Psychiatric Association, 1994). To meet the *Diagnostic and Statistical Manual of Mental Disorders* (4th edition) (DSM-IV) criteria, these problems must occur repeatedly during the same year. By this definition, anyone who smokes cigarettes regularly can be said to have this disorder.

Addiction

Addiction is a complicated matter. Although the word implies that the person involved is captive to a drug, the process is, in fact, much more complicated and involves more than simple physical dependence.

There are many ways to understand the effects of abused substances on the individual. There are two diagnostic systems in current use, the *ICD-10 Classification of Mental and Behavioral Disorders: Clinical Descriptions and Diagnostic Guidelines* (World Health Organization, 1992) and the DSM-IV (American Psychiatric Association, 1994). Both describe the mental and physical disorders associated with substance abuse.

Addiction also is called *dependence.* There are many aspects to being dependent on a psychoactive substance. DSM-IV (American Psychiatric Association, 1994) states that to be given this diagnosis a person must demonstrate at least three of the following seven characteristics occurring at any time over a 12-month period:

1. *Physical tolerance:* The person demonstrates tolerance to the substance (i.e., larger and larger amounts of the drug are needed to achieve intoxication or other desired effects).
2. *Withdrawal symptoms:* The person experiences withdrawal when

not taking the drug so that avoiding this experience becomes a motivation for taking the drug.

3. *Out-of-control use:* The use of the substance is out of control so that it is taken in larger amounts and over a longer time period than the person intends.

4. *Persistent desire:* The person has a persistent desire for the drug or is unsuccessful in being able to control use.

5. *Focus on the substance:* The person spends much time focused on getting the substance, taking it, or recovering from using it. Thoughts and conversation are often concerned with the drug.

6. *Interference with life:* Frequent intoxication or withdrawal interfere with work, social life, family life, or other activities, or use has become physically hazardous.

7. *Persistent use:* The person continues to use the drug despite understanding that the addiction is causing social, psychological, or physical problems or is leading to dangerous activities (e.g., driving when drunk).

OTHER SUBSTANCE ABUSE–RELATED TERMINOLOGY

The authors have provided explanations for other terms appearing in this book. The following is a list of terminology related to use, misuse, and abuse of drugs and alcohol:

Chemical dependence An addiction to a psychoactive substance (e.g., alcoholism, narcotics addiction), which may include narcotics, alcohol, and nicotine.

Codependent A person associated with an addicted person, usually a family member, who has become involved with the addiction process and whose behavior has become influenced by the addict's behavior. The codependent is often described as "enabling" the addict because of behaviors that help the addict avoid the consequences of his or her actions.

Delirium Delirium is described as a clouding of consciousness in which the individual loses clarity in awareness of the environment. Ability to focus attention on the environment is impaired. Behavior patterns can include disturbances in perception or hallucinations, incoherent speech, disturbances in the sleep/wake cycle, and alterations in the usual psychomotor pattern (e.g., activity level). Usually memory is affected and the person may be disoriented as to time and space. The condition develops rapidly and can fluctuate over a short period of time. Delirium has an organic basis and, when it is related to substance abuse, is usually related to the use of high quantities of the substance or to an abrupt cessation of use. Different drugs may produce different patterns of delirium.

Dementia   Dementia involves significant loss of cognitive abilities in which social and occupational functioning are affected. Memory loss is a critical symptom. Other symptoms can be loss of critical judgment, loss of concrete thinking, and disorders of higher cortical functioning (e.g., loss of speech, specific motor functions). Dementia results from an organic cause (e.g., alcoholism) and is permanent rather than transitory.

Dependence   A physical addiction to a substance. Dependence comes about as a result of use of the drug in significant quantities for a period of time (which may vary by individual). An individual can become physically dependent on a drug without deliberately abusing the drug. For example, narcotics given for pain can lead to dependence without the individual intending for this to occur. However, when there is no psychological involvement in the use of the drug, withdrawal is usually less of a problem.

Intoxication   A substance-specific syndrome due to recent ingestion of a psychoactive substance. More than one substance may produce similar or identical syndromes. In addition, intoxication is characterized by maladaptive behavior during the waking state due to the effects of this substance on the central nervous system (e.g., belligerence, impaired judgment, impaired social or occupational functioning).

Psychoactive substance   A chemical that has a psychological effect (i.e., causing intoxication, euphoria, hallucinations, depression, or other alterations in mood or cognitive status).

Psychological addiction   Subjective term focusing on a user's need of a drug to reach his or her maximum level of functioning or state of psychological "well-being."

Tolerance   A biological process that occurs as a person becomes dependent on a chemical. As the body adjusts to the habitual presence of the drug (tolerance), a greater quantity ("dose") becomes necessary to produce the same effects as previously were experienced at a lower dose.

Withdrawal   When tolerance (dependence) on a substance has occurred, discontinuing the use can lead to a state of "withdrawal" or abstinence syndrome. The nature of this withdrawal depends on the action of the drug to which the individual was addicted. Most significant forms are associated with dependence on a central nervous system depressant (e.g., alcohol, narcotics).

CONCLUSION

A better understanding of what causes an individual to become addicted to a particular drug or drugs is beginning to point toward alternative and more effective rehabilitation strategies. Each individual is unique in the process of addiction and his or her requirements for rehabilitation. Regardless of the etiologies, the powerful effects of drugs on the lives of children, families, and the individual using the drug must be ameliorated through research and expansion of community treatment programs.

REFERENCES

American Psychiatric Association. (1994). *Diagnostic and statistical manual of mental disorders* (4th ed.). Washington, DC: Author.

Brecher, E.M., & Editors of Consumer Reports. (1972). *Licit and illicit drugs.* Boston: Little, Brown.

World Health Organization. (1992). *The ICD-10 classification of mental and behavioral disorders: Clinical descriptions and diagnostic guidelines.* Geneva, Switzerland: Author.

I

THE CHILDREN
AND THEIR FAMILIES

1

Children of Parents Who Abuse Drugs and Alcohol

Claire D. Coles

Abuse of drugs and alcohol by parents can have very negative consequences for children. This always has been true (Sullivan, 1899); however, since the 1980s, this problem and its consequences have become the focus for heightened concern among educators, health professionals, social service providers, and legislators, as well as the general public. Much of this concern was fueled by the cocaine epidemic of the 1980s with its associated social disruption, crime, and violence; but the problems associated with addiction existed before "crack" existed and will continue when the cocaine epidemic burns itself out. The assumption that parental addiction has negative consequences is evident in the growth of the Adult Children of Alcoholics (ACOA), a self-help movement, which is concerned with repairing the effects of being reared by parents with an addiction. In addition, it is now clear that the child can be affected more directly as a result of substance abuse by pregnant women.

At the present time, it is clear that there are negative effects of substance abuse on fetal development and family function and that these consequences must be addressed. However, the publicity surrounding the use of drugs and alcohol by pregnant women has created hysteria and confusion, which can harm more than help exposed children. In trying to find simple answers to the difficult questions of maternal addiction, the media have provided us with a new myth—the "crack baby"—and have substantially distorted the

3

scientific information about alcohol effects and fetal alcohol syndrome (FAS) so that prenatal alcohol exposure is sometimes considered to be a sole cause for criminal behavior and other unusual outcomes.

Even those interested in getting accurate information may not find this an easy task. In the 1980s and 1990s, the scientific and clinical literatures on this topic have burgeoned, flooding health care professionals, educators, legislators, and social agencies with information, some of it useful, much of it conflicting and confusing. Despite the difficulties in understanding the research literature, those who work with the victims of addiction, both the parents and the children, were and are anxious to understand these effects so that they can provide the help that is necessary.

However, understanding takes work. The physical and behavior problems seen in children with prenatal exposure to drugs and alcohol are the result of many related factors, and focusing only on the mother's drug taking may not lead to adequate solutions. The following case study is presented to illustrate the complexity, as well as the grievousness, of the problem.

Leya and Marla

Leya and Marla, shy and elf-like, fraternal twin girls, were 3 years, 10 months old. Physically, they were slight, dark-skinned, and had an open expression due to their wide-spaced brown eyes. Pediatric and psychological assessment later indicated that both girls had all the characteristic features of fetal alcohol syndrome (FAS) including growth retardation—their weight was less than the 5th percentile, and their head circumference, less than the 2nd—dysmorphic facial features (i.e., low set ears, absent philtrum, small eye openings), and intellectual deficits (I.Q. scores = 52 and 53) when tested with the Stanford-Binet (3rd ed.) intelligence test (Terman & Merrill, 1972).

Throughout their 23-year-old mother's pregnancy, she drank up to 32 drinks (16 ounces of absolute alcohol) a week and often "binged" on weekends. She also smoked at least a pack of cigarettes a day and used marijuana several times a week.

She already had two other children. Leya, who was born first, had a birth weight of 1,800 grams (less than 4 pounds) and a cardiac defect; Marla weighed 1,650 grams (3½ pounds) and had a cleft lip and palate. Both were small for their gestational age (SGA). During their first year, Marla had surgery for her cleft lip and palate, and Leya was admitted to the county hospital at 6 months old with failure to thrive. During the time when most children double their weight, Leya had gained only a few pounds over her birth weight and was seriously ill. As often happens, Leya gained weight successfully in the hospital and was discharged to her mother's care, only to be readmitted with the same diagnosis at 15 months. As a result of this admission, the county child welfare office was brought in to supervise the twins after Leya was discharged from the hospital. Examination of hospital emergency room records in the following months indicated that the twins' mother was treated repeatedly for physical injuries due to beatings and, on one occasion, a gun shot wound. It was noted that she was intoxicated during these admissions.

As the mother's addiction became more serious, the county intervened and the twins' were removed from their mother's care. Following a policy that is intended to preserve families as well as control cost, the authorities placed the twins with their mother's family. In those days, just before "crack houses," the mother's family ran a "shot house" where liquor was dispensed illegally by the drink. Later it appeared that the twins were neglected and sexually abused while in this environment and the county removed them from this placement and put them in foster care. In foster care, the twins' behavior was a concern to both foster parents and case workers. The twins were referred for developmental testing and diagnosis of their FAS. The behaviors that concerned their caregivers included "slowness," clumsiness, delayed language development, sexual acting out behaviors, and disturbances in sleeping and eating. In addition, Leya was very noncompliant and refused to cooperate with either caregivers or medical personnel. Both children showed hypervigilant behavior—an extreme wariness and a suspicion of the motives of the adults they encountered.

It was evident that the children experienced the cognitive and behavior effects of early neglect and abuse as well as the apparent sexual abuse. The twins also experienced the effects of neglect by the social agencies that should have been serving them. There were months of delay in intervention after the first hospitalization for failure to thrive, and delay in placing the children in a good foster home. The school system the twins attended later could not provide adequate compensatory education. Because of the beneficial effects of their foster home and therapeutic intervention in the preschool period, the twins' test performance (on the Stanford-Binet, 4th ed.) rose to the low borderline range. Because their IQ scores, which were now around 70, were too high to be considered mental retardation, the twins were refused special education services and have had to repeat first grade three times.

When the twins were 4½ years old, their mother had a third daughter, Keisha, who was exposed to both alcohol and cocaine, and who weighed 1,350 grams (less than 3 pounds) when she was born at full term. She had the features of FAS and a cardiac defect. Due to the twins' history, this child was immediately placed in foster care but the foster mother was unable to obtain adequate medical care for this child, who weighed 9 pounds when she was 6 months old. The children's biological mother refused to accept referral to a treatment program and was lost to follow-up.

The twins' story is not pleasant. And, if their social and educational environment does not improve, predictions for their future are not optimistic. Unfortunately, their history is typical of those of many children of substance abusers and illustrates the multiple negative influences that combine to produce such situations. To help the twins and their siblings and to prevent other children from having similar experiences, it is necessary to understand how their problems come about and to take actions to prevent such things in the future.

To understand the many factors involved and to develop solutions, it is necessary to address certain questions about parental addiction and prenatal exposure. The questions to be discussed in this chapter include:

- What is the extent and nature of drug and alcohol use by pregnant women?
- What are the effects of drug and alcohol exposure on the fetus and the developing child?
- What is the range of effects seen in a child as a result of prenatal exposure?
- How does maternal substance abuse affect the fetus and the infant?
- Does use by the father affect the child's outcome?

• What is the role of the environment during pregnancy and for the child, pre- and postnatally?

DRUG AND ALCOHOL USE BY PREGNANT WOMEN

Although there has been a great deal of concern about the growing problem of drug abuse during pregnancy, the actual extent of use of legal and illegal drugs during pregnancy is not completely understood. The National Institute on Drug Abuse (NIDA) (1992) conducts a household survey every few years to track the trends in drug and alcohol use in different groups of the population, but there has been no similar survey specifically of pregnant women.

Based on our current knowledge, it is difficult to identify accurately the risk of exposure in a given individual. Instead, it is necessary to examine information from a number of different sources to try to form a picture of prevalence of drug abuse during pregnancy in the United States. In a study published in 1989, the National Association for Perinatal Addiction Research and Education (NAPARE) surveyed 36 hospitals nationwide and found that about 11% of women who delivered had indications of substance abuse. However, this figure included all kinds of drugs. Examination of the existing literature (Day, Cottreau, & Richardson, 1993) suggests that there are differences in the pattern and extent of drug and alcohol use in different parts of the country and in women of different ethnic groups and social classes. For instance, although only about 1% of women report ever using heroin, heroin use is relatively common in inner-city neighborhoods in the northeast and Washington, D.C., but not in rural areas or in the south (NIDA, 1992). In Atlanta, even among women being treated for addiction to cocaine and alcohol, heroin use is uncommon (Smith, Dent, Coles, & Falek, 1992).

Another impediment to an easy understanding of these issues is the changes that occur in the patterns of drug use over time. For example, in the early 1980s, cocaine was the drug choice of the "trendy" and the wealthy. By the end of that decade, with the advent of "crack" cocaine, the preponderance of use of this drug was by low-income minorities while casual use by middle-class individuals had declined (NIDA, 1992). Because of concern about the effect of cocaine exposure on infants, several studies have been done to determine the incidence of cocaine use by pregnant and postpartum women. Recent cocaine use is usually identified through urine screening in prenatal clinics or following delivery. In some inner-city hospitals, use of cocaine was found to be as high as 18% (self-report) or 9% (urine screen) (Zuckerman et al., 1989), while in other regions it was as low as 5%. Even within the same hospital, rates vary among different groups. In 1989 and 1990, a medical records review of deliveries in a large inner-city hospital in Atlanta found that, among full-term infants, the rate of cocaine-positive urine screens was about 5%. Among those infants in the neonatal intensive care units the rate was much higher, reaching 25% in some groups of very low birth weight infants.

There is also a great deal of variability in the rate of use among different kinds of drugs. In a study in Florida published in 1990 (Chasnoff, Landress, & Barrett), evidence of marijuana use was found in 14.4% of white, predominantly middle-class women and 6% of black, predominantly lower-class women. Evidence of cocaine use was found in 1.8% and 7.5%, respectively. In a population study done by the Centers for Disease Control in Rhode Island (Hollingshead et al., 1990), similar differences in the rate of use among different groups of the population were identified, marijuana: 3.4% and 2.0%, respectively, and cocaine: 1.1% and 8.2%, respectively.

Although attention has been directed at the use of illegal drugs such as cocaine and heroin, the most commonly used, and abused, substances are alcohol and cigarettes, both in the general population and by pregnant women. According to the NIDA household survey (1992), 61.5% of American women of all ages reported drinking alcohol during the previous year and 44.1% in the last month. Cigarette use was similar, with 29.7% reporting use in the last year and 25.5% in the last month. Use during pregnancy, particularly of alcohol, is much lower. Most women spontaneously reduce alcohol use during pregnancy (Russell, 1985) and, since the problems associated with alcohol exposure have become better known, many women not addicted to alcohol avoid drinking altogether. Although cigarette smoking is known to cause lower birth weight, smoking reduction or cessation appears to be less common.

Based on research and experience, Rosett and Weiner (1984) estimated that 5%–10% of pregnant women drank at levels high enough to place their fetuses at risk. Fortunately, FAS does not occur that frequently. However, it has been estimated that FAS has an incidence of .3–1 per 1,000 live births (Abel & Sokol, 1991) in the general population. Some groups, such as Native Americans, may have much higher rates (May, Hymbaugh, Aase, & Somet, 1982).

The Effects on the Fetus and the Developing Child

There has been a great deal of rumor and speculation about how alcohol, cocaine, and other drugs affect the embryo and fetus during gestation and what the manifestations of these effects are in the neonate, infant, and developing child. Although it is difficult to study this problem in humans and difficult to apply the results of animal studies to children, research carried out since the 1960s provides some answers to these questions.

In thinking about the effects of drugs and alcohol on the child, it is important to remember that different drugs may have different effects on both mother and child because of their biochemical actions. It is also important to discriminate between the teratogenic or toxic effects of a given drug and the effects of the lifestyle associated with addiction to legal or illegal drugs. Much of the scientific research using animal models and epidemiological studies carried out in human populations has focused on the question of the teratogenic effects of specific drugs; that is, research has been directed at answering questions such as, "If all other factors are held constant, does exposure to cocaine cause physical damage to the fetus?" or "Does exposure to alcohol during pregnancy affect attention at 6 years if all possible confounding factors are controlled statistically?"

In contrast in clinical studies, children, similar to the twins in the case study, are affected by multiple factors, and it is difficult in practice to separate the effects of the drug from those of the many other things that are affecting their lives. This book discusses both kinds of effects.

Range of Effects of Prenatal Exposure

The range of effects reported in women abusing drugs and for their exposed children is very wide, as seen in Figure 1.1. At one extreme are infertility and nonviability because women who abuse alcohol and heroin are known to have problems with fertility (Russell, 1985) as well as with sexual functioning. Amenorrhea is common and a higher incidence of sexually transmitted diseases (STDs) is associated

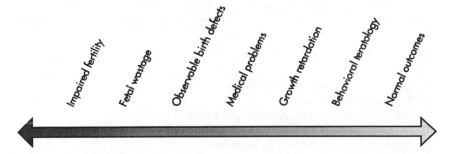

Figure 1.1. Reproductive effects of substance abuse by women range from impaired fertility through teratogenic risks to the offspring to normal outcomes in infants.

with reduced fertility. When the pregnancy is established, fetal wastage is more common than in the general public. Incidence of spontaneous abortions is elevated among all groups of substance abusers (Anokute, 1986) and fetal death and still births are more common. In the neonatal period, sudden infant death syndrome (SIDS) is approximately five times higher than average among all groups of substance abusers (Regan, Ehrlich, & Finnegan, 1987). If the infant survives, severe effects can include physical defects, growth retardation, and neurological damage (Scialli, 1992). At the other extreme, in most children, exposure appears to be associated with developmental outcomes in the normal range (Coles & Platzman, 1993).

Given that there can be such a wide range of outcomes, the following is an important question that has not been answered completely: What determines a particular outcome in a particular mother and child and, therefore, determines the severity of the outcome? Table 1.1 lists some of the factors that are believed to contribute to the impact of drugs on the fetus and the child. Those factors contributing to effects on offspring prenatally exposed to drugs and alcohol are believed to include genetic vulnerability, which suggests that some individuals may have more tendency to be affected by exposure than others. The type of drug used affects the probable outcome (see Table 1.2). Also important is the way the drug is used—the exposure history. Included in the exposure history are the drug dose (i.e., the amount of drug consumed), duration of drug use (i.e., the length of time that the drug is used during gestation), and pattern of use (i.e., whether the drug is used daily or in a "binge" pattern). Other, less direct, influences include the mother's health and medical history, the availability and use of prenatal care and medical care when the child is born, postnatal caregiving factors, the immediate family environment, and the general social environment (i.e., socioeconomic status) (Vorhees, 1986). Without consideration of the developmental process itself and the many factors that are known to affect it, it may be difficult to understand why such

Table 1.1. Factors affecting outcome in children prenatally exposed to drugs and alcohol

1. Genetic and/or physical vulnerability
2. Drug type and drug action
3. Type of exposure: dose, duration, and timing
4. Maternal health, access to health services, and prenatal care
5. Pregnancy complications (e.g., prematurity)
6. Status and process variables
7. Availability of services: prevention, education, and treatment

Table 1.2. Consequences of exposure to specific drugs in pregnancy

Drug	Problems noted	Comments
Alcohol	Fetal wastage	Extensively studied
	Facial dysmorphia	Full FAS only in alcoholics
	Persistent growth retardation	Many associated behavior problems
	Central nervous system damage/intellectual deficits	Many nonspecific physical problems
	Cardiac abnormalities	
	Neonatal withdrawal	
	Failure to thrive	
	Vision and hearing problems	
	Long-term effects	
Cannabis (marijuana)	Lower birth weight	Well studied
	Neonatal behavioral effects	
Cigarettes (nicotine)	Lower birth weight	Well studied
		Usually "catch up" growth postpartum
Cocaine (crack)	Spontaneous abortion	Numerous other effects still under study
	Abruptio placenta	
	Preterm birth	
	Lower birth weight	
	Neonatal behavioral effects	
	Enters breast milk	Infant cocaine intoxication
	Birth defects[a]	
	Neonatal withdrawal[a]	
	Sudden infant death syndrome[a]	
	Long-term effects[a]	
Methamphetamine	Effects similar to cocaine	
Opiates (heroin and methadone)	Pregnancy complications	Extensively studied
	Lower birth weight	Birth weight normal with methadone
	Perinatal complications	
	Severe withdrawal	Withdrawal worse with methadone
	Sudden infant death syndrome	No long-term effects on growth or development
Phencyclidine (PCP)	Hypertonic tone[a]	Limited information available
	Neurological abnormalities[a]	
	Tremors/jitteriness[a]	
	Persistent effects in infancy[a]	

[a]Effects suggested but not confirmed in systematic research.

various outcomes have been observed among exposed children and how these factors are related to substance abuse.

Effects of Different Drugs on the Infant and Child

Although it is clear that there are many factors affecting outcome, we do know something about the impact of specific drugs. Table 1.2 summarizes current knowledge about this impact. It should be noted that information is much more comprehensive for alcohol and the opiates than it is for cocaine, which has been studied for a much shorter period of time.

THEORIES ON EFFECTS OF PRENATAL EXPOSURE TO DRUGS AND ALCOHOL

There are several theories that explain the process by which effects of prenatal exposure to drugs and alcohol might occur in a child. Some of these theories include the teratogenic model, the toxic model, the maternal functioning model, the sociological model, and the interactive model.

Teratogenic Model

The teratogenic model explains negative consequences of prenatal exposure in terms of direct damage to the fetus caused by exposure during gestation. This model assumes that both physical defects and behavior problems observed neonatally and during later childhood are the direct result of exposure to a teratogen, which leads to observable deficits in cognitive, emotional, and behavioral outcomes (Wilson, 1977).

It is popularly assumed that prenatal exposure to alcohol and other drugs is always associated with negative outcomes. This assumption rests on the idea that these psychoactive substances are teratogens; that is, they are chemicals that cause damage to the developing fetus leading to physical birth defects. This view has arisen, in part, because there are a number of common teratogens, including mercury and lead, and drugs like thalidomide and Accutane, which cause well-documented birth defects in both humans and animals. In addition, research and clinical observation have made it clear that alcohol, one of the most commonly abused drugs, is also a teratogen. However, it is not clear that all drugs that are used for recreational reasons are teratogens. Twenty years of research have revealed no birth defects associated with exposure to opiates or marijuana. Nor, at the present time, is there convincing evidence that cocaine, despite early reports, causes physical anomalies in babies.

Toxic Model

A second way of conceptualizing the effects of drug and alcohol abuse during gestation focuses on the toxicity of abused substances. The toxic model assumes that the use of certain drugs affects the mother physically either acutely (e.g., causing vascular constriction) or chronically (e.g., causing impaired liver function or altered endocrine function), which then leads to physical consequences for the infant. The speculation that the putative negative effects of cocaine result from vascular disruptions (Volpe, 1991) is based on this type of assumption.

Similarly, attributing behavior problems in children to the effects of second-hand cigarette smoke or cocaine fumes is a toxic model because it assumes that behavioral deficits may be caused by inhalation of toxic substances.

Maternal Functioning Model

Another way to understand negative effects of maternal drug use on offspring is to attribute the viability of the offspring to maternal status. In the maternal functioning model, the child's status is affected indirectly by the mother—by her health during gestation, her personal habits, and her caregiving competence. All of these things are negatively affected by the addiction process. For instance, because there is a relationship between lack of prenatal care and infant outcome, this has become a focus in studies of the outcome of pregnancy in women identified as drug users (Levy & Koren, 1990; Randall, 1991). Women who do not receive prenatal care may have untreated infections or nutritional deficiencies that can affect the fetus's development. Lack of prenatal care is associated with lower birth weight as well as preterm birth.

Sociological Model

An alternative theory for the effects of drug abuse in pregnancy is the sociological model. This model assumes that effects result from social factors including access to prenatal care and the effects of poverty, racism, and similar factors. The discrepancy in results of exposure to teratogens, which is apparently due to social class (see below), is supportive of this model. For instance, FAS is identified much more frequently among lower-class individuals and minorities. This difference may be due to real differences in incidence of this problem, to ascertainment bias on the part of health care professionals, or to an increased vulnerability in economically deprived individuals to the effects of teratogens.

Interactive Model

The interactive model assumes that development results from the interaction of multiple factors and that examination of outcome must attend to all of these various factors. Investigation of effects using this model can lead to the use of very large samples and statistical analyses involving regression or model building. Although this theory is more likely to be "true" than are the others, it is difficult to apply in practice because of practical issues and expense. It also can be difficult to understand.

DRUG AND ALCOHOL ABUSE BY THE FATHER

Although concern usually focuses on maternal substance use and abuse, the question of the effects on the offspring of paternal use is beginning to be examined. This is a realistic concern both because of possible direct effects of the father's use and because men who abuse drugs and alcohol are much more likely to associate with women who do so as well (i.e., assortative mating).

There are several ways in which drug and alcohol abuse could affect fathering. First, substance abuse can interfere with endocrine function and affect both potency and sperm viability. In animal models, when males are alcoholized, there is reduced fertility and evidence of damage to the sperm such that there is a high incidence of pregnancy loss.

It is not clear whether changes in characteristics of offspring of men who use alcohol is analogous to the effects seen in offspring of women drinking during pregnancy. In an epidemiological study of the children of men who were drinking heavily at the time of conception, lower birth weights were noted (Little & Sing, 1986). Animal models have been used to study the effects of alcohol and have noted behavior differences in offspring (Abel & Bilitzke, 1990) but it is hard to explain what the mechanism of these effects might be.

Finally, there have been many studies of the children of alcoholic fathers. Behavior effects in these children suggest that there may be a genetic cause for some of the behaviors of the sons (but not the daughters) of alcoholic fathers (Monteiro & Schuckit, 1988). These effects include increased hyperactivity, tremors, alterations in electroencephalogram (EEG) results, and other physiological reactions. In addition, there is a good deal of evidence to suggest that living with an alcoholic father produces a number of behavior and emotional problems in both sons and daughters (see Chapter 2).

THE CHILD'S CONTEXT: ENVIRONMENTAL EFFECTS

When a baby is defined as having FAS or being a "crack baby," it suggests that the conditions at birth will define the rest of the child's life. Unfortunately the rest of his or her capabilities and experiences are ignored. Much of the empirical research on the effects of prenatal exposure has been from the "teratogenic" perspective, rather than from the broader perspective of the child's environment. For that reason, many different professionals have looked at the prenatal exposure only, rather than at the many other factors that affect the child's environment or at the interaction between the biological and the environmental influences. However, to understand the status and behavior of affected children, it is necessary to take a broader view and look at the world in which they live.

The environment of children prenatally exposed to drugs and alcohol includes many influences that should be evaluated, ranging from the addictive substances themselves (which affect both the prenatal and the postnatal environment) to what are called "status" and "process" variables (Bradley et al., 1989). "Status" variables are those like socioeconomic status (SES), which exert broad, although indirect, influence over a whole class of individuals. In contrast, "process" variables are the aspects of the environment that are experienced more directly and specifically by the child. Process variables include things like particular behaviors of family members, the caregiver's style, and specific and significant events, such as loss of a parent, which affect the developing child. It has been demonstrated that these process factors are more effective in predicting children's developmental status than are the more general "status" variables like social class and parent occupation (Bradley et al., 1989).

Although drug and alcohol use may affect social class in a general sense, it is likely that addiction will affect more strongly the "process" area. For example, one important process factor is the interaction patterns between mother and child (or parents and child). These patterns have been investigated in drug-abusing families (Burns, Chetnick, Burns, & Clark, 1991; Davis, 1990). In these studies, the nature of the interactions with parents, as well as other directly experienced factors, often appear to have more effect on outcomes like emotional and cognitive development than does prenatal exposure to specific drugs.

For this reason, to understand the process of development in children prenatally exposed to drugs and alcohol, it is necessary to examine the environmental factors that are associated with the use of psychoactive drugs by pregnant women and parents and to understand how these affect the developing child. Although drug and alcohol use are found in all strata of society, a number of factors have been identified as more common in women who are addicted or who use drugs and alcohol abusively.

PROBLEMS COMMONLY IDENTIFIED AMONG ADDICTED WOMEN

Low Socioeconomic Status

Many people believe that abuse of drugs and alcohol is more common among the poor and among minorities. Although this belief is probably only a stereotype, it is often true that, for practical reasons, the women and children included in research studies on prenatal substance abuse are from lower SES groups. In the United States, for cultural and economic reasons, these groups are disproportionately from the ethnic minorities and from the urban areas. It may be that these women are more likely to use drugs and alcohol; however, it also is possible that they are more likely to be identified as users because of public attitudes or because of the way in which research is conducted—that is, in university hospitals and public health clinics (Coles, 1992). For this reason, to understand the effects of drugs on children, it is important to control the effects of social class because being of low SES affects the course of development in children both overall and in specific areas in a variety of ways (i.e., IQ scores, language skills) (Sameroff, Seifer, Brocas, Zak, & Greenspan, 1987).

Two frequently observed patterns are of particular relevance in explaining the experience of children prenatally exposed (Aylward, 1992). First, the pattern of cognitive development in low SES children as measured by standardized tests of infant cognitive development involves an accelerated decline beginning in the second half of the first year (see Figure 1.2). The pattern, in fact, is strikingly similar to that seen in research studies in children of mothers who use alcohol and drugs (Coles & Platzman, 1993; Kaltenbach & Finnegan, 1992; Platzman, Coles, Rubin, & Smith, 1986). This pattern is seen even when the child has not been exposed to any other risk factors, including prenatal drug and alcohol exposure. Therefore, it is clearly possible that the effects of low SES may be mistaken for the effects of drug exposure.

Second, a great deal of research on infants at high risk (Aylward, 1992; Zeskind & Ramey, 1981) has demonstrated that there is an interaction between "risk" status in infancy, which is associated

Mean Bayley scores by drinking group

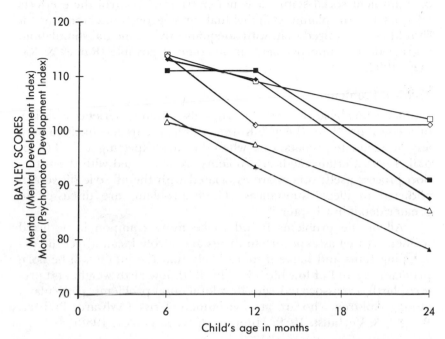

Figure 1.2. The effects of different durations of prenatal alcohol exposure on infants' mental development (MDI) and motor development (PDI) in an economically disadvantaged population. Although there is more deficit of prenatal alcohol exposure when the mother drinks for a longer period in pregnancy (stopped versus continued) than when the mother does not drink (never), the decline in scores associated with social class is much greater than the effects of substance abuse. Scores can be interpreted by comparing to a middle-class population average of 100. (■ = MDI–Never; □ = PDI–Never; ◆ = MDI–Stopped; ◇ = PDI–Stopped; ▲ = MDI–Continued; △ = PDI–Continued)

with biological insults (e.g., low birth weight), and the environmental "risk" resulting from low social status. The classic pattern of environmental exacerbation of biological deficits observed in such children is described by Aylward (1992). In study after study, given the same biological conditions in the neonatal period, by school age, the middle-class child will be without observable effects, while the lower-class child will show significant impairments (Drillien, Thompson, & Burgogne, 1980).

Because of such findings, it is clearly vital that the effects of social class be taken into consideration in evaluating individual children's outcomes as well as in studies of groups of children exposed to drugs. Research studies should include contrast groups drawn from the same SES groups so that SES effects will not be attributed to drug exposure. However, because there is a transactional effect between biological risk and SES, it may be that, even with a group of equivalent social status, it is not possible to control these effects adequately. In planning individual and group interventions, it should be recognized that, with adequate environmental stimulation, a great deal of improvement in outcome is possible (Ramey & Ramey, 1992).

Medical Problems

Women who abuse alcohol and drugs also often experience a variety of medical problems (Levy & Koren, 1990) and are less likely to have any or adequate prenatal care when they are expecting a child (Randall, 1991). Certain medical problems are associated with the addiction process itself; others are associated with the lifestyle of women addicted to illegal substances. These problems are discussed in greater detail in Chapter 2.

All of the problems found to be more common in addicted women, as well as exposure to drugs and alcohol, can affect the developing fetus and make it more likely that the infant will be born prematurely and of low birth weight. Both low birth weight and preterm birth are associated with developmental problems, particularly among children who are at environmental risk (Aylward, Pfeiffer, Wright, & Verhulst, 1989; Hunt, Cooper, & Tooley, 1988).

Comorbidity

It has been observed that women who are addicted to psychoactive drugs are likely to have a number of associated mental health and social problems (Smith, Raskind-Hood, Coles, & Sowemimo, 1992). Many of them have been reared in families made dysfunctional by substance abuse. In addition, many women in treatment report histories of physical and sexual abuse during childhood as well as sexual and physical abuse during adulthood (Wallen & Berman, 1993). As a result, such women may exhibit the symptoms of posttraumatic stress disorder (PTSD) including anxiety, depression, physiological reactions, acting out behavior, and other related symptoms (American Psychiatric Association, 1994). These problems probably contribute to the development of addiction and interfere with recovery. Unfortunately, such histories also are known to be associated with difficulties in parenting and an increased prevalence of abuse and neglect in their own children (Bays, 1990). Because preschool and school-age children who are abused and neglected exhibit symptoms similar to those that are attributed to the effects of cocaine and alcohol in some studies (Pynoos & Eth, 1985; Salizinger, Feldman, Hammer, & Rosario, 1993), it is important to consider the effects of these problems in treating children. Rather than assuming that children's observed behavior can be attributed to the effects of prenatal exposure on brain chemistry, it would be parsimonious first to rule out current environmental stressors.

Mood Disorders

Depression and associated problems are common in adults addicted to alcohol and drugs. Alcohol and the opiates are central nervous system (CNS) depressants, and their use is associated with mood disorders. Cocaine addiction also is associated with depression although the mood fluctuations are likely to be more extreme, ranging from intense euphoria during intoxication to severe depression during withdrawal that may last for weeks. Comparison studies of treated and untreated young women who use cocaine found that approximately one third reported suicidal ideation or suicide attempts as well as significant social problems. (Smith, Dent, Coles, & Falek, 1992; Smith, Raskind-Hood, Coles, & Sowemimo, 1992)

In studies of the effects of maternal depression on parenting and child outcome, significant effects on emotional and developmental status have been identified. Children show effects on both emotional development, in less secure attachments (Radke-Yarrow, Cummings, Kulzynski, & Chapman, 1985) and cognitive development, in decrements in performance on cognitive tests (Sameroff, Seifer, & Zak, 1982). Field, Healy, Goldstein, and Guthertz (1990) present data that suggest that these effects may result from differences in the early pattern of interaction between mother and child.

Finally, women who are addicted to alcohol and drugs are often in situations characterized by high stress and low social support. Some women have become alienated from families because of the addiction process or other problems. Other women have partners who are themselves addicts or who are physically or emotionally abusive. Research on the relationship between stress and drug use has indicated that stressful life events in the absence of social, financial, and emotional support contribute significantly to relapse in individuals who abuse drugs (Leukefeld & Tims, 1989). Women who are addicted and socially isolated are likely to experience stress and depression during pregnancy and postpartum and may have a more difficult time in caring for children than other women because of these problems. There is evidence that children of women who are addicted pre- and postnatally are at higher risk for abuse and neglect (Bays, 1990; Kelley, 1992; Regan, et al., 1987) and for developing antisocial behavior and depression as early as the preschool period (Fitzgerald et al., 1993). Children who are abused and neglected are at higher risk for developmental delay (Allen & Wasserman, 1985). Neglected children are also at risk of failing to form an attachment to caregivers as well as all the problems associated with such failure (Ainsworth, Blehar, Waters, & Wall, 1978).

SUMMARY

It is clear that children who have parents who are substance abusers are at risk for many problems. In addition to the direct physical impact of prenatal exposure, there are significant environmental factors to be considered when investigating the developmental effects of prenatal drug and alcohol exposure. Unfortunately, environmental issues have, for the most part, not received the same attention as have the teratogenic effects of various drugs. It can be hoped that this oversight will be corrected in future research. However, in practical terms, those who work with children and families cannot afford to ignore these factors in planning for prevention, evaluation, and treatment.

REFERENCES

Abel, E.L., & Bilitzke, P. (1990). Paternal alcohol exposure: Paradoxical effect in mice and rats. *Psychopharmacology, 100*(2), 159–164.

Abel, E.L., & Sokol, R.J. (1991). A revised conservative estimate of the incidence of FAS and its economic impact. *Alcoholism: Clinical and Experimental Research, 15,* 514–524.

Ainsworth, M.D.S., Blehar, M.C., Waters, E., & Wall, S. (Eds.). (1978). *Patterns of attachment: A psychological study of the stranger situation.* Hillsdale, NJ: Lawrence Erlbaum Associates.

Allen, R., & Wasserman, G.A. (1985). Origins of language delay in abused infants. *Child Abuse and Neglect, 9,* 335–340.

American Psychiatric Association. (1994). *Diagnostic and statistical manual of mental disorders* (4th ed.). Washington, DC: Author.

Anokute, C.C. (1986). Epidemiology of spontaneous abortions: The effects of alcohol consumption and cigarette smoking. *Journal National Medical Association, 78,* 771–775.

Aylward, G.P. (1992). The relationship between environmental risk and developmental outcome. *Developmental and Behavioral Pediatrics, 13*(3), 222–229.

Aylward, G.P., Pfeiffer, S.I., Wright, A., & Verhulst, S.J. (1989). Outcome of low birthweight infants over the last decade: A meta-analysis. *Journal of Pediatrics, 115,* 515–520.

Bays, J. (1990). Substance abuse and child abuse: The impact of addiction on the child. *Pediatric Clinics of North America, 37*(4), 881–904.

Bradley, R.H., Caldwell, B.M., Rock, S.L., Barnard, K.E., Gray, C., Siegel, L., Ramey, C.T., Gottfried, A.W., & Johnson, D.L. (1989). Home environment and cognitive development in the first 3 years of life: A collaborative study involving six sites and three ethnic groups in North America. *Developmental Psychology, 25*, 217–235.

Burns, K., Chetnik, L., Burns, W.J., & Clark, R. (1991). Dyadic disturbances in cocaine-abusing mothers and their infants. *Journal of Clinical Psychology, 47*(2), 316–319.

Chasnoff, I.J., Landress, H.J., & Barrett, M.E. (1990). The prevalence of illicit drug use or alcohol use during pregnancy and discrepancies in mandatory reporting in Pinellas County, Florida. *New England Journal of Medicine, 322*, 1202–1206.

Coles, C.D. (1992). How the environment affects research on parental drug exposure: The laboratory and the community. In NIDA Research Monograph: *Measurement Issues in Epidemiological, Prevention, and Treatment Research on the Effects of Prenatal Drug Exposure on Women and Children, 117*, 271–292.

Coles, C.D., & Platzman, K.A. (1993). Behavioral effects of prenatal exposure to alcohol and drugs. *International Journal of the Addictions, 28*(13), 1393–1433.

Davis, S.K. (1990). Chemical dependency in women: A description of its effects and outcome on adequate parenting. *Journal of Substance Abuse Treatment, 7*, 225–232.

Day, N.L., Cottreau, C.M., & Richardson, G.A. (1993). The epidemiology of alcohol, marijuana, and cocaine use among women of childbearing age and pregnant women. *Clinical Obstetrics and Gynecology, 36*(2), 232–245.

Drillien, L.A., Thompson, A.J.M., & Burgogne, K. (1980). Low birthweight children at early school age. A longitudinal study. *Developmental Medicine and Child Neurology, 22*, 26–47.

Field, T., Healy, G., Goldstein, S., & Guthertz, M. (1990). Behavior state matching and synchrony in mother/infant interactions of nondepressed versus depressed dyads. *Developmental Psychology, 26*(1), 7–14.

Fitzgerald, H.E., Sullivan, L.A., Ham, H.P., Zucker, R.A., Bruckel, S., Schneider, S., Schneider, A.M., & Noll, R.B. (1993). Predictors of behavior problems in three-year-old sons of alcoholics: Early evidence for the onset of risk. *Child Development, 64*(1), 110–123.

Hollingshead, W.H., Griffin, J.F., Scot, H.D., Burke, M.E., Coustan, D.R., & Vest, T.A. (1990). Statewide prevalence of illicit drug use by pregnant women-Rhode Island. *Morbidity and Mortality Weekly Report 39*(14), 225–227.

Hunt, J.V., Cooper, B.A.B., & Tooley, W.H. (1988). Very low birthweight at 8 and 11 years of age: Role of neonatal illness and family status. *Pediatrics, 82*, 596–603.

Kaltenbach, K.A., & Finnegan, L.P. (1992). Prenatal opiate exposure: Physical, neurobehavioral, and developmental effects. In M. Miller (Ed.), *Development of the central nervous system: Effects of alcohol and opiates* (pp. 36–46). New York: Wiley-Liss.

Kelley, S.J. (1992). Parenting stress and child maltreatment in drug-exposed children. *Child Abuse and Neglect, 16*, 317–328.

Leukefeld, C.G., & Tims, F.M. (1989). Relapse and recovery in drug abuse: Research and practice. *International Journal of the Addictions, 24*(3), 189–202.

Levy, M., & Koren, G. (1990). Obstetric and neonatal effects of drugs of abuse: Emergency aspects of drug abuse. *Emergency Medicine Clinics of North America, 8*(3), 633–652.

Little, R.E., & Sing, C.F. (1986) Association of father's drinking and infant's birthweight. *New England Journal of Medicine, 314*(25), 1644–1645.

May, P.A., Hymbaugh, K.J., Aase, J.M., & Somet, J.M. (1982). Epidemiology of fetal alcohol syndrome among American Indians in the Southwest. *Social Biology, 30,* 374–387.

Monteiro, M.G., & Schuckit, M.A. (1988). Populations at high alcoholism risk: Recent findings. *Journal of Clinical Psychiatry, 49*(9) (Suppl.), 3–7.

National Association for Perinatal Addiction Research and Education, 1988. (1989, October). Innocent addicts: High rate of parental drug abuse found. *ADAMHA News.*

National Institute on Drug Abuse. (1992). *National household survey on drug abuse: Population estimates, 1991, revised.* (DHHS Publication No. ADM 92-1887). Washington, DC: U.S. Government Printing Office.

Platzman, K.A., Coles, C.D., Rubin, C.P., & Smith, I.E. (1986, March). *Developmental profiles of infants with fetal alcohol syndrome and fetal alcohol effects.* Paper presented at the Southeastern Psychological Association Annual Meeting, Orlando, FL.

Pynoos, R.S., & Eth, S. (1985). Children traumatized by witnessing acts of personal violence: Homicide, rape or suicide behavior. In S. Eth & R.S. Pynoos (Eds.), *Post traumatic stress disorder in children* (pp. 17–43). Washington, DC: American Psychiatric Association.

Radke-Yarrow, M., Cummings, E.M., Kulzynski, L., & Chapman, M. (1985). Patterns of attachment in two- and three-year-olds in normal families and families with parental depression. *Child Development, 56,* 884–893.

Ramey, C.T., & Ramey, S.L. (1992).Effective early intervention. *Mental Retardation, 6,* 337–345.

Randall, T. (1991). Intensive prenatal care may deliver healthy babies to pregnant drug abusers. *Journal of the American Medical Association, 265*(21), 19–20.

Regan, D.O., Ehrlich, S.M., & Finnegan, L.P. (1987). Infants of drug addicts: At risk for child abuse, neglect, and placement in foster care. *Neurotoxicology and Teratology, 9,* 315–319.

Rosett, H.L., & Weiner, L. (1984). *Alcohol and the fetus: A clinical perspective.* New York: Oxford University Press.

Russell, M. (1985). Alcohol abuse and alcoholism in the pregnant woman: Identification and intervention. *Alcohol Health Research World, 10,* 28–31.

Salizinger, S., Feldman, R.S., Hammer, M., & Rosario, M. (1993). The effects of physical abuse on children's social relationships. *Child Development, 64*(1), 152–168.

Sameroff, A.J., Seifer, R., Brocas, R., Zak, M., & Greenspan, S. (1987). Intelligence quotient scores of 4-year-old children: Social-environmental risk factors. *Pediatrics, 79,* 343–350.

Sameroff, A.J., Seifer, R., & Zak, M. (1982). Early development of children at risk for emotional disorder. *Monographs of the Society for Research on Child Development, 47*(7), 1–82.

Scialli, A.R. (1992). *A clinical guide to reproductive and developmental toxicology.* Boca Raton, FL: CRC Press, Inc.

Smith, I.E., Dent, D.Z., Coles, C.D., & Falek, A. (1992). A comparison study of treated and untreated pregnant and postpartum cocaine-using women. *Journal of Substance Abuse Treatment, 9,* 343–348.

Smith, I.E., Raskind-Hood, C., Coles, C.D., & Sowemimo, D. (1992, June). *Working with a complexity of issues: Co-morbidity in addicted women.* Paper presented at the Committee for Problems in Drug Dependency Annual Meeting: Keystone, CO.

Sullivan, W.C. (1899). A note on the influence of maternal inebriety on the offspring. *Journal of Mental Science, 45,* 489.

Terman, L.M., & Merrill, M.A. (1972). *Stanford-Binet Intelligence Scale* (3rd ed.) (Form L–M). Boston: Houghton-Mifflin.

Volpe, J.J. (1991). Effect of cocaine use on the fetus. *New England Journal of Medicine, 327*(6), 399–407.

Vorhees, C.V. (1986). Principles of behavior teratology. In E.P. Riley & C.V. Vorhees (Eds.), *Handbook of behavioral teratology,* (pp. 23–48). New York: Plenum Press.

Wallen, J., & Berman, K. (1993). Possible indicators of childhood sexual abuse for individuals in substance abuse treatment. *Journal of Child Sexual Abuse, 1*(3), 63–74.

Wilson, J.G. (1977). Current status of teratology. In J.G. Wilson & F.C. Fraser (Eds.), *Handbook of teratology, 1,* (pp. 47–74). New York: Plenum.

Zeskind, P.S., & Ramey, C.T. (1981). Preventing intellectual and interactional sequelae of fetal malnutrition: A longitudinal, transactional and synergistic approach to development. *Child Development, 52,* 213–218.

Zuckerman, B., Frank, D.A., Hingson, R., Amaro, H., Levenson, S.M., & Kayne, H. (1989). Effects of maternal marijuana and cocaine use on fetal growth. *New England Journal of Medicine, 320,* 762–768.

2

Addiction and Recovery: Impact of Substance Abuse on Families

Claire D. Coles

Substance abuse is usually a family problem. Not only the person who is chemically dependent, but all those who come into regular contact with the individual who is addicted are affected, especially family members. In addition, it has long been recognized that alcoholism "runs in the family" (i.e., the children of parents who are alcoholics are more likely than other children to abuse alcohol themselves when they reach adulthood) (Schuckit, 1991). It also is believed that families with substance abuse problems are dysfunctional and, for this reason, do not provide the optimal environment for rearing children (Bijur, Kuron, Overpeck, & Scheidt, 1992; Woodside, 1986).

Delia and Mario
Early in his second grade year, 7-year-old Mario was transferred from one public school to another. Initially, his teacher noticed that he was quiet and withdrawn but did not have a behavior problem. However, he had difficulty concentrating on his work, and on his first tests he was not able to perform as well as most of the children his age. After a few weeks, he became increasingly restless and began fight-

25

ing with the other boys. His teacher had difficulty controlling him in class. She suspected that he had attention-deficit/hyperactivity disorder (ADHD), but when she tried to reach his parents, she discovered that he had been living with his maternal aunt since his mother was arrested earlier in the fall.

His mother, Delia, now 27, had a troubled history. She was one of seven children who grew up in a low-income, minority ghetto in an urban area. Her mother, an alcoholic, died in her early 40s of cirrhosis of the liver. Like many substance abusers, Delia's mother felt most comfortable with people who had similar habits and had married a man who also drank heavily. After her mother died, Delia moved in with her father's relatives, with whom she lived until adolescence. During childhood, Delia was abused both physically and sexually but received no treatment despite failing grades at school, frequent absences, and persistent behavior problems. In addition to her mother, Delia's maternal grandparents and one uncle were alcoholics. Family members also smoked heavily and used marijuana recreationally. Delia began smoking cigarettes when she was 10 years old and recalls taking her first drink a few years earlier. She reported that the men who abused her sexually when she was a young teenager gave her marijuana and other drugs, which helped her feel less depressed.

Delia's first child was born when she was 15 and she began to receive Aid to Families with Dependent Children (AFDC) at that time. Mario was born when she was 20 years old and his little sister 3 years later. When Delia came to the attention of the authorities because of the birth of a premature infant with a urine test positive for cocaine, she had experienced six pregnancies and delivered four children. By this time, she had experimented with a number of different illegal drugs as well as alcohol and nicotine. Delia's youngest infant was placed in foster care and the other three children with relatives. The oldest child, a boy, has begun to skip school regularly and has been in minor legal troubles. His family is concerned that he spends too much time with local gang members. Mario is depressed, failing in school, and having behavior problems. His 4-year-old sister is reported to have no problems thus far.

There are several notable things about the story presented in this case study. To an observer, the extent to which drug and alcohol abuse damages the lives of both abusers and family members is striking, but often the people themselves do not recognize the association between substance abuse and what is happening to them. For this family, the negative consequences continue troubling one generation after another; however, there are other factors of great importance including other types of psychopathology and social dysfunction that often accompany substance abuse, as well as the denial of family members and other observers (e.g., Mario's teacher and Michael's psychiatrist in the case study on pp. 45–46) who often fail to recognize that substance abuse is related to the problems they encounter.

To help in understanding such families, in this chapter, the following questions are addressed:

- How do different kinds of substances affect those who use them?
- What causes addiction?
- Are there cultural, ethnic, and gender differences in substance use and addiction?
- How does addiction affect families and children?
- What is involved in treatment and recovery from addiction and substance abuse?

ADDICTIVE AND ABUSED SUBSTANCES

People find ways to misuse many substances, both naturally occurring (e.g., marijuana, opiates) and those created in laboratories (e.g., methamphetamines, barbiturates). Substances that can produce physical and psychological sensations that alter consciousness in some manner and that at least some people find pleasurable are called psychoactive drugs. The most widely used and abused substances in the United States are nicotine and alcohol (National Institute on Drug Abuse, 1992), which are legally available after a certain age. The next most widely misused are probably a variety of prescription drugs that are obtained either legally or illegally. Drugs in this category include amphetamines (e.g., methamphetamine, Ritalin, "speed," "crank"), barbiturates ("downers"), synthetic opiates (e.g., Demerol, Percocet), "tranquilizers" and "muscle relaxants" (e.g., Valium), and sleeping pills (e.g., Seconal). An illegal drug, marijuana ("grass," "dope," "rope," "reefer"), has been used widely for years and probably is used by 5%–15% of the population in the United States (National Institute on Drug Abuse, 1992). Finally, there are a variety of illicit drugs that are used by a small percentage of the population. Heroin ("snow," "skag") has been used by approximately 0.2% of the population and there was an epidemic of heroin use in the 1960s. In the 1980s, cocaine ("coke"), which has been used mostly by the wealthy, became financially available to the less affluent and the "crack" epidemic arose. Crack is a form of cocaine that has been chemically treated to increase purity and to make it more easily and rapidly absorbed. According to the National Institute on Drug Abuse Household Survey (1992) about 2%–5% of the population reported using cocaine in the last year, although use is higher in some groups than in others.

Table 2.1 shows which common drugs fall into various classifications of psychoactive drugs. Prescription drugs and over-the-counter drugs can fall in many classifications.

EFFECTS OF DIFFERENT DRUGS

Physiological Addiction

Some drugs are very physiologically addictive. Frequent exposure to significant quantities of these drugs rapidly leads to dependence and when the drug is no longer taken, withdrawal is obvious and unpleasant. Some widely known drugs in this category are narcotics (e.g., heroin, codeine, opium, Percodan), alcohol, Valium, and barbiturates. These drugs are central nervous system (CNS) depressants, and the subsequent withdrawal symptoms resemble those of influenza, although there also may be hallucinations and unpleasant

Table 2.1. Classifications of psychoactive drugs

Class	Examples
Central nervous system depressants	Alcohol, hypnotics, antianxiety drugs
Central nervous system sympathomimetics	Cocaine, amphetamine, methylphenidate
Opiates	Heroin, morphine, methadone, prescription analgesics
Cannabinols	Marijuana, hashish
Psychedelics/ hallucinogens	Lysergic acid diethylamide (LSD), mescaline, psilocybin
Solvents	Aerosol sprays, glue, tolulene, gasoline, paint thinner
Over-the-counter	Substances that contain atropine, scopolamine, antihistamines
Other	Phencyclidine (PCP), bromides

Adapted with permission from Schuckit, M.A. (1989). *Drug and alcohol abuse: A clinical guide to diagnois and treatment* (3rd ed.). New York: Plenum.

physical sensations (e.g., delirium tremens [DTs], which are associated with alcohol withdrawal).

Possibly the most common highly addictive drug is nicotine. It is so powerful in its action that smokers feel compelled to smoke at frequent intervals during the day despite social sanctions against smoking and strong evidence that this practice is carcinogenic. Withdrawal from this drug is unpleasant and lasts a long time, although it is not life threatening nor as acute as withdrawal from narcotics and alcohol.

Psychological Addiction

Drugs also can be psychologically addicting. Psychological addiction is a subjective term that describes the user's need to have the drug in order to reach what is seen by the user as a maximal level of functioning or to achieve a state of psychological well-being. (Clearly, others might not agree with the addict's interpretation of the effects of the drug.) Some drugs, like cocaine, have such a powerful positive reinforcement associated with use, that they probably are addictive through a process of classical conditioning (i.e., by becoming associated with a powerful positively reinforcing physical experience). However, in the case of cocaine, there may be other physical factors as well. It has been documented that there is a cocaine withdrawal (Gawin & Ellinwood, 1988) that occurs when an individual stops using the drug. This is usually described as a "crash" because the individual becomes depressed and physically exhausted. This period may last 6–10 weeks after the last use of cocaine, following which the user often experiences an upsurge in the desire for the drug that can interfere with recovery. Table 2.2 shows some of the effects of the various categories of drugs on those who take them.

WHAT CAUSES ABUSE AND ADDICTION?

Most people have an opinion about what causes alcoholism and drug addiction (Easthope, 1993). Sometimes this theory is based on academic knowledge or personal experience. Often, it is based on common knowledge and media accounts. Understanding the reasons for addictive behavior is important because, to some extent, how we understand the reasons for addiction affects how we deal with people with such problems and how we design prevention and treatment efforts.

The cause of addiction and drug abuse can be seen as the responsibility of the individual, of the environment or social group, or as a combination of these factors (Easthope, 1993). The theories of

Table 2.2. Psychoactive consequences of abuse of various drugs

Substance	Intoxication	With-drawal	Delirium	With-drawal delirium	Delusional disorder	Mood disorder
Alcohol	X	X		X		X
Amphetamine and related substances	X	X	X		X	
Cannabis	X				X	
Cocaine	X	X	X		X	
Hallucinogen	X (halluci-nosis)				X	X
Inhalant	X					
Nicotine		X				
Opioid	X	X				
Phencyclidine (PCP) and related sub-stances	X		X		X	X
Sedative, hyp-notic, or anxiolytic	X	X		X		

Adapted with permission from Schuckit, M.A. (1989). *Drug and alcohol abuse: A clinical guide to diagnosis and treatment* (3rd ed.). New York: Plenum.

addiction, which are summarized in Figure 2.1, can be classified in this way.

Moral Turpitude

Historically, the moral turpitude viewpoint has been predominant. This theory assumes that abuse of drugs and/or alcohol results from individual weakness or sinfulness. Abuse of drugs and alcohol, although common throughout history, was proscribed by various authorities. Many religions proscribe use of psychoactive substances completely (e.g., Islam). Other faiths (e.g., some Native American faiths, certain Christian faiths) have limited the use of drugs to liturgical purposes. Whatever the method chosen for dealing with the use of intoxicants, abuse or addiction was generally regarded as sinful or taboo and attributed to weakness or immorality on the part of the addict. This view of alcoholism is seen clearly in the Temperance movement in the United States in the 19th and early 20th century. This feeling about addicts persists today. In a study carried out in 1991 by Good, Strickland, and Coles, 26% of the general public, 20% of health care professionals, and 40% of the addicts themselves agreed with the view that addicts were immoral and that legal rather than therapeutic methods should be used to deal with them.

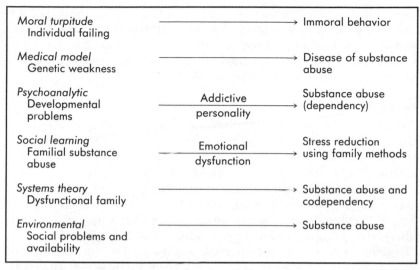

Figure 2.1. Brief theories of substance abuse.

Medical Model

The most commonly espoused view of reasons for addiction among health care professionals, "addictionologists," and alcohol and drug treatment professionals is the "medical model." This model views substance abuse as a disease with the cause often ascribed to a genetic defect. This also is an individual weakness model but in this case the weakness is not attributable to moral failure or sinfulness but to physical weakness that is beyond the control of the individual. Some treatment professionals have compared alcoholism to diabetes. Blum et al. (1990) reported evidence that alcoholism is related to presence or absence of the A1 allele of the dopamine D_2 receptor. Similar studies now are being carried out with cocaine addicts and other drug users, although the evidence for such a relationship is very limited. However, most authors (e.g., Gordis, Tabakoff, Goldman, & Berg, 1990) caution that drug and alcohol abuse, which are very common, are not genetically simple phenomena but, instead, result from complicated processes that include both physical and environmental factors.

Psychoanalytic Theory

A final individual model is the psychoanalytic theory. This view attributes substance abuse to an individual's addictive personality, which makes the person vulnerable to abuse of various chemical substances as well as other habits such as eating disorders (e.g., anorexia), sexual acting out (i.e., sexaholic), and excessive devotion to work (i.e., workaholic). Problems in the resolution of childhood trauma, which interfered with the development of a healthy personality, are seen as the cause of an addictive personality.

Social Learning Theory

Another theory of addiction derived from psychological theories is the social learning model. This theory assumes that the child who is reared in an environment where substance abuse is common will be affected in two ways. First, the child is likely to experience stress as a result of nonoptimal rearing patterns that may persist until adolescence and adulthood. Second, the child learns from observation of his or her family and the general culture that substance use and abuse are appropriate ways to deal with stress. Then, following these "models" of behavior and internalizing them, the individual acts in ways similar to those he or she has observed. Because behaviors associated with substance abuse are often reinforcing in the short term, they tend to be maintained despite the probability of long-term negative consequences.

Systems Theory

Systems theory views substance abuse as the result of a "dysfunctional" family system. In this perspective, the addictive behavior of one or more individuals in the system results from the dynamics of the system, rather than from individual actions or motivation. In addition to the substance abuser (usually the husband), there is a co-dependent (usually the wife) and other family members who maintain the addictive behavior by "enabling" the substance abuser. This view of addiction is also common among addiction treatment professionals and often forms the basis for psychotherapy (Berenson, 1976).

Environmental Theory

The environmental theory of substance abuse attributes use to the situations in which an individual lives. Interpersonal, cultural, organizational, and physical environments have all been investigated for their effects on the development, maintenance, and cessation of addiction as well as the likelihood of relapse (Davis & Tunks, 1990–1991). Interpersonal factors affect the individual most intimately. These include family, peer, and social group influences that interact with the effects of the larger cultural factors, such as social class and ethnic group, to produce attitudes and behaviors. Legal drug use is affected both by these factors and by the greater social norms and cultural values that produce conventional patterns of use. However, illegal drug use appears to be more influenced by the microenvironment, (i.e., by peer and family factors) (Khavari, 1993). Studies have found that illicit drug use often results from a combination of peer influence and stressful family situations, particularly those with low cohesion or structure (Khavari, 1993). However, larger social factors also have effects. Social problems resulting from social inequities can lead to stress and despair and when drugs become widely available in such a situation, they are used by members of minority and financially underprivileged groups to relieve their feelings. In addition, among individuals at high risk who have limited access to the usual occupational roles in this culture, involvement with drugs and drug dealing may seem like a reasonable alternative occupation.

GENDER, CULTURAL, AND ETHNIC DIFFERENCES

Addiction can manifest itself differently in different groups; to use the same criteria for judgment in all cases may lead to errors. Men and women, people in different regions of the United States, and people from different ethnic and religious backgrounds have different attitudes about substance use and show different behaviors.

Gender Differences

Males are approximately five times more likely to receive a diagnosis of alcoholism or drug addiction than are females (Robins & Regier, 1991). This statistic seems to indicate that men are more vulnerable to the effects of drugs and alcohol than are women. However, as the National Institute on Drug Abuse Household Survey (1992) cites, men report much higher levels of both drug and alcohol use across all ethnic and regional categories and are, therefore, exposed to substances of abuse more frequently and more heavily. There are also consistent regional differences in substance use, but across the United States, males report drinking alcohol and using drugs more than females. Table 2.3 shows the pattern of use in men and women in different regions of the United States. Please note that these tables do not show addictive behavior but reported drug use.

However, differences in the amount of use probably do not account completely for the reported differences in incidence of addiction. Sandmaier (1980) reported that female alcoholics are often misdiagnosed as depressed. She suggested that cultural factors accounted for the difference because alcoholism in women is less socially acceptable than in men. However, this difference also may

Table 2.3. Reported substance use by men and women in different regions

Drug	Gender	Northeast Ever (%)	Northeast Last year (%)	North central Ever (%)	North central Last year (%)	South Ever (%)	South Last year (%)	West Ever (%)	West Last year (%)	Total U.S. Ever (%)	Total U.S. Last year (%)
Alcohol	Male	90.3	78.4	91.6	76.9	86.2	64.9	90.0	76.1	89.0	72.7
	Female	83.6	69.5	83.5	67.3	75.1	55.7	83.8	68.4	80.6	63.8
Cigarettes	Male	72.8	32.8	80.4	37.3	77.3	35.2	78.1	32.8	77.3	34.7
	Female	65.2	28.7	70.2	30.0	68.1	30.2	71.0	29.5	68.5	29.7
Marijuana	Male	39.3	12.2	38.5	12.0	33.5	10.2	43.0	14.2	37.8	11.8
	Female	29.5	7.3	28.0	6.4	25.3	7.0	36.6	9.0	29.0	7.3
Cocaine[a]	Male	16.3	4.1	12.2	3.7	11.1	3.1	20.2	6.2	14.3	4.1
	Female	9.1	1.8	7.5	1.8	6.8	1.7	14.7	3.2	9.0	2.0
Heroin[b]	Male	1.4	0.3	1.3	0.2	1.0	0.2	1.9	0.1	1.9	0.2
	Female									1.5	0.2

Sedatives	Male	4.3	0.5	3.4	0.7	4.6	1.2	7.2	1.3	4.8	1.0
	Female	2.3	1.1	3.9	1.1	3.3	0.8	6.2	1.6	3.8	1.1
Stimulants	Male	5.6	1.2	7.4	1.2	7.3	1.4	13.4	2.4	8.2	1.5
	Female	3.4	0.3	5.2	1.0	5.9	1.5	9.7	1.7	5.9	1.2
Inhalants	Male	5.9	1.0	5.4	1.5	6.4	1.7	10.7	2.1	7.0	1.6
	Female	3.3	0.7	3.7	0.8	3.5	0.9	5.9	1.4	4.0	1.0

From National Institute on Drug Abuse. (1992). *National household survey on drug abuse: Population estimates, 1991* (rev. ed.). Rockville, MD: Author.

[a]Includes "crack."

[b]Separate totals for male and female heroin use are unavailable by region.

have occurred because the diagnosis of addiction was developed based on the behavior of males. When these diagnostic characteristics are applied to females, the results may not be accurate.

Male and female substance abusers often show different patterns of behavior. Obviously, men and women with substance abuse problems show a range of behaviors. As with most comparisons of male and female behavior, the similarities probably are greater than the differences. However, there are certain behavior patterns that tend to differentiate the behavior of addicted men from that of addicted women. In part, this may be because of social differences and, in part, because of physical differences.

Addicted men are more likely to show antisocial behaviors including violence directed against others, reckless disregard of their own safety and others, inability to sustain relationships, and criminal activity. For this reason, they often are diagnosed with Antisocial Personality Disorder (American Psychiatric Association, 1994). Addicted men also often have difficulties with maintaining their occupational functioning and show academic and work dysfunction. Automobile accidents and arrests for driving under the influence (DUI) are much more common among men. Not surprisingly, given these behaviors, legal difficulties are also more characteristic of male substance abusers than female substance abusers. This is particularly true when the substance being used is illegal.

In contrast, women are more likely to show depressive symptoms. They also have a higher rate of suicide. Both of these symptoms might result from cultural differences in the stereotyped behavior of men and women. However, these emotional problems may result also from differences in circumstances. Women who abuse substances generally lose their social support and find themselves isolated and without resources. For example, although wives of alcoholic men usually stay with their mates, 9 of 10 husbands of alcoholic women leave the marriage (Reed, 1985). Female alcoholics more often than male alcoholics have significant physical problems and neurological damage as a result of abuse. Although there has been little research on why women have more physical problems, Frezza et al. (1990) have reported that prolonged alcohol abuse leads to an impairment of the body's ability to produce alcohol dehydrogenase, which is an enzyme that helps in the metabolism of alcohol. These researchers also found that the production of dehydrogenase was more impaired in women who drank heavily than in men. This deficiency allows a greater concentration of alcohol to enter the blood stream and the liver. This gender difference may explain why women are more likely to have liver damage and why they develop cirrhosis more rapidly than men with similar patterns of use.

Cultural and Ethnic Differences

There are differences in the rate of use of various drugs among different groups in the United States, as well as in different regions (National Institute on Drug Abuse, 1992). Table 2.4 presents the results of a survey of drug and alcohol use among different ethnic groups. However, these summary scores, which "average" the responses of individuals of particular groups, probably present a much too simplified picture. Study of cultural and ethnic differences in substance use and abuse is difficult because of the many differences in these various groups in the United States. For instance, all groups of White or "Anglo" Americans are not the same in cultural background or attitudes toward substance use. Immigrant Italian families in New York City probably have different customs regarding alcohol use than do Baptists in Mississippi. To take another example, it is not possible to talk about use by Hispanics without consideration of class differences, differences in country of origin, and whether the individual is a recent immigrant or has been born in the United States. Research that goes beyond labeling by ethnic group indicates that there are significant differences in rates and patterns of alcohol use among various Hispanic groups living in the United States—Cuban, Latin American, Puerto Rican, and Mexican—so that is is impossible to generalize to "all Hispanics" (National Institute on Alcohol Abuse and Alcoholism [NIAAA], 1993). Therefore, although surveys indicate that White, well-educated men in the Northeast have a higher probability of use, particularly of alcohol, and low-income, Black women in the Southeast have the lowest probability of use, it is not possible to know about people's individual use based on their ethnic origin or other demographic characteristics.

Nevertheless, it is important to understand that members of different ethnic and cultural groups may have different attitudes about substance use that can affect their behavior and influence their response to a problem with addiction. For instance, if "macho" male behavior is the cultural norm and this value is associated with being able to drink heavily, such behavior may not be seen as inappropriate by family members even when it is having negative consequences.

RECOVERY FROM ALCOHOLISM AND DRUG ABUSE

Addiction is a fearful thing. It brings with it the specter of loss of control and of loss of a loved one to a physically and emotionally destructive process. Many people believe that a person who has been addicted never recovers from it although they may become "sober." Alcoholics often refer to themselves as "recovering" rather than

Table 2.4 Reported substance use by men and women in three ethnic groups

		Ethnic group					
		White		African American		Hispanic	
Drug	Gender	Ever (%)	Last year (%)	Ever (%)	Last year (%)	Ever (%)	Last year (%)
Alcohol	Male	90.6	73.6	84.2	66.1	86.0	75.0
	Female	83.2	66.6	74.7	54.5	68.9	54.9
Cigarettes	Male	79.8	34.3	70.2	36.2	70.7	35.8
	Female	72.2	30.7	61.3	28.6	50.7	24.8
Marijuana	Male	37.6	11.1	44.4	17.1	34.4	12.5
	Female	30.2	7.4	28.6	8.2	20.1	5.0
Cocaine[a]	Male	14.2	3.8	15.7	5.3	15.1	5.2
	Female	9.5	1.8	7.5	2.7	7.3	2.3
Heroin[b]	Male	1.2	0.1	1.9	0.4	1.5	0.4
	Female						

Sedatives						
Male	5.0	1.0	3.3	1.1	4.2	0.9
Female	4.2	1.1	2.9	1.2	1.8	0.6
Stimulants						
Male	9.1	1.6	3.3	1.0	6.5	1.0
Female	6.7	1.2	3.3	0.9	3.1	1.1
Inhalants						
Male	7.3	1.6	4.9	1.4	6.3	1.3
Female	4.1	0.9	2.9	1.2	3.3	1.1

From National Institute on Drug Abuse. (1992). *National household survey on drug abuse: Population estimates, 1991* (rev. ed.). Rockville, MD: Author.

[a] Includes "crack."

[b] Separate totals for male and female heroin use are unavailable for ethnic group.

"recovered." How and why addicts recover and which ones do are currently subjects for research (NIAAA, 1993). However, while research goes on, many different approaches to treatment are being used. These approaches can be categorized as physical methods, which are based on a biological and medical model; psychological methods, which try to change the individual's behavior or the system from which the person comes; and social methods, which use social coercion or persuasion.

Physical Methods

Drug Therapy   As a society, Americans often turn to medications for help in solving problems. (It may be for this reason that Americans have a problem with substance abuse.) Drugs are often used as therapy in the treatment of addiction. This is particularly true during the initial stages of detoxification when the addict is no longer taking the substance of abuse and may go through an uncomfortable withdrawal period. Drugs may be used during this time to reduce the negative symptoms of withdrawal. Benzodiazepines (e.g., Valium, Ativan) are used to manage alcohol withdrawal (Liskow & Goodwin, 1987), and certain opiates and other sedatives may be used in opiate withdrawal. For example, paregoric is given to newborns who are experiencing severe withdrawal symptoms (Finnegan & Kaltenbach, 1992), and nicotine patches have gained great acceptance in the treatment of cigarette smoking because they reduce the symptoms of nicotine withdrawal.

Drugs are used in other ways in treatment. During recovery from alcoholism, disulfiram (Antabuse) may be used. This is an alcohol-sensitizing agent that causes an individual to react with noxious physical symptoms if he or she drinks alcohol. These symptoms include flushing, nausea, vomiting, and cardiovascular changes (NIAAA, 1993).

Addiction to various opiates including opium, morphine, and heroin has troubled society repeatedly during different eras. For example, the invention of the hypodermic needle in 1840 led to an upswing in opiate use. Although there were morphine maintenance clinics in the early 1900s, it was not until the development of methadone in the 1960s that this type of treatment became common (Weddington, 1990–1991). At this time, an epidemic of heroin abuse was in progress and addiction was becoming defined as a medical disorder (Dole & Nyswander, 1965). Methadone, an artificial opiate with some of the biochemical properties of heroin but without the pleasurable psychoactive properties of that drug, could be substituted for it. Although addicts remained addicted to methadone and had to report daily to a treatment clinic to receive the drug, they were no longer dependent on the illegal drug heroin and could be rehabilitated socially. Initially, methadone maintenance was seen as an adjunct to counseling and rehabilitation; however, because of cost, it is now often the only service offered narcotic addicts over the long term.

Acupuncture Acupuncture, a traditional Chinese treatment, currently is being studied for effectiveness as a treatment for addiction. In fact, it is one of the four accepted treatment protocols used in drug treatment in New York City.

Psychological Methods

Therapies based on behavior processes are often used in the treatment of addiction. In part, this is so because of theories that personality development and learned behavior are etiological factors in addiction and, in part, because of a belief that social and group factors contribute to the addiction and would, presumably, contribute to the recovery.

Group Therapy Group therapy is usually a part of traditional "28-day" treatment programs for addicts. After detoxification, addicts are kept in inpatient treatment and participate in a number of different group therapies that are intended to produce changes in attitude or behavior.

Family Therapy Family therapy focuses on the addict's immediate family as a usual part of the treatment process. Families of addicts are often seen as negatively affected by their experience with the addict. In addition, many therapists believe that treating the family, particularly the spouse, of the addict contributes to long-term abstinence (McCardy et al., 1986). Without changes in the environment, many addicts have difficulty maintaining sobriety.

Individual Psychotherapy Individual psychotherapy can be an important part of maintaining recovery, although it is not usually seen as the way in which recovery is brought about. Most therapists believe that it is inappropriate to conduct therapy with an addict who is still using drugs because so many of the behaviors that are observed are the result of the alcohol or drugs rather than underlying personality processes.

However, it is very likely that addiction is comorbid with many emotional problems that eventually require treatment. For example, it has been observed (Wallen & Berman, 1993) that many women who abuse alcohol and drugs were sexually abused as children. When sober, the women often reexperience the anxiety and other symptoms of posttraumatic stress disorder as well as the low self-esteem that led to the initial drug and alcohol use. Therapy at this point can prevent relapse as well as lead to better emotional and social functioning.

Classical Conditioning A treatment based on learning theory involves classical conditioning. Using this method, the substance that was abused is paired with a noxious stimulus like an emetic, which causes nausea and vomiting, or with an electric shock, which is painful. Over time, the individual receiving such treatment should build up a conditioned avoidance response to the substance. This outcome generally occurs, but it is often specific to the setting in which treatment occurred and not very effective in the outside world where the negative contingencies are much more remote and where the addict has more control.

In cocaine addiction, which is probably maintained by a classical conditioning process, treatment often focuses on identifying the "cues" or environmental factors that "trigger" craving for cocaine. Such triggers may include a cocaine pipe, a particular physical setting, or a time of day when use was habitual. The recovering addict is then given strategies for dealing with these cues without using the drug. Interestingly, similar factors are at work in the maintenance of nicotine use, and many people who try to stop smoking find that they have to change other habits to avoid cuing a desire for a cigarette.

Social Methods

A number of social methods have been tried to reduce or eliminate addiction or to help the recovering addict remain sober.

Legal With some regularity, American society attempts to solve drug-related social and medical problems using legal methods. The two most commonly used legal methods for dealing with substance abuse are prohibition and prosecution.

Although drug use has been common in America for centuries, in the beginning of the 20th century, more emphasis began to be placed on legal methods of control (Weddington, 1990–1991). In 1914, as the result of a persistent problem with opiate abuse, the Harrison Act was passed instituting criminal penalties for the importation, sale, or possession of opiates except for legitimate medical uses. In 1918, the 18th Amendment to the Constitution launched the United States into the "Great Experiment" of Prohibition. The Volstead Act of 1919 prohibited the manufacture and consumption of alcohol. Although the Volstead Act was repealed by 1933, the prohibition of opiates persisted. Currently, a legal rather than a treatment approach is the main focus of government efforts to control the use of cocaine and marijuana.

Prosecution of sellers and users of drugs and alcohol has been more or less enthusiastic at different points in time probably due to cultural and social trends. Because marijuana use was so common among middle-class young people and culturally accepted during the late 1960s and early 1970s, several states decriminalized its use (e.g., Alaska). In contrast, during the 1980s and 1990s, legal methods have been used against pregnant drug users to prevent prenatal exposure to cocaine, and enforcement of laws against marijuana use and driving when intoxicated has been much more vigorous.

Medicalization and Hospitalization Another social approach is to declare addiction a disease and to provide medical care for addicts. This approach is currently very popular. Addicts are frequently hospitalized, although once they have been detoxified, there is little justification for this expensive form of treatment. For most addicts, outpatient treatment is equally effective and much less expensive. However, the outpatient approach has not been very successful in treating cocaine addicts, and residential treatment is being tried as an alternative.

Rehabilitation Originally, rehabilitation was designed to help those who, because of their addiction, had lost their occupation and family support, and had few choices remaining to them when sobriety was finally achieved. This pattern is often observed in older addicts. However, advocates of rehabilitation point out that many addicts, particularly adolescents and people in their 20s, have never been habilitated at all. Unfortunately, because of the long period of drug use during development, these people lack the life skills to function adequately in society. Even if such people become sober after detoxification and a month of hospitalization and acute treatment, they are often not ready to function independently in society. Halfway houses, residential programs, and retraining programs have been established to provide the type of "aftercare" that many addicts need in order to become functional adults.

Self-Help Groups One of the major factors in recovery from addiction are self-help groups. The original addiction-focused, self-help group was Alcoholics Anonymous (AA), which was founded by a recovering alcoholic. There are now a number of other groups including Narcotics Anonymous (NA); Cocaine Anonymous (CA); AlAnon, a group for relatives of alcoholics; Alateen, for teenage children affected by alcoholism; and even Alatot for young children, who are brought by their caregivers. In addition, this model has been used in the establishment of a number of other programs directed at different conditions (e.g., Overeaters Anonymous). Because these groups have, as basic tenets, 12 steps that the recovering person is supposed to follow, they generally are called "12-Step Programs." Although these programs often do not allow research to be carried out with their members, it is widely believed that they are very effective in helping people overcome addiction. For this reason, many programs include a 12-Step Program as part of the aftercare plan.

FAMILIAL PATTERNS OF DRUG AND ALCOHOL ABUSE

Addictive behavior seems to be more common in some families than in others. Children of alcoholics have a 4 times higher risk of becoming alcoholics than children of nonalcoholics (Schuckit, 1991). This finding may indicate either that children learn these patterns of substance abuse at home or that there is a biological or genetic basis for alcoholism. Twin studies and adoption studies have been used to investigate this question. Twin studies are used because identical twins are siblings who share the same genetic makeup while fraternal (nonidentical) twins are no more genetically similar than other brothers and sisters. However, both types of twins share the same rearing environments and should, therefore, have the same behaviors if the caregiving environment is responsible for the behavioral trait. Therefore, by comparing the risk for becoming alcoholic in identical and fraternal twins, it is possible to compute the relative effects of genetic and environmental influences (Schuckit, 1981). The probability of showing the same trait as the parent is called "heritability."

Another way this issue is studied is through adoption studies of children of parents who are substance abusers. Adoption studies look at the rates of substance abuse in the children who have been separated from their biological parents and adopted compared to the rates in both sets of parents (biological and adoptive). Studies of this sort have found a higher rate of alcoholism in adopted children whose biological parents are alcoholics (Cadoret, Cain, & Grove, 1980) than would have been expected based on the rates in their adoptive families. These studies suggest that there may be a genetic component to alcoholism. However, the pattern of results also indicates that the process is complicated and not controlled by a single gene and that there are important environmental factors at work as well (Schuckit, 1991).

That environmental factors are also very important is shown by another statistic. Offspring of substance abusers, particularly alcoholics, are much more likely than others to be abstainers, who avoid substance use completely. In fact, they are more likely to be abstainers than to be alcoholics (Harburg, DiFranceisco, Webster, Gleiberman, & Schork, 1990). This finding suggests that, based on their early experiences with alcohol, adult children often make the decision to avoid using this substance completely. So, rather than being helpless in the face of a genetic predisposition to addiction, the majority of offspring choose to avoid imitating the problems they observed in their parents. This finding raises questions about co-factors that are probably present in individuals who become addicted themselves.

Lisa and Michael

Lisa was 16 years old when she accepted a lift home from a party on the back of a motorcycle driven by her intoxicated boyfriend. In the resulting accident, her pelvis was crushed and she received multiple fractures in both legs, injuries that required several operations and a year lost from school. After the accident, when the police called her parents, her mother was home but her father, a surgeon, was not. He was in the hospital recovering from a suicide attempt. His diagnosis was depression. Lisa, who had been an "A" student at a private school, had not told anyone at school about her father although her friends knew that she was drinking heavily and using pills on the weekends. Neither parent appeared to be aware of her problems. Her father, Michael, had been addicted to alcohol and prescription drugs since he was involved in a malpractice suit several years previously.

Michael was the only child in a middle-class family. He graduated from an Ivy league university and an eastern medical school and married a pretty, somewhat younger and less educated woman. He always described his marriage as a "rescue" because his wife came from a "dysfunctional" family with an alcoholic father who had deserted his wife and daughters. Both Michael and his wife drank socially, although Michael had some anxiety about drinking due to his own father's heavy alcohol use. When he was in his early 40s, Michael was sued by a patient and, although he won the case in court and his practice was unaffected, he became depressed and began drinking more heavily. His marriage began to deteriorate and his teenage children became withdrawn and uncommunicative at home. Around this time, Michael began an affair with his nurse, who became pregnant, and he began to use the prescription drugs that were available to him to control stress. Eventually, as problems increased, he consulted a psychiatrist colleague, who prescribed a number of psychotropic medications for depression and anxiety. Michael never mentioned his substance abuse to his psychiatrist, who never questioned him about these issues. Michael's wife informed the psychiatrist of her husband's drug and alcohol abuse and questioned him about possible interactions with the antidepressants and antianxiety drugs he was prescribing, but Michael received no treatment for substance abuse and his medication was not changed. Eventually Michael attempted suicide, slashing his wrists in his bathroom but timing the attempt so that his son could discover him when he came home from school. Michael recovered after receiving inpatient treatment for substance abuse and depression although he and his wife were divorced. Lisa recovered from the motorcycle accident and eventually entered a prestigious college where she was on the dean's list. During her freshman year, she began dating an attractive young man who drank heavily but denied having any problems with alcohol.

Children whose parents abuse substances can be affected in a variety of other ways; however, the extent of the effects depends on the extent to which the child's environment is affected. This depends on how "dysfunctional" the family is or becomes, how much other pathology is present, the extent to which addiction affects the family's financial status, and how the relationship between parent and child is maintained or impaired. Therefore, understanding the effects of addiction on the family and providing ways to prevent negative consequences on the children requires knowledge of many factors.

Effects of parental substance abuse on children have been studies both by clinicians involved in treatment and by professional researchers. Because of their different foci and approaches to the problem, these groups have sometimes come to different conclusions. The clinical or treatment literature and the publications of the Adult Children of Alcoholics (ACOA) movement present one picture (Brown, 1991; Sher, 1991) and the research literature sometimes presents another (Sher, 1991). In addition, some groups have been studied more than others and there is very limited understanding of the specific problems experienced by children of users of illicit drugs despite considerable concern about them.

Clinical Observations of Effects on Children

In the 1960s and 1970s, attention turned from an exclusive focus on the addict (usually a male alcoholic) to a greater understanding of effects on the family (Steinglass, 1980) and the children (Cork, 1969).

From observations of families and children of addicts and alcoholics presenting for treatment, it is widely believed that parental substance abuse is associated with a higher incidence of abuse, neglect, cognitive and academic problems, hyperactivity, and emotional problems in children. Two patterns of dysfunctional families have been described as associated with addiction; these are the "enmeshed" family, which is stereotypically that of the middle-class alcoholic, and the "unorganized" family, which is stereotypically that of the lower-class drug addict. However, these are indeed stereotypes and should be treated with caution.

Enmeshed Families Families of middle class alcoholics are often described as enmeshed because they limit contact with others outside the family who might provide social support or stimulation for the children. This pattern is believed to be due to unspoken rules that operate in such families, which include "Don't talk, don't trust, don't feel" (Emshoff & Anyon, 1991). These rules have been developed to protect the current organization of the family and support the denial of the substance abuse that is common in such families. Within these highly self-involved families, children's needs may be ignored because the family's attention is focused on the parent who is abusing substances. Often that parent's behavior has to be monitored carefully to avoid negative consequences. For example, much family effort may be expended to avoid provoking a violent reaction from a parent who is intoxicated. Because the family may be dependent on the alcoholic as a breadwinner, much effort may be expended to hide the consequences of the alcoholic's behavior from employers or others outside their family.

The family lives of addicts are often characterized by inconsistency and uncertainty. Discipline may be dependent on whether on not the addict is drinking or abusing drugs. Family rules may apply in one situation and be forgotten in others. A parent who is affectionate and considerate when sober may be violent and inconsiderate when intoxicated. Promises made in one state may not be remembered in others.

It also is widely assumed that parental addiction is associated with higher rates of abuse and neglect of children. Parents who abuse drugs and alcohol are concerned with obtaining drugs or with hiding the consequences of their addiction and may not have the time, energy, and judgment that are required for competent parenting. In addition, many drugs (e.g., alcohol, cocaine) are disinhibiting; that is, use of these drugs may either impair judgment or provide the excuse for acting impulsively so that the individual who would not usually react violently may do so when drinking or using certain drugs. Similarly, much sexual abuse of children occurs in families where substance abuse is common. The drug abuse may be disinhibiting or may be used as an excuse for conduct the abuser wishes to indulge in anyway.

Unorganized Families Families where substance abuse is a problem also may be dysfunctional in other ways. A family pattern that seems to be related to certain types of drug abuse is the "unorganized" pattern. This pattern is often seen among underprivileged individuals but can be observed in middle- and upper-class families as well, so social class should not be used as a sole guideline. In the unorganized (or underorganized) family, the family structure may be more open because of a lack of consistent rules about behavior, lack of supervision of children, single-parent status, financial problems, and similar factors. Children in such situations are often neglected because there may be no adult available to care for them when their parent is abusing drugs and alcohol, and they may be abused sexually due to lack of appropriate supervision. In this type of family, children's basic needs can be overlooked because no one may be taking responsibility for providing for them (Aponte, 1974). Children in such families can have many different responses; however, one pattern that is often seen is the "parentified" child who takes on the care of younger siblings as well as of the incompetent parent. It is not uncommon, in such situations, for school-age children to assume the care of toddlers and infants despite their lack of adult skills.

There is also concern about intellectual and emotional development in families of parents who are substance abusers. For obvious reasons, family environment may not support or facilitate the child's learning. Academic goals for the child may be subservient to more immediate needs for drug seeking and other activities. Children are often described as lacking in self-esteem and as having more psychopathology than other children (Emshoff & Anyan, 1991). Because children have learned that the addicted and abusive parent is not trustworthy, they may fail to trust other people they encounter, which will limit their ability to interact in the world. Like their parents, children may deny their own problems and others' problems and regard being strong in the face of problems as an ideal. This pattern leads to a denial of the person's feelings and a tendency to assume responsibility for caring for others.

Another problem that arises in families where children are neglected is the failure to establish an appropriate attachment to a caregiver during the first few years (Zeanah, Mammen, & Lieberman, 1993). Children without such psychological attachments can grow up without feelings of empathy for other people, and this situation may interfere with appropriate personality development leading to what is called "sociopathic" behavior. It may be for this reason, among others, that Richards, Morehouse, Seisax, and Kern (1983) find that children's outcome is less positive when the mother, rather than the father, is the one addicted because the mother is more likely to be the child's caregiver. Finally, children from families with an addiction are at very high risk for becoming addicted themselves.

Research on the Children of Addicted Families

Although the patterns described above are commonly seen in clinical settings, research support for a specific relationship between such observations and substance abuse has been limited. Sher (1991) has reviewed the research literature on the psychological effects of alcoholism on children in the family.

In reviewing this literature, Sher points out some of the methodological problems in doing research on this topic. An initial problem comes in identification of a group of children or "adult children" who can be described as children of addicts or substance abusers. Although this may seem a simple problem, the difficulty is in defining alcoholism or drug abuse, retrospectively (after the fact). The identification is usually made by questioning offspring about parental and family substance-abuse patterns and relying on this information for classification. A second problem arises in finding an appropriate group to sample. If people are selected from those applying for treatment from mental health providers, there is a built-in bias because people who come for treatment are, by definition, experiencing problems. There may be other individuals from similar families who are not experiencing distress and not being identified for this reason.

The age at which people are selected for inclusion is also of concern. Because problems can arise at different times, if no problems are identified in a group of adolescents, it might be argued, for instance, that the difficulties will not appear until later, during adulthood.

Even when these methodological considerations are taken into account, there are findings of interest resulting from research studies. ACOAs and children whose parents abuse other drugs have been reported to be at higher risk (Bernardi, Jones, & Tennant, 1989; Bijur et al., 1992) and to have a variety of subsequent problems in emotional development (Woodside, 1986). However, when studies of children of alcoholics and other addicts are compared to studies of children of parents with other types of psychopathology, it is clear that there are similar problems with children of most parents who show significantly deviant behavior. Indeed, it seems as though the kinds of emotional problems shown by ACOAs (e.g., depression, low self-esteem) do not appear to be specific to children of alcoholics. Rather, these problems appear to be common to people who are reared in dysfunctional families.

One of the most frequently identified problems in ACOAs is attention-deficit/hyperactivity disorder (ADHD). For this reason, many people (Goodwin, Schulsinger, Hermansen, Guze, & Winokur, 1975; Wood, Wender, & Reimherr, 1983) have speculated on the relationship between this disorder and alcoholism and other forms of substance abuse. In some cases (Gold & Sherry, 1984) it is assumed that prenatal exposure to drugs and alcohol leads to attention deficits. Others believe that substance abuse may be a self-medication for the problems associated with ADHD. However, as Sher (1991) notes, problems in discriminating ADHD from conduct disorder as well as insecure attachment and other disorders make it difficult to rely on findings in this area. This is clearly an area that should be viewed with caution and will require more research.

In contrast, there does seem to be a strong relationship between conduct disorder and parental alcoholism and drug abuse. Children of addicts are more likely than children in the general population to receive a diagnosis of conduct disorder and often show the individual behaviors (e.g., skipping school, stealing, poor impulse control) associated with this disorder. However, in studies that have controlled for other parental factors (e.g., divorce, parental pathology, poverty), the relationship is no longer apparent (Offord, Allen, & Abrams, 1978). A similar pattern is seen in studies of parental depression and anxiety. These findings suggest that substance abuse is one disorder that can interfere with parenting significantly and that other conditions that interact with substance abuse must be taken into consideration as well in understanding the effects of parental addiction in children.

Academic achievement and school performance also have been investigated in such children. In general, these studies have shown that the ACOAs function within the normal range, but generally do less well than controls who come from more functional families (Knop, Teasdale, Schulsinger, & Goodwin, 1985; Wilson, McCreary, Kean, & Baxter, 1979). The reasons for these differences have not been identified; however, it is possible to speculate that children in such families find that the stresses of their daily lives interfere with their concentration on academics.

Protective Factors There is evidence that many children growing up in families plagued by substance abuse have significant problems in development and can experience negative consequences in adulthood. However, many children do not experience such consequences and function normally in adulthood. For that reason, protective factors that ameliorate negative outcomes in these children at high risk also have been studied. The results of such studies suggest that children who have better outcomes have had more peer support, are more likely to have had a supportive and nurturing relationship with the nonaddicted parent and to have lived in a family with structure and routines. Negative outcomes were related to having fewer financial resources, greater disorganization, and to earlier parental loss as a result of divorce, death, or other factors (Emshoff & Anyan, 1991).

The Family in Recovery

When the parent who abuses drugs and alcohol begins the recovery process, there are profound effects on the family. Although having a sober parent is certainly a much better situation ultimately, there are a number of short-term problems that can arise.

Reorganization During the parent's addiction, the family is often organized around the substance abuse. Children and spouses develop coping patterns that are appropriate to that situation. Children may learn to make their own decisions about how to conduct their social lives and the amount of freedom they want. When the parent stops using drugs or alcohol, the family has to change many of the coping strategies that were used before to accommodate to the changes in the recovering parent. When the parent begins to "act like a parent" again, the child may not relish restrictions on former freedoms or loss of power within the family. This is a good time for family therapy to help in making this adjustment.

Allowing Time for Healing The substance abuser who has participated in major dysfunctions in the family often returns to resentful and angry children. It is impossible, at this point, to have things the way they were before the addiction became severe. The family has to come to forgiveness of the addict's past behavior and the addict has to allow the family members to do this in their own time.

Making Recovery Part of Daily Living Because recovery has to be continued for the rest of the addict's life, the process and the rituals have to be incorporated into the family's daily routine. For instance, if the recovering alcoholic is going to AA meetings several times a week, the family should find a way to accommodate this commitment. Changes also can be made in routines that previously were associated with drug abuse. Therefore, if adult social life previously involved heavy drinking at neighborhood parties, the family has to develop alternative social outlets.

Need for Support Even when the addict has recovered and completed treatment, need for support of sobriety continues. This support may include 12-Step groups, family and individual therapy, and encouragement from the family. It is important that the family recognize that not only the addict but other family members may need help through this time.

THE QUESTION OF INTERPERSONAL VIOLENCE

Parental addiction usually is considered a risk factor for child and marital abuse (Bays, 1990; Leonard & Jacob, 1988.) Bays (1990) noted that there is an increased incidence of violence in such families and that abuse and murder are more common when both marital partners are intoxicated. This increased level of interpersonal violence can be attributed to changes in the status of the abuser (e.g., brain damage, sleep deprivation), to the social situations associated with intoxication, or to cultural expectations about behavior during periods of intoxication.

Other research suggests that sexual and physical abuse in childhood may be associated with later substance abuse (Boyd, 1993; Widom, 1993). Miller (1993) found patterns of early abuse to be more common in women receiving alcoholism treatment than in women requiring other kinds of mental health services. In a different population, Boyd (1993) reported a relationship between early sexual abuse, depression, and later crack cocaine use in young black women. Kilpatrick (1990) found many relationships between being a victim of violent crime and alcohol and drug use.

These ideas about the relationship between violence and substance abuse have the appeal of common sense and are supported by cultural attitudes that have prevailed since colonial times, at least

(Pleck, 1987). However, modern researchers caution that the relationship between addiction and interpersonal violence is a complex one (Fagan, 1993; Widom, 1993) and that many other factors contribute to these outcomes including cultural expectations, social stresses, and personal expectations. In reviewing these issues, Widom(1993) concluded that, although it seems likely that a relationship will be found, there does not yet exist sufficient methodologically sound research to completely explain the relationship between violence and addiction.

SUMMARY

This chapter provides an overview of the problems found in children growing up in families affected by drug addiction and alcoholism. To provide information to guide helpers, misused drugs and their effects, the possible etiologies of drug and alcohol use, as well as common treatment methods are reviewed.

- Addiction and abuse of drugs and alcohol involve misuse of a variety of legal and illegal substances that, although they differ in their effects, are all psychoactive; that is, they affect the central nervous system and cause alterations in consciousness.
- There are various reasons for drug and alcohol abuse, and there is no one theory that explains all addiction. Some focus on the individual addict as the source of the problem, some on the family, and some on the environment.
- Treatment of alcoholism and drug abuse can be approached from a therapeutic perspective leading to medical or psychological intervention, or from a legalistic perspective leading to laws regarding use and prosecution of users.
- The impact of substance abuse on the child and the family can be discussed from both clinical and research perspectives. Although there is clear evidence that growing up in a family troubled by addictions leads to emotional problems, research suggests that other kinds of family dysfunction have similar outcomes.

REFERENCES

American Psychiatric Association. (1994). *Diagnostic and statistical manual of mental disorders* (4th ed.). Washington, DC: Author.
Aponte, H. (1974). Psychotherapy for the poor: An eco-structural approach to treatment. *Delaware Medical Journal, 46,* 134–136.
Bays, J. (1990). Substance abuse and child abuse: The impact of addiction on the child. *Pediatric Clinics of North America, 37,* 881–904.

Berenson, D. (1976). Alcohol and the family system. In P.J. Guerin (Ed.), *Family therapy: Theory and practice* (pp. 284–297). New York: Gardner Press.

Bernardi, E., Jones, M., & Tennant, C. (1989). Quality of parenting in alcoholic and narcotic addicts. *British Journal of Psychiatry, 154,* 677–682.

Bijur, P.E., Kuron, M., Overpeck, M.D., & Scheidt, P.C. (1992). Parental alcohol use, problem drinking, and children's injuries. *Journal of the American Medical Association, 267,* 3166–3171.

Blum, K., Nobel, E.P., Sheridan, P.J., Montgomery, A., Ritchie, T., Jagadeeswaran, P., Nogami, H., Briggs, A.H., & Cohn, J.B. (1990). Allelic association of human dopamine D_2 receptor gene in alcoholism. *Journal of the American Medical Association, 263,* 2055–2060.

Boyd, C.J. (1993). The antecedents of women's crack cocaine abuse: Family substance abuse, sexual abuse, depression and illicit drug use. *Journal of Substance Abuse Treatment, 10,* 433–438.

Brown, S. (1991). Adult children of alcoholics: The history of a social movement and its impact on clinical practice and theory. In M. Galanter (Ed.), *Recent Developments in Alcoholism* (Vol. 9, pp. 267–285). New York: Plenum.

Cadoret, R.J., Cain, C.A., & Grove, W.M. (1980). Development of alcoholism in adoptees raised apart from alcoholic biologic relatives. *Archives of General Psychiatry, 37,* 561–563.

Cork, M. (1969). *The forgotten children.* Toronto, Ontario, Canada: Addiction Research Foundation.

Davis, J.R., & Tunks, E. (1990–1991). Environments and addiction: A proposed taxonomy. *International Journal of the Addictions, 25,* 805–826.

Dole, V.P., & Nyswander, M.E. (1965). A medical treatment for diactylimorphine (heroin) addiction: Treatment with methadone hydrochloride. *Journal of the American Medical Association, 193,* 645–650.

Easthope, G. (1993). Perceptions of the causes of drug use in a series of articles in the International Journal of the Addictions. *International Journal of the Addictions, 28,* 559–569.

Emshoff, J.G., & Anyan, L.L. (1991). From prevention to treatment: Issues for school-aged children of alcoholics. In M. Galanter (Ed.), *Recent developments in alcoholism, Vol. 9: Children of alcoholics* (pp. 327–346). New York: Plenum.

Fagan, J. (1993). Set and setting revisited: Influences of alcohol and illicit drugs on the social context of violent events. In S.E. Martin (Ed.), *Alcohol and interpersonal violence: Fostering multidisciplinary perspectives* (Monograph 24) (pp. 161–191). Rockville, MD: Institute on Alcohol Abuse and Alcoholism, United States Department of Health and Human Services.

Finnegan, L.P., & Kaltenbach, K.A. (1992). Neonatal abstinence syndrome. In R.A. Heokelman, S.B. Friedman, N.M. Nelson, & H.M. Seidel (Eds.), *Primary pediatric care* (2nd ed., pp. 1367–1378) St. Louis, MO: C.V. Mosby.

Frezza, M., di Padova, C., Pozzato, G., Maddalena, T., Baraona, E., & Leiber, C.S. (1990). High blood alcohol levels in women: The role of decreased gastric alcohol dehydrogenase activity and first-pass metabolism. *New England Journal of Medicine, 322,* 95–99.

Gawin, F.H., & Ellinwood, E.H. (1988). Cocaine and other stimulants: Action, abuse, and treatment. *New England Journal of Medicine, 318,* 1173–1182.

Gold, S., & Sherry, L. (1984). Hyperactivity, learning disabilities, and alcohol. *Journal of Learning Disabilities, 12,* 3–6.

Good, L.N., Strickland, K.E., & Coles, C.D. (1991, June). *Knowledge and attitudes of public and professionals about substance abuse in pregnancy.* Paper presented at the Committee on Problems on Drug Dependency Annual Meeting, Richmond, VA.

Goodwin, D.W. (1985). Alcoholism and genetics. *Archives of General Psychiatry, 42,* 171–174.

Goodwin, D.W., Schulsinger, F., Hermansen, L., Guze, S.B., & Winokur, G., (1975). Alcoholism and the hyperactive child syndrome. *Journal of Nervous and Mental Diseases, 160,* 349–353.

Gordis, E., Tabakoff, B., Goldman, D., & Berg, K. (1990). Editorial: Finding the gene(s) for alcoholism. *Journal of the American Medical Association, 263,* 2094–2095.

Harburg, E., DiFranceisco, W., Webster, D.W., Gleiberman, L., & Schork, A. (1990). Family transmission of alcohol use: II. Imitation of and aversion to parent drinking (1960) by adult offspring (1977)—Tecumseh, Michigan. *Journal of Studies on Alcohol, 51,* 245–256.

Khavari, K.A. (1993). Interpersonal influences in college students' initial use of alcohol and drugs—the role of friends, self, parents, doctors, and dealers. *International Journal of the Addictions, 28,* 377–388.

Kilpatrick, D.G. (1990, August) *Violence as a precursor of women's substance abuse: The rest of the drugs-violence story.* Paper presented at Topical Mini-Convention of Substance Abuse and Violence at the 98th Annual Convention, American Psychololgical Association, Boston, MA.

Knop, J., Teasdale, T.W., Schulsinger, F., & Goodwin, D.W., (1985). A prospective study of young men at high risk for alcoholism: School behavior and achievement. *Journal of Studies on Alcohol, 46,* 273–278.

Leonard, K.E. & Jacob, T. (1988). Alcohol, alcoholism, and family violence. In V.B. VanHasselt, R.L. Morrison, A.S. Bellack, & M. Hersen (Eds.), *Handbook of family violence* (pp. 383–406). New York: Plenum.

Liskow, B.I., & Goodwin, D.W. (1987). Pharmacological treatment of alcohol intoxication, withdrawal, and dependence: A critical review. *Journal of Studies on Alcohol, 48* (4), 356–370.

McCardy, B.S., Noel, N.E., Abrams, D.B., Stout, R.L., Nelson, H.F., & Hay, W.M. (1986). Comparative effectiveness of three types of spouse involvement in outpatient behavioral alcoholism treatment. *Journal of Studies on Alcohol, 47,* 459–467.

Miller, B.A. (1993). Investigating links between childhood victimization and alcohol problems. In S.E. Martin (Ed.), *Alcohol and interpersonal violence: Fostering multidisiplinary perspectives* (National Institute on Alcohol Abuse and Alcoholism Research Monograph No. 24, pp. 315–323. Rockville, MD: United States Department of Health and Human Services.

National Institute on Alcohol Abuse and Alcoholism. (1993). *Eighth Special Report to the U.S. Congress on Alcohol and Health from the Secretary of Health and Human Services.* Rockville, MD: U.S. Department of Health and Human Services, Public Health Service, National Institutes of Health.

National Institute on Drug Abuse. (1992). *National household survey on drug abuse: Population estimates, 1991* (rev. ed.). Rockville, MD: U.S. Department of Health and Human Services, Public Health Service, Alcohol, Drug Abuse, and Mental Health Administration.

Offord, D., Allen, N., & Abrams, N. (1978). Parental psychiatric illness. *Journal of the American Academy of Child and Adolescent Psychiatry, 17,* 224–238.

Pleck, E. (1987). *Domestic tyranny: The making of American social policy against family violence from Colonial times to the present.* New York: Oxford University Press.

Reed, B.G. (1985). Drug misuse and dependency in women: The meaning and implications of being considered a special population or minority group. *International Journal of the Addictions, 20*(1), 13–62.

Richards, T.M., Morehouse, E.R., Seisax, J.S., & Kern, J.C. (1983). Psychosocial assessment and intervention with children of alcoholic parents. In D. Cook, C. Fewell, & J. Riolo (Eds.), *Social work treatment of alcohol problems* (pp. 131–142). New Brunswick, NJ: Rutgers Center of Alcohol Studies.

Robins, L.N., & Regier, D.A. (Eds.). (1991). *Psychiatric disorders in America: The epidemiological catchment area study.* New York: Free Press.

Sandmaier, M. (1980). *The invisible alcoholics: Women and alcohol use in America.* New York: McGraw-Hill.

Schuckit, M.A. (1981). Twin studies on substance abuse: An overview. In L. Gedda, P. Paris, & W. Nance (Eds.), *Twin research, Vol. 3: Epidemiological and clinical studies* (pp. 61–70). New York: Alan R. Liss.

Schuckit, M.A. (1989). *Drug and alcohol abuse: A clinical guide to diagnosis and treatment* (3rd ed.). New York: Plenum.

Schuckit, M.A. (1991). A longitudinal study of children of alcoholics. In M. Galanter (Ed.), *Recent developments in alcoholism, Vol. 9: Children of alcoholics* (pp. 5–19). New York: Plenum.

Sher, K.J. (1991). Psychological characteristics of children of alcoholics: Overview of research methods and findings. In M. Galanter (Ed.), *Recent developments in alcoholism, Vol. 9: Children of alcoholics* (pp. 301–326). New York: Plenum.

Steinglass, P. (1980). A life history model of the alcoholic family. *Family Processes, 19*(3), 211–226.

Wallen, J., & Berman, K. (1993). Possible indicators of childhood sexual abuse for individuals in substance abuse treatment. *Journal of Child Sexual Abuse, 1*(3), 63–74.

Weddington, W.W. (1990–1991). Toward a rehabilitation of methadone maintenance: Integration of relapse prevention and aftercare. *International Journal of the Addictions, 25,* 1201–1221.

Widom, C.S. (1993). Child abuse and alcohol use and abuse. In S.E. Martin (Ed.), *Alcohol and interpersonal violence: Fostering multidisciplinary perspectives.* (National Institute on Alcohol Abuse and Alcoholism Research Monograph No. 24). Rockville, MD: U.S. Department of Health and Human Services.

Wilson, G.S., McCreary, R., Kean, J., & Baxter, C. (1979). The development of preschool children of heroin addicted mothers: A controlled study. *Pediatrics, 63,* 135–141.

Wood, D., Wender, P.H., & Reimherr, F.W. (1983). The prevalence of attention deficit disorder, residual type, or minimal brain dysfunction, in a population of male alcoholic patients. *American Journal of Psychiatry, 140,* 95–98.

Woodside, M. (1986). Children of alcoholics: Breaking the cycle. *Journal of School Health, 56,* 448–449.

Zeanah, C.H., Mammen, O.K., & Lieberman, A.F. (1993). Disorders of attachment. In C.H. Zeanah (Ed.), *Handbook of infant mental health* (pp. 332–349). New York: Guilford.

3

Helping Families with Multiple Needs

Claire D. Coles and G. Harold Smith

Society expects that all children will arrive at the school door ready to learn. Educational programs are developed with some basic assumptions about children—that children will have the social skills necessary to get along with peers at an age-appropriate level, the cognitive competence to understand the lessons, and a history of interaction with adults that will lead them to accept the teacher as an authority figure with benign intentions. To be successful in this first interaction with the greater world, children need basic adaptive skills that will enable them to feed themselves, use the bathroom independently, and put on and button their coats during the winter. Ideally, children will have been encouraged in their normal curiosity and desire to learn by a supportive home environment. Most fundamentally, children must be ensured of a home and a caregiver, clothes, and food to eat to develop typically.

But all children do not have such things. For one reason or another, many children come from families that are so beset by problems and have so few resources that these fundamental assumptions cannot be met. In some families in which one or both parents are addicted to drugs or alcohol, children often lack those things most of us consider essential. Working with such children and their families challenges professionals in ways for which they may not have been prepared. These challenges arise from several sources—the characteristics of individual families, the nature of the addiction process

57

and the way in which it is dealt with by American society, multiple social factors (e.g., racism, poverty) often associated with addiction, as well as the characteristics of the (helping) systems that become involved and the reactions of the professional helpers themselves (Thom, 1994).

Antonio and Linda Martin

Antonio Martin was 5 years old and enrolled in the community's Head Start program when he was identified by the program staff as having difficulty learning. Although Antonio had not received any formal testing, his acting out behavior and poor academic performance were sufficient to recommend him to a class for children with mild intellectual disabilities. Antonio was referred to a developmental pediatrician because of his poor attention. The pediatrician had seen him previously and diagnosed a genetic disorder that had caused a mild facial dysmorphia. Antonio did not have an attention disorder, but was referred to a psychologist. There were two reasons for the referral. First, the physician believed that the suspicion of mental retardation should be validated through psychological testing; and second, because Antonio's mother, Linda Martin, was experiencing a great deal of difficulty in coping with Antonio's behavior, the physician thought she might benefit from counseling.

Mrs. Martin explained during the assessment process that Antonio's behavior had gotten much worse since his father was arrested and jailed for shooting his girlfriend during a drug deal. She said that Antonio had been very attached to his father, who spent a lot of time with him. Since his father's arrest, Antonio had gone from being "a good boy, to a sad boy, and now a bad boy." With her husband in prison and her own family living in a different part of the state, Mrs. Martin had little social support and no one to talk to about Antonio's problems and her own depression. Although she was a bright woman with some college education, lack of child care and work experience prevented her from getting a job. Also, because she had been sexually and physically abused as a child, she did not feel confident in her decisions about discipline with her own children. In addition to Antonio, Mrs. Martin had 3 other children: a son, age 7, and 2 daughters, ages 4 years and 18 months. Mrs. Martin said that her biggest concern about Antonio's behavior was that he did not obey her immediately when she gave him a command. The counselor gently explained that children this age often did not obey immediately, particularly if they were tired or distracted by other things. Mrs. Martin replied that she understood, but given the drive-by shootings in her inner-city neighborhood, she wanted to be sure that whenever she heard gunfire close by, the children would immediately get down on the floor to avoid being hit by a bullet. Feeling out of her depth, the counselor acknowledged that this was a sensible approach given the situation.

Formal psychological testing indicated that Antonio was of normal intelligence and had no indications of attention deficits. He did have some articulation problems due to oral malformations associated with his genetic problem, and speech therapy was recommended. Mrs. Martin was noted to be depressed as a result of her social situation and her personal history of physical and sexual abuse. She was referred for psychotherapy for her emotional problems and social work services to help her find child care so that she could look for a job.

Clarissa Brown

Clarissa is 14 years old and is the older of 2 children of Sam and Rebecca Brown. Her sister, Dawn is 10 years old. Rebecca has been in and out of treatment programs for alcoholism several times. Each time she appears to be making a good recovery, but relapses after a relatively short period of time. Sam has filed for divorce because of his wife's continuing problems with alcoholism. Rebecca has moved out of the home and is staying with a friend who also is addicted to alcohol and is in relapse. Sam has been working two jobs in order to maintain the family's standard of living, and has left Clarissa to take care of Dawn. Clarissa has been falling asleep in class and not completing homework assignments. Even though she is a bright child with above-average intelligence, she is in serious danger of failing several of her courses. Her homeroom teacher spent time with Clarissa over a period of several days. When she felt that a comfortable and trusting relationship had developed between the two of them, she asked Clarissa if there were any problems at home. Clarissa began to sob and shared with the teacher that her parents were divorcing as a result of her mother's alcoholism, that she felt overwhelmed by her responsibility to care for Dawn, and that she felt her own life was hopeless. Clarissa told her teacher that since her mother had left, her mother had been calling Dawn at all hours, leaving Dawn in tears each time. Dawn refused to tell her sister or father what her mother said on the telephone. Clarissa also reported that her father had been bringing "girlfriends" home to spend the night. According to Clarissa, these women used vulgar language and ordered her and her sister to do personal chores for them.

With support from her teacher, Clarissa agreed that her confidences should be shared with the school's guidance counselor. The guidance counselor recognized that Clarissa was at very high risk for a number of negative outcomes, including suicide. He immediately contacted Clarissa's father and asked for an appointment. Mr. Brown expressed a sincere desire to meet with the counselor, but because of his work schedule and the danger of losing his job no appointment could be set. At that point, the counselor initiated a referral to the community's child protective service based on suspected neglect of the two children.

Working with families like these can leave professionals feeling overwhelmed by the immensity and extensiveness of some of the problems involved. Often, it is difficult to know where to begin the process of understanding or how to help most effectively. To help in understanding families with multiple needs and the resources that are available to them as well as how working with them affects professionals, this chapter discusses the following topics:

- How to assess a family's multiple needs and resources
- How to recognize and overcome barriers to work effectively with families with multiple needs
- How to identify resources in the community and negotiate in "the system"
- How to recognize the effect of families with multiple needs on helpers and to avoid burnout

ASSESSING NEEDS AND RESOURCES

What are addicted families and families with multiple problems like? First, every family has unique characteristics, and to provide help effectively, professionals must begin with a comprehensive assessment of the child at risk and the family. Because it is the family's *problems* that will bring them to the attention of professionals, it is important to examine what *resources* exist as well so that these can be mobilized to help in recovery.

Substance abuse, when it comes to our attention, is often focused on as the *cause* of an individual's or a family's problems, but as discussed in previous chapters, there are often many other issues in addition to addiction that need to be addressed before the child and the family can function adequately. In some cases, these conditions preceded the problems with substance abuse and, in fact, may have contributed to the person becoming addicted. Early histories of poverty, violence, child abuse, and family dysfunction are often reported by adults who are addicted (Windom, 1993) and are believed to increase the probability of substance abuse. In contrast, negative consequences (e.g., an increased likelihood of disease, legal problems, financial problems) may result from drug and alcohol abuse.

Individuals living in poverty seem to be vulnerable to negative effects of drug abuse, perhaps because of the lack of protective factors. Even without the stress of parental addiction (Lief, 1985), the social factors, including poverty, the stigma of racism, and the problems that can result from single-parent status, are often associated with poorer development outcomes and academic failure in children (Craig, 1992; Culp et al., 1991). Garbarino (1990) discusses these ecological factors and notes that economic issues have a large role in the "dynamics of early risk" (p. 89), such that people who are limited in their access to monetary resources will evolve "systematic patterns of deprivation" (p. 89), which affect most areas of the child's life within the family, at school, and in the neighborhood. Because these effects are so pervasive, Garbarino argues that, in a sense, "the underclass represent a kind of ecological conspiracy against children" (p. 89).

People in such problematic circumstances may be vulnerable to substance abuse because it can represent a temporary release from the stresses of this kind of life (Staples, 1990). In addition, involvement with illegal drugs can be seen as a way to improve economic status when there are few other opportunities to make an adequate income.

It can be difficult to distinguish the effects of addiction itself from the effects of these other factors. Even if problems with substance abuse can be overcome, many of the other problems confronting the family will remain and must be addressed if the family is to succeed in providing for their children.

Multidisciplinary Assessment

In evaluating a child and family with multiple needs, a multidisciplinary approach is usually necessary. Although the child may be identified at school through developmental delays or academic or behavior problems, many systems must be addressed to ensure that intervention will be effective. A good assessment includes a medical work-up with vision and hearing screening, a social history and needs assessment, age-appropriate psychological and educational testing, and, perhaps, specialized evaluations (e.g., speech language therapy, physical therapy). Some families and children have had, or will need, extensive social services or involvement with various agencies to provide housing; improve health, nutrition, social functioning, and mental health; or deal with a variety of other problems.

At the same time that needs are identified, resources also should be examined. There may be extended family members who can provide for the child. The parent who is presently addicted and dysfunctional may have education and skills that can be used if the alcohol and drug treatment is successful. The child who is failing at school may have sufficient intellectual ability to succeed if given adequate support. Similarly, there may be community resources, either public or private, that can be used to support and empower this family.

Once assessment is completed, intervention is necessary. Various professionals have to be willing to work together to identify appropriate sources of help, and to design and implement intervention strategies. Although it is easy to make such a suggestion, it is often much more difficult to follow through on it in the "real world."

RECOGNIZING AND OVERCOMING BARRIERS

People who need help most are often the most difficult to help. Middle class people who have a problem with addiction usually have a number of support systems still in place that can be used in order to help in overcoming the problems of addiction. However, families with fewer resources present a much more difficult task.

Families usually come to the attention of a *gatekeeper,* who could be a preschool teacher, a nurse in a well-baby clinic, a doctor in an emergency room, or a child protective services worker who is called in by the neighbors. This person then has to decide to follow up on the observation and to involve other professionals in the process of helping this family.

Effects of Parental Addiction

It is most common for those who are substance abusers to associate with mates who are also abusers (i.e., *assortative mating*) so that, in many cases, both mother and father are impaired. However, as discussed in Chapter 2, males are more likely than females to use drugs and alcohol abusively so that having a father who is an addict is probably the more common problem for children in families affected by drugs and alcohol. Typically men who are addicted to drugs and alcohol demonstrate an increase in violent and unstable behavior, vocational problems that can lead to loss of jobs and increased financial problems, legal problems that include automobile violations (e.g., charges of driving under the influence of drugs or alcohol), and the probability of medical problems (see Table 3.1).

Table 3.1. Medical problems commonly associated with alcoholism

Liver
   Alcoholic steatosis (fatty liver)
   Alcoholic hepatitis and fibrosis
   Cirrhosis

Pancreatitis

Cardiovascular injury
   Alcoholic cardiomyopathy
   Hypertension
   Hemorrhagic strokes

Immune system impairment
   Cancers of mouth and upper respiratory tract
   Liver cancer

Endocrine abnormalities
   Impaired gonadal function in males (impotence, testicular atrophy, infertility)
   Impaired reproductive function in females (amenorrhea, early menopause, failure
      to ovulate)
   Sexual dysfunction

Neurological disorders
   Wernicke-Korsakoff syndrome
   Alcoholic dementia
   Organic mental disorder

From U.S. Secretary of Health and Human Services. (1993). *Eighth special report to the U.S. Congress on alcohol and health: Effects of alcohol on health and body systems.* Rockville, MD: U.S. Department of Health and Human Services, National Institutes of Health, National Institute of Alcohol Abuse and Alcoholism.

If the child's father is addicted and his mother is not, the mother may be able to "buffer" the child to the extent to which she is not herself impaired by her association with her spouse. However, when a child's mother is negatively affected by the addiction of her spouse, the child may assume a surrogate spouse or a parentified role to fill in the missing part of the family unit. The child may feel forced by the spouse who is not addicted to help meet the adult's emotional needs, which can be an intolerable burden for some children.

Single-Parent Responsibility

In many families with multiple needs, the mother alone is responsible for the child's care and may have little social support to help her in this task. If the father is impaired or absent, the family is often living in poverty. The lower social status of women and the responsibilities of child care often prevent even competent mothers from receiving an adequate salary. If the mother is addicted, there are some common problems she may encounter that can interfere with drug and alcohol treatment for her as well as interfere with interventions intended to treat or prevent children's disabilities or remediate academic difficulties. These common problems include: financial restraints, limited transportation, available child care, social support, poor health, and different values.

Financial Restraints Most families with multiple needs who come to the attention of schools and social agencies do not have adequate financial resources. The lack of financial resources places limitations on time, mobility, flexibility in scheduling, and on most service choices. When money is extremely limited, families may not be able to eat regularly enough for children to maintain an alert state at school or to have a coat in the winter. They may not have regular medical care, dental care, eye care, or immunizations.

As Beckwith (1990) notes, in order to help children in families at high risk, it is often necessary to attend to the most basic, most practical issues of living and survival. A family that does not have the money to buy food or children's shoes is not likely to be able to respond to instructions from a physical therapist about positioning a child with gross motor delays, or to work with a counselor to improve behavioral management skills, or to help a child with homework. Greenspan (1990) has described a *service pyramid* that graphically represents the hierarchy of needs that must be met in a family before intervention services can be effective (see Figure 3.1).

Limited Transportation Professionals who have scheduled their scarce time find it frustrating when parents (usually mothers)

Figure 3.1. The service pyramid: preventive intervention services. (From Greenspan, S. [1990]. Comprehensive clinical approaches to infants and their families: Psychodynamic and developmental perspectives. In S.J. Meisels & J.P. Shonkoff [Eds.], *Handbook of early childhood intervention* [p. 165]. New York: Cambridge University Press; reprinted by permission.)

have difficulty keeping appointments or regularly bringing their children to school or other programs. One reason for such behavior is the lack of convenient access to transportation. Families with multiple needs often do not have cars and may find it difficult to use public transportation. For example, a woman with several toddlers may find it very difficult to get to a program many miles away if several bus transfers are required. Similarly, a mother may be in an outpatient drug treatment program that requires her to appear promptly at 8:30 A.M. every day or risk dismissal from the program. If she has to wake up several young children, take them to a sitter or child care program, and then travel by public transportation, she might drop out of drug treatment rather than face failing to appear on time.

The following are some approaches that have been used in trying to alleviate the problem of transportation:

1. Locating in, or bringing services to, areas of high need
2. Providing Medicaid transportation or school vans to bring children to programs or appointments
3. Providing bus tokens to offset cost of transportation
4. Using "outreach" as part of service coordination and early intervention services more frequently

When such resources are not available, professionals may need to resort to more unconventional means. These methods can include scheduling appointments at unusual times (e.g., seeing clients on Saturday morning) or rescheduling meetings repeatedly despite missed appointments.

Available Child Care In the United States, there is limited, high-quality, reasonably priced child care available for any group of parents. For this reason, concern for their children and lack of alternative caregivers often limits parents' activities. Concern for dependent children certainly can keep women from entering or completing drug treatment (Brown, 1992). The effect of this limitation has been demonstrated by a study in California (Beckman & Amaro, 1986) that showed that provision of child care services led to increases in the number of women in treatment programs. Once women complete drug and alcohol treatment and are in recovery, similar problems with child care can interfere with completing job training programs and may keep mothers from entering the work force.

Programs that provide on-site child care services are more successful in keeping parents involved, in filling appointments, and in preventing people from dropping out. A second way in which this problem has been addressed is through residential drug treatment programs. The Comprehensive Addiction Rehabilitation Programs (CARP) in Atlanta, Georgia, is an example of an addiction program providing residential services for women in treatment as well as care for their preschool children (see Chapter 9). However, there are many other such programs currently in place throughout the United States, many of them sponsored by the federal Centers for Substance Abuse Prevention (CSAP) and Substance Abuse Treatment (CSAT). One of the earliest established of these was Operation PAR (Parental Awareness and Responsibility) in Pinellas County, Florida.

Social Support It is clear that children and their parents need support from their own families and their communities to develop optimally. However, many addicts have limited access to social support from their families or friends as well as from the usual agencies that provide services to young mothers. Health care and social agencies and social organizations, such as churches, which can be resources for most people, may be seen as dangerous by addicts who are afraid of being reported to authorities or of receiving social censure for their behavior. In addition, because the addiction process itself often absorbs them to the exclusion of other activities, women's behavior may alienate family and nonaddicted friends and acquaintances. As a result, many of these families have few places to turn for help either on a daily basis or in emergencies. This isolation can further impoverish their lives and their children's lives.

This social isolation or association only with other addicts is a difficult problem to address when the addiction is ongoing. However, once in recovery, women can be integrated back into the community through a process of habilitation and aftercare. Children, whether their parents are in recovery or not, can be encouraged to participate in social activities, groups for children of alcoholics, and school programs.

Poor Health Many addicts are in poor health as a result of their lifestyles and lack of access to health care or because they do not use the health care resources that do exist (see Tables 3.1 and 3.2). In addition, many addicts have other emotional problems (see

Table 3.2. Medical complications common in women abusing substances

Infections
 Bacterial endocarditis (subacute)
 Cellulitis
 Hepatitis
 Phlebitis
 Pneumonia (acute and chronic)
 Septicemia
 Tetanus
 Tuberculosis

Acquired immunodeficiency syndrome (AIDS)

Urinary tract infections (UTIs)
 Cystitis
 Pyelonephritis
 Urethritis

Sexually transmitted diseases (STDs)
 Condyloma acuminatum
 Gonorrhea
 Herpes
 Syphilis

Other problems
 Anemia (iron and folic acid deficiency)
 Hypertension
 Poor dental hygiene
 Sclerotic veins
 Tachycardia
 Vitamin deficiencies, especially B complex and C

From Coles, C.D., & Finnegan, L.P. (1989). *Substance abuse in pregnancy: Reproductive and developmental risk.* Unpublished paper; reprinted by permission.

Chapter 1) that can interfere with their adaptive functioning and parenting abilities.

Different Values The assumption that a child or a family needs help is based on certain beliefs and standards. For example, a mother with an addiction whose child has a learning disability may have a different understanding of the reasons for, and ramifications of, the child's problems than do the professional helpers with whom she comes into contact. A woman who did not finish high school and has no relatives or acquaintances who did well at school may not view her child's academic achievements in the same way as the child's teacher. Instead, her major concerns may be that the child behaves well and helps out at home with younger children. Similarly, a suggestion that infant language can be stimulated by reading to the child may seem nonsensical to a depressed mother who herself reads at a primary level.

IDENTIFYING RESOURCES AND NEGOTIATING THE "SYSTEM"

It is clear that children in families affected by substance abuse often need help from sources outside their own families. However, where that help can be found is not always clear, nor once it has been identified, is it always easy to ensure that it is received.

Services for Children

Children with diagnosed disabilities, and, sometimes, those who are considered to be at risk because of environmental or biological factors (including those with family substance abuse), are eligible for early intervention (EI) services beginning at birth. (For a discussion of the laws and regulations governing special education services, see the Introduction to this volume.) Intervention for children younger than 3 years and their families is considered vital because this period forms the basis for the child's later cognitive and emotional development (Greenhough et al., 1993; Halpern, 1993). The first early intervention programs were designed for treatment of children with physical and mental disabilities with an emphasis on sensory and motor stimulation (Harris, 1987; Stedman & Eichorn, 1964). Later, intervention was directed at prevention of social retardation associated with poverty (Bryant & Ramey, 1987; Ramey & Ramey, 1992).

Whatever the reasons for the child's risk status, it is clear that in families with multiple needs the difficulties experienced by the family may interfere with the goals of the early intervention program. Beckwith (1990), in a discussion of how parenting affects the intervention process, notes that in these families substantial modifications may be required in an agency's usual procedures for referral, assessment, and service delivery. In many cases, basic survival needs must be addressed before any other efforts can be undertaken. Then, practical problems, like those previously discussed, must be taken care of to allow the family access to resources. Often, in addition to these practical issues, emotional problems in the family, between parent and child and between parents, must be treated to ensure that appropriate intervention with children can be undertaken. Some professionals have difficulty dealing with these issues and feel that they have no obligation to serve those who will not cooperate with their own treatment. However, without attention to these basic requirements, many families will not be able to follow through with plans meant to help their children.

Preschool Age (3–5 Years) In most states, services to preschool children, ages 3–5 years, are provided by local education agencies under the leadership of state departments of education. Service delivery models vary and may reflect a combination of alternatives designed to maximize available resources and address constraints of population diversity, geographic considerations, and program philosophies addressing parental and family responsibilities (see Table 3.3).

School Age (6–21 Years) Service provision to school age children at high risk has received more attention over a longer period of time than to the younger age groups. Consequently, these services are usually more well-established than programs for children of preschool age. The basic impact of PL 101-476, the Individuals with Disabilities Education Act of 1990 (IDEA), on family services for this group was to formalize the need for involvement of parents or guardians in the referral, assessment, placement, and programming decisions for their child. Children and youth in foster placement, a situation that is common among children of parents with addiction, must be provided with a *surrogate parent* who is responsible for monitoring services and consenting to proposed plans presented by local education agencies. Local school districts are required to offer a continuum of services to students with disabilities. These may include offering and monitoring support services in the student's regular classroom setting, providing resource services either in the classroom or through "pull-out" models, which involve pulling out the child from his or her regular classroom for certain subjects or for special services, and providing special education classes that serve the student for the majority of the school, or providing specialized center programs for students with disabilities. Students may be served

Table 3.3 Service delivery models for preschool interventions

Model	Program provisions	Staff	Requirements
Home-based	Provide direct services to children and parenting training to caregiver in home setting.	May be professionally licensed or certified and/or paraprofessional staff under professional supervision. Home-based models typically emphasize use of nonprofessional staff under supervision.	Consistent caregiver in home capable and willing to follow-through on developmental services to the child.
Center-based	Provide services to children at central location. Transportation may be provided to children or may be responsibility of child's caregivers. Follow-up support to families is typically provided at center or through home visits by staff.	May be professionally licensed or certified and/or paraprofessional staff under professional supervision. Disciplines of staff will vary according to program model and services provided.	If transportation is not provided by program, caregivers are responsible for bringing child to center for services.
Community-based	Children are enrolled in one agency with collaborative services provided by other cooperating agencies directly to child and/or family.	May be professionally licensed or certified and/or paraprofessional staff under professional supervision. Disciplines of staff will vary according to program models and services provided.	Child must qualify for enrollment into lead agency, which may be dependent upon economic criteria, age, developmental levels, commitment of family involvement, and/or other factors.

From Smith, G.H. (1993). Intervention strategies for children vulnerable for school failure due to exposure to drugs and alcohol. International Journal of the Addictions, 28(13), 1448; reprinted by permission.

Services	Frequency	Advantages
Emphasis is typically on helping parent improve parenting and to support access to community resources for related child and family service needs.	Services usually provided on weekly schedule with paraprofessional staff alternating with professionally licensed staff for assessment and family counseling services.	Provides for long-term positive outcomes as caregiver helps meet needs of child through improved parenting skills. Close monitoring of home conditions and identifying need for expanded community agencies resources and involvement.
Range of services will vary according to model and funding sources. Developmental programming, therapeutic services, and family support usually provided.	Services may be provided on daily basis or on weekly schedule. Frequency of home and family services varies.	Allows service agency to concentrate staff and other program resources at central location to maximize services to children and their families. Support multidisciplinary program of services to child based on locating resources at one location.
Services will vary and may be direct for developmental programming, therapeutic services, and family support. Indirect support through consultation with agency staff. Participation of staff in inservice training programs is usually available.	Direct services to child provided on varying schedule. Therapeutic services usually provided on weekly basis. Frequency of home and family services varies.	Broadens community resources for special needs children with wider array of service options for children and their families. As staff are helped to meet needs of targeted clients, potential capability of meeting needs of other children is expanded.

through a combination of these service systems appropriate to the student's individualized education program and services required for educational benefit.

Related services that permit the student to participate in and benefit from educational services also are required and include medical services, therapies, and specialized training. These services are provided by the district or through collaborative or contract agreements with public or private agencies. All services must be made available at no cost to parents.

Family services, which are required for infants, are not included as a requirement in IDEA for school-age children and youths. However, because of the real need for such services, many districts have expanded resources to offer parenting training, support groups, and opportunities for parents to participate in local school activities. Local education agencies are beginning to expand services to children and their families beyond educational services through collaborative relationships with community health and social service agencies. These *community-based programs* may be located in local schools and may, as a result, offer a significant resource to local communities by providing the means for more effective service delivery by the cooperating agencies. Because schools are located in neighborhoods and are often more accessible and familiar to families, services can be provided to people who might not otherwise receive them.

Decisions and interpretation of IDEA and its accompanying regulations by the federal Office of Civil Rights and by case law, which developed as a result of decisions by various state and federal courts, have had a significant impact on how services are provided to students and the responsibilities of local school districts to provide resources to students. In most cases, local education agencies have continued to expand services with broader options and alternatives to students.

Other Services for Children Most urban and suburban communities have a variety of services available. (Availability in rural communities may vary.) However, access to many services depends on the family's resources. Obtaining health care, for example, depends on whether family members have insurance through employers or are eligible for assistance through the federal Medicaid program, whose provisions vary by state. For those who do not have insurance through employment and who do not meet the criteria for Medicaid, many health care and related services (e.g., dental care, psychological counseling) are unavailable, in a practical sense, because of their cost.

Children who qualify for special educational services can receive some noneducational services through public school systems working in collaboration with community health and social service agencies. However, children whose educational disabilities are not severe enough to meet legal criteria (see the Introduction to this volume) for services may still require help to achieve reasonable academic and social goals but may be unable to receive these through the school system. If parents are able to pay for remedial services privately or if there are services available through other agencies or programs, the child still may be served. However,, those who are most in need often do not have the acumen to identify such resources within a confusing and bureaucratic system or the financial means to pay for them if they can be found.

Meeting Parents' Needs

Alcohol and Drug Treatment   In vulnerable families in which addiction is an issue, alcohol and drug treatment may be necessary before the family is capable of using other assistance and resources that may be offered. Such treatment can be obtained privately by those who have insurance and through public programs by others. Generally, drug treatment includes a period of acute care during which the person is withdrawn from addictive drugs (i.e., narcotics, alcohol, and cocaine, but not usually nicotine) followed by a "28-day" inpatient program. Ideally, this acute care is followed by an after-care program that often involves required attendance at 12-Step programs like Alcoholics Anonymous. In some cases, inpatient treatment is replaced by an outpatient program that allows working people to retain their jobs. Outpatient programs have been demonstrated to be more effective than the more traditional inpatient programs for some clients (Cummings, 1991). However, for certain drugs and for highly dysfunctional individuals, inpatient programs may be more effective (Buddle, Rounsaville, & Bryant, 1992). In general, the more the individual is impaired, the longer and more intensive the treatment may need to be (Charuvastra, Dalali, Cassuci, & Ling, 1992).

For many women who have used cocaine during pregnancy, residential treatment is recommended during recovery. Residential treatment usually lasts from 3 months to a year and involves not only drug and alcohol treatment but also vocational rehabilitation, psychological counseling, and other services that allow the woman to function effectively when she leaves drug and alcohol treatment.

Despite the great need for services, many individuals from families with multiple needs do not have adequate insurance to provide them with appropriate treatment, and the available public programs are often limited in size. In the last few years, as attention has focused on the effects of maternal substance abuse as well as on the cocaine epidemic, there has been an increase in treatment resources. However, the available treatment slots still are exceeded greatly by the number of people needing treatment (Brown, 1992). For example, in Atlanta in 1994, a public drug treatment program that can serve 3,000 clients a year receives 9,000 applicants (M. Cone, personal communication, May 15, 1994).

In addition to restrictions in size, sometimes the existing programs are not suitable for all individuals. Current methods of drug and alcohol treatment were developed when the middle-age, white male alcoholic was the prototypical addict. In the 1960s and 1970s, methadone treatment for narcotics abusers also focused primarily on males, although they were generally younger and economically less advantaged. Based on experience with such individuals, a treatment culture evolved that adheres to a number of principles about treatment of addiction. Because many such programs are staffed by counselors and administrators whose primary "training" for their positions was recovery from their own addiction, these beliefs are deeply ingrained and often difficult to change.

Because men with an addiction, like many men in this culture, use denial as a defense mechanism and have been reared to deny their feelings, many addiction programs include a confrontational approach designed to break through these emotional defenses and force the addicts to acknowledge the negative effect of their behavior on themselves and others. In addition, because the older male addicts usually have left jobs and careers as well as families behind, recovery often focuses on *rehabilitation* so that these formerly functional people can be returned to their previous status. Because of cultural values, treatment focus tends to be on individuation and independent action in contrast to interdependency, with dependency seen as characteristic of the *addictive personality*. Finally, because men usually do not have direct responsibility for children, provisions for child care are not made.

To treat minorities and women effectively, modifications have to be made in many programs (Creigs, 1989; Hanson, 1985). Reed (1985) notes that, for programs to serve women, the classic, confrontational style has to be modified because women with an addiction, in contrast to men, have different personality dynamics—they often have low self-esteem and tend to self-blame. In addition, such women often have been victims of violence. For these reasons, the confrontational style may be very threatening to them and may produce results contrary to those seen in men. Another difference is that, by the time they enter treatment, women's social support networks are often much less available than are those of men in similar circumstances. This discrepancy occurs because women, more often than men, have partners who are also substance abusers and who may have ambiguous feelings about their recovery. In addition as previously mentioned, women, to a greater extent than men, may be alienated from the usual sources of social support.

Another innovation needed in treatment for women is inclusion of explicit policies against sexual harassment by either other clients or staff. Since addicted women often have histories of abuse as well as low self-esteem, it is necessary for policies to be in place to protect them from problems in these areas and to teach them to rely on other resources for achievement. Finally, because young women with an addiction often have never functioned adequately (i.e., never worked, never finished school, never acted as an adult), focus must be on *habilitation*, or the development of social and occupational skills that will support them in recovery.

Similar cultural differences exist in dealing with various minority groups whose values and customs differ from those of the majority. For these reasons, specialized programs have been developed to work with African Americans, Latinos, and Asian Americans, as well as women (Hanson, 1985).

Mental Health As was mentioned in Chapters 1 and 2, many parents who abuse substances require psychological and psychiatric services to deal with both their own history of abuse and neglect and their current problems. Although there are many providers of such services, traditionally trained psychotherapists and physicians often have little knowledge of, or experience with, addiction and substance abuse. Medical schools and graduate training programs usually do not deal with these topics or deal with them in a very cursory manner. In addition, the techniques of counseling and psychotherapy were designed for work with verbally fluent, middle-class people with adequate financial resources and accessible social support systems, rather than with members of families with intensive needs, who are often frustrating to work with. Fortunately, beginning in the 1980s, there has been increased interest in the problem of addiction and there is now a medical speciality called Addiction Medicine, which requires training and board certification. Similar improvements in training have occurred in other fields, particularly social work. However, many professionals, particularly educational professionals, who are often the first ones to come in contact with a problem through children, have little training in dealing with families with an addiction or with identification of the effects on children of the problems associated with addiction (Craig, 1992).

Parenting Many children from families at high risk are being reared by parents who do not have the basic skills to parent adequately (Lief, 1985). Problems in parenting arise for many reasons and effective remediation requires that these problems be identified. Some parents have limited intellectual skills, and although they may try hard, they have difficulty understanding children's needs. Others were reared without being parented adequately themselves and, for this reason, lack the models and the skills that most people learn in their own families. Other parents have emotional problems that prevent them from functioning as nurturing parents or perceiving their own children's behavior accurately. Finally, when the addiction process is acute, the search for, and involvement with, the drug may interfere with parenting activities.

For these reasons, parenting classes are often recommended to help parents understand typical child development, plan nutritious meals, provide adequate health care, and discipline appropriately. Even after recovery from addiction, parents may have unexpected problems dealing with children who have been neglected previously and may be acting out their own feelings regarding their parents' previous and current behavior.

Other Services Because many families have so few resources, they need a variety of other services to ensure that they will be able to function adequately and provide for their children. In low-income, inner-city populations, many people who are addicted to cocaine, heroin, or alcohol do not have high school diplomas, and because many had children while still teenagers themselves, they have no employment history and few marketable skills. In addition, literacy levels are often low. For example, in a survey done at an inner-city hospital, the average literacy level of adults was the fifth grade (Coles, 1992).

In other cases, because of the lifestyle associated with the addiction to illegal drugs, parents may be in poor health. In some inner-city neighborhoods, life expectancy is much lower than in the rest of the United States. In addition, parents may need help in obtaining available resources such as Women, Infants and Children (WIC), a supplementary nutrition program for pregnant women and infants, or Supplementary Security Income (SSI), which makes additional resources for poverty-level children with disabilities available, to provide the medical and educational services such children need. Families may need a range of services to provide for their basic needs before the children's educational and emotional needs can be adequately addressed.

SYSTEMS AND THEIR INTERACTIONS

Usually, in working with families with multiple needs, effective intervention and improvement require the interaction of several educational, medical, social service, and legal systems. In addition to early intervention and special education services for children, parents may need substance abuse treatment and medical services. Other social systems may become involved as well; for example, child protective services or the legal and justice systems. This complicated involvement with many educational and social systems often can become confusing for all concerned, including both professional helpers and families.

Sometimes the needs of different systems and their personnel collide and sometimes there are legal, economic, and other constraints on what can be done.

Kevin and His Family
Kevin was a quiet, well-behaved, 9-year-old boy with shiny, straight blond hair and large blue eyes. Although not a good student, his grades were not bad enough to suspect a learning disability, and his behavior was generally reserved and respectful. However, by January of his fourth grade year, he had been absent for several weeks because of illness and other unexplained reasons. He did not return to school after Christmas. His teacher first called his parents, who were not available, and then discussed his case with her colleagues. She discovered that he had 5 siblings, 2 sisters who were ages 7 and 5, in lower grades and twin brothers in preschool, who were absent also. All of these children had missed school frequently, and the twins, who were frail and sickly, had developmental delays. There was also an infant sister.

Because their parents were unavailable, the children's case was reported to the county child protective services, who were already familiar with the family. It was discovered that the children had been deserted. Their mother, who was addicted to drugs and alcohol, was hospitalized following delivery of a seventh child, who was diagnosed with fetal alcohol syndrome (FAS), and her current boyfriend was missing. Kevin's father had left many years previously. Kevin and his 7-year-old sister, Meg, were caring for the four younger children themselves. Because they had no money, Kevin had been going to grocery stores and begging for food and scavanging through the garbage. He also had been begging for money and collected enough money to buy milk and diapers for his infant sister who was cared for by Meg. An investigation of the family situation indicated that Kevin and his sisters, in addition to being neglected, had been physically and sexually abused by their mother's boyfriend as well as other men.

The children were placed in a children's shelter immediately and then, after a number of weeks in the shelter, foster homes were found that would take several siblings together. The twins and the newborn were placed with one family and the four other children were placed with a childless couple, the Greens. However, the staff of the agency in charge of adoptive and foster placement, who hoped that the Greens would adopt all four children, did not inform the foster parents of the abuse history nor did they tell the Greens that there were concerns about fetal alcohol effects. In the rural county in which they all lived, the Greens learned of the possibility of drug and alcohol effects from the family who had taken the affected newborn.

The Greens eventually decided that they wanted to adopt Kevin and his sisters. As part of this process, they brought the four children to a multidisciplinary center for medical and psychological evaluation. Because the Greens were unaware of the abuse history, they were concerned that the academic problems and acting out behaviors shown by Kevin and Meg since their placement were the result of attention-deficit/hyperactivity disorder (ADHD), which they believed was associated with alcohol exposure. Although they had to give consent for treatment, the county agency did not inform the multidisciplinary center of the children's social and educational history. In evaluation of the children, significant emotional problems were noted. Meg's behavior was of particular concern. She refused to go to bed at night and often awoke screaming. In addition, she appeared to be experiencing "rage" attacks during which she would be uncontrollably angry. Because the abuse history was not known, these reasons for her behavior were not evident and arrangements were made for a neurological examination and an electroencephalogram (EEG) to rule out the possibility of a seizure disorder.

Just before this appointment, the Greens discovered that Kevin was sexually molesting Meg and his other sister. Professionals at the multidisciplinary center, in compliance with the law, immediately informed the county child protection service and sent Meg and her other sisters to be evaluated by a children's hospital child abuse team. Kevin was given a series of personality tests and evaluated by a program for juvenile perpetrators. These evaluations revealed extensive and severe emotional problems, and the juvenile perpetrator program recommended that he not be returned to the foster home because there was no way to guarantee that the abuse of his sisters would not continue. Placement in a residential treatment facility was recommended for him despite the potential effects of the separation from his sisters and the Greens, to whom he was attached.

However, the county took no action to remove Kevin from the Greens' home, and the educational and mental health agencies responsible for his education and medical care stated that there were no public residential treatment facilities available and no funds provided for private placement. In addition, the adoptive workers denied previous knowledge of the children's history of abuse. Acting under a legal mandate, the multidisciplinary center's staff and professionals at the hospital where the children were evaluated for sexual abuse threatened to report this situation to the state oversight agency. A period of mutual misunderstanding and hostility followed.

Kevin was eventually removed from his original foster home and placed in one that did not have other children. He is still not receiving appropriate therapeutic services although he is being given medication. The Greens have adopted his sisters, who are receiving educational and therapeutic interventions because of their adoptive parents' persistence. The twins and the baby with FAS remain in foster care and receive EI services.

Most of the professionals—teachers, social workers, psychologists, and physicians—who were aware of the these children's experiences, reacted to the situation with significant distress. There was a reluctance to accept that Kevin was irrevocably damaged by his experiences and that he would have to be taken out of his foster home. There was considerable anger at the county agencies for the way in which the case was handled and at the "system" because there were not adequate resources available to provide appropriate treatment for Kevin. The staff of the county agency responded that their behavior was not the result of malice or incompetence but of the lack of resources, including inadequate staffing, lack of access to appropriate treatment facilities, and little training in the recognition of and response to such situations.

Although extreme, this story suggests the difficulties that can be encountered when a family requires intervention from many sources. In most cases, problems are less obvious and outcomes more positive. However, it is important to be aware of the ways in which different professionals and systems understand these problems. Different systems have different rules and these may not be compatible with one another at all times. For example, EI programs see women as mothers, as good or bad parents, who are more or less able to support their children's progress. As a result, staff have limited patience with and training about working with parents disabled by addiction. In contrast, addiction treatment programs see mothers primarily as addicts and often have limited understanding of the effect of motherhood on a woman's emotions and behavior.

These differences in emphasis grow out of the goals and purposes of these different agencies. Most early intervention programs have a strong emphasis on family involvement. Their methods stress this approach, and staff members' belief systems are organized around services for children and parents. Parents' roles in such a system are rather narrowly defined. Although EI teams understand that the family must be supported in order to help improve the child's development, they may not be sympathetic with mothers who behave in immature, needy ways or whose focus is on their own recovery rather than their children's needs. Finally, treatment is often organized around training the parent to act as a therapist for the child to stimulate physical, cognitive, and emotional development. Inherent in this belief system is a point of view that the child's special needs and vulnerabilities make a focus on the child paramount.

In contrast, most substance abuse treatment programs, until very recently, required that parents be separated from children for detoxification and treatment. The belief system associated with substance abuse treatment required that, during the first part of treatment, addicts must be separated from outside contacts in order to break connections with the old, addicted lifestyle. Therefore, addicts often were forbidden to contact anyone outside the treatment center including young children.

Recently, some residential substance abuse treatment programs, understanding the need to deal with both mothers and children, have incorporated therapeutic nurseries into their programs. The result is that the two groups of professionals must learn how to work together and resolve any philosophical differences that arise. In one outpatient substance abuse program in northern California, which had previously served male alcoholics, the addition of a federally funded demonstration program for pregnant women and their children led to many changes in the way services were provided—vans became available to provide transportation, a child day care center was set up, and lunch was included with outpatient services because women were pregnant and young children were hungry. More radically, therapists began to provide nurturing as well as substance abuse treatment and 12-Step programs to pregnant young women who had never received adequate parenting themselves. Initially, male addicts and traditional substance abuse professionals were angry at what they considered coddling of the women, but eventually they decided that the changes were an improvement and began to see that male addicts might benefit from a similar change of emphasis as well.

There are many other examples of confusion among systems; however, the important point for professionals is to understand the need to remain aware of these potential problems and to avoid the complications they cause whenever possible.

EFFECTS OF WORKING WITH FAMILIES WITH MULTIPLE NEEDS

Despite the best efforts to provide for individuals of families with multiple needs, a number of things can interfere with services to children. In addition to frequent problems involving inadequate services, lack of coordination among service providers often leads to confusion and inefficiency (see Chapter 8). Sometimes, providers are not sufficiently trained to work effectively with these families, and their own well-meaning ignorance or unacknowledged prejudices can interfere with treatment or educational outcomes. Some more specific problems have been identified as commonly encountered in working with substance abusers and their families. If those professionals who work with them are aware of these potential issues, they can be more effective in their efforts and can avoid potential pitfalls.

Triangulation

Triangulation is a concept from systems theory that views people as part of complex organizations or systems. Families, agencies, organizations, and communities all are examples of systems. Teachers, psychologists, social workers, special educators, and health care professionals all work within systems—schools, clinics, and social agencies—

that serve families at high risk. Within a larger system, there are
various subsystems, hierarchies, and triangles. The triangle is seen
as the smallest stable unit, a three-person, emotional configuration
(Bowen, 1976). When there is little stress, the triangle is stable, usually with a comfortably close pair and one person who is involved in
a less central way. The classic example of this relationship is the family in which father and mother are the pair who are both in a relationship with their child (see Figure 3.2). However, when there is
stress, the dynamics of the relationship may shift with the outsider
(the third point of the triangle) coming into a too close relationship
with one of the original pair, and the other member being excluded
or having a reduced role. In a family, when parents are in conflict,
one of the children may be drawn into the triangle, forming a closer
relationship with a parent than is desirable. An extreme example of
this kind of pattern occurs in incestuous families, but it occurs in less

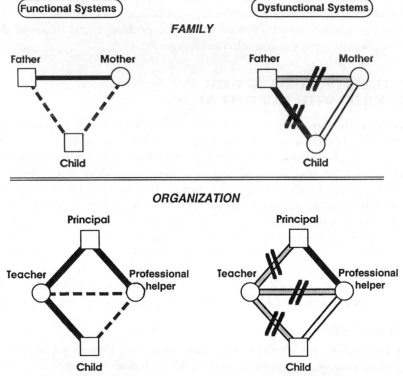

Figure 3.2. Triangulation in dysfunctional systems. The bonds between the people involved in
the dysfunctional systems are as follows: ▬▬▬ Strong relationship, ══╫╫══ Conflict,
▬ ▬ ▬ ▬ Less involved relationship, and ═══════ Inappropriately involved relationship.

toxic forms in many other families. In families with an addiction, a child may be "parentified" to help with adult responsibilities because the parent with an addiction can no longer assume them and has been reduced to a dependent role.

In highly disorganized families, such as some single-parent families living in poverty, there is no parent dyad, so other individuals, grandmothers, older children, or boyfriends or girlfriends, are often pulled into triangles with the parent and child. In such situations, when the family becomes involved with agencies or the legal system, parents may be excluded either through their own actions or by legal or social agencies. When there are a number of service providers and educators involved with a family, there are many opportunities for triangulation. Police, courts, social agencies, and school personnel all can be drawn into triangles with parents with an addiction and their children. When helpers are pulled into a triangle, conflict often is transferred from the family, where it originated and eventually must be resolved, to the helping system. The concerned teacher, substance abuse counselor, or protective service worker can be drawn into conflict about visitation or custody or other aspects of the relationship between the mother and child, which frees the addict from having to face the consequences of her actions. Similarly, the teacher who focuses on the mother's problems can avoid understanding any difficulties involved in her own interactions with the student. Similar interactions occur within organizations, particularly organizations that are under the type of stress that occurs when there are many families with multiple needs to be helped.

Triangulation is a common strategy, but not an effective one, for coping with in-system problems in agencies and schools as well. When a system is functional, problems are resolved through one-to-one interactions without involving third parties. For example, when there is a disagreement between two supervisors about a managerial issue or about how to resolve the conflict between the lack of resources and a child's need for services, in a functioning system, this problem will be resolved through direct negotiation between the two supervisors. In a dysfunctional system, a triangulation will occur, in which a teacher or other service provider will be pulled into a triangle so that the managers can avoid confrontation. Although the immediate tension between the two supervisors is resolved in this way, the problems usually continue.

Countertransference

Analysts first used the term *countertransference* to describe the emotional reactions of the helping professional or service provider to the student, patient, or client. The term comes from another term, *transference,* that is used to describe the client's emotional reaction to the therapist. Both terms refer to sometimes-unconscious feelings that develop during a helping interaction. In these interactions, the student, patient, or client is in the less powerful role of the person needing and seeking help from the more powerful professional person. As a result of the nature of this relationship, clients often develop strong feelings about professionals, often similar to those they felt about other authority figures, including parents, spouses, and teachers. During these interactions, a transference of feelings occurs that may confuse or exaggerate the present situation with the emotional reactions that belong to other contexts.

Helping professionals, however, also may have reactions to the client or the student that are affected by their own feelings and needs. These feelings are called countertransference. If the countertransference feelings are not monitored carefully, they can interfere with professional plans and activities. Imhof, Hirsch, and Terenzi (1983) note that dealing with individuals with high needs, such as addicts, often produces strong feelings of this type. Children, particularly young children and adolescents, also arouse very strong feelings, both positive and negative, in those who work with them.

Imhof et al. (1983) discuss how this process can affect the interaction between the helper and the family and interfere with professional effectiveness. If countertransference is occurring, the professional should pay more attention to the dynamics of the situation in order to avoid this significant problem. The following is a list of individual reactions that may indicate countertransference is occurring:

1. *Bad behavior on the part of the professional (i.e., acting in ways that are not professional)* Exhibiting frequent lateness, forgetfulness, or mistakes in judgment or getting bored with the person to be helped is bad professional behavior. Concrete examples are the protective service coordinator who does not make a planned home visit because she is too tired to drive across town or a teacher who does not remember to carry out a behavioral modification plan consistently and then complains that behavior modification does not work. The behavior of the adoptive workers in the case study of Kevin and his family are probably the result of this type of reaction.
2. *Overprescription of medication* Prescribing too much medication for treatment is a particular risk for physicians. In situations of this kind, the physicians may feel sorry for people who appear to be suffering, or feel helpless in the face of unsolvable prob-

lems. To compensate, they may overprescribe medication, including antidepressants and Ritalin, when alternative treatments or no treatment might have been more appropriate.

3. *Pseudoparenting* Pseudoparenting occurs when professionals, who are trying to help difficult clients, begin to take on the role of the "good" parent or the "bad" parent. In some cases, this behavior results from their own feelings, but often it comes as a reaction to the demanding or dependent behavior of the people with whom they are working. Obviously, when dealing with children, it is easy to fall into this role. The teacher, for example, might feel that he or she is better qualified to parent a particular child than the mother who is seen as neglectful or disturbed. By interfering in this way, the teacher can take away the parent's authority without solving the original problem.

4. *"You and me against the unjust world"* When the professional "overidentifies" with the client it may result in a bond between the two against society. For example, the professional may begin to see the addict as a social rebel who is challenging an unjust world or as a neglected child who has a right to violent or outrageous reactions. If the professional shares some characteristics with the person who needs help (i.e., life history, ethnic background, sexual orientation), this reaction may occur more readily. In such situations, a disgruntled or angry professional may tolerate or encourage "acting out" on the part of the student or client instead of setting appropriate limits.

5. *Taking responsibility for the other's outcome* It is very gratifying to the professional to see improvement and very upsetting to watch failure; thus, it is very easy to take responsibility for the client's outcome. Helpers who begin to see the accomplishments and failures of the people they are working with as their own rather than the other person's can become ineffective. A common pattern is for the professional to become elated by an improvement and to react punitively when the person they are working with fails to meet expectations.

Countertransference can occur in a system as well as in an individual. The following is a list of systemic reactions that may indicate countertransference is occurring:

1. *Systemic countertransference* Sometimes, the countertransference goes beyond the individual helper and affects the whole school, agency, or treatment center. When this happens, the entire system may organize itself around its reaction to a particular child or family. This type of problem can arise, for example, when a

child becomes the identified "bad kid" in a class or when a parent's behavior becomes a major focus of outrage for the staff of an early intervention center. This problem usually develops when there is stress in the system (e.g., when the facility is understaffed, when there is concern about budget cuts, or when the population being served is very impaired or difficult). Under such circumstances, the negligent behavior of a mother with an addiction whose child has fetal alcohol syndrome may begin to arouse a great deal of hostility in staff members. This hostility may then be expressed toward the mother in such a way that eventually she stops bringing the child to the center for treatment. The staff is then relieved of some of their stress and the mother is no longer faced with emotionally painful results of her alcohol abuse in pregnancy. However, the child's development is further impaired and any opportunity to improve as a result of early intervention is lost.

2. *Societal countertransference* Countertransference also can be applied to the general society. When dealing with families at high risk, the individuals in the family are often stereotyped by professionals (e.g., "bio-underclass," "piss-poor protoplasm," "crack baby") and seen as the cause of their own problems or as, in a profound sense, less worthy. The well-documented phenomenon of "blaming the victim" (Ryan, 1971) is a similar process in which the anxiety aroused in others by the victim's experience is resolved by placing the blame for the misfortune on the victimized person.

For similar reasons, those who work with addicts often describe them as manipulative and sociopathic, thus placing responsibility both for the addiction and for treatment failure on the addict. It is often difficult to overcome these reactions because, to do so, requires that the teacher, therapist, or physician examine his or her own motives and feelings and separate these emotions from more balanced reactions to the person with whom he or she is working. Unfortunately, it is often difficult for people to face their own negative feelings and less-than-admirable behaviors. Therefore, to be effective in working with families with multiple needs, professionals must be able to attend to their own issues regarding racism, sexual politics, poverty, incest, and other forms of child abuse, as well as addiction.

Burnout

The most significant pitfall for those working with families and difficult social conditions is a phenomenon called *burnout* (Kurland & Salmon, 1992; Maslach, 1982). This problem occurs among human services professionals, such as teachers, police officers, social workers, physicians, and therapists. It is defined by Maslach (1982) as a "syndrome of emotional exhaustion, depersonalization, and reduced [feelings of] personal accomplishment." Professionals who are burnt out may experience physical and emotional exhaustion. Those with this condition no longer may have sympathy, respect, or positive feelings for the people with whom they work and may begin to treat them in impersonal and derogatory ways. Under these conditions, the professional is no longer working competently and decision making can become rigid and ineffective (McGee, 1989). Working with families with intensive needs and with addicts can, in the most extreme cases, lead to what has been called secondary posttraumatic stress disorder (PTSD) in professionals who may even experience some of the symptoms of PTSD. Such professionals may react with sleeplessness, hypervigilance, anxiety, and other symptoms of stress.

Coping Strategies Professional helpers should be aware of the risk of being affected by the stress associated with their jobs. There are strategies for reducing this risk. To maintain professional and personal balance, it is important to do those things that provide adequate internal and external support.

Professional skills can be maintained and enhanced through ongoing professional interactions, continued education, and support by appropriate supervision and/or mentoring. When professionals become aware that some problems have developed, it is necessary to ask for supervision from peers and mentors in order to clarify their thinking. For this reason, it is vital to have a working environment that allows and encourages such professional support.

In addition, it is important for professionals to have realistic goals for the people they are trying to help and to have access to adequate resources when needed. The system in which the interaction takes place (e.g., school, training center, clinic) should be supportive of the faculty or staff, and clear organizational goals that are not in conflict with this support and with the ongoing professional activities should be set.

Finally, it is important for service providers to keep their own lives and alternative activities apart from their work and to devote time to these activities. Service providers also should remember that despite the difficulties involved in working with families affected by substance abuse, there are often positive outcomes.

Reprise: Antonio and Linda Martin
Antonio and his family initially came to the attention of professionals when he was referred for medical assessment of

his genetic disorder. However, he also was referred to Head Start, which he qualified for initially due to his status as economically "at risk." The family also encountered "the system," when his father, a drug dealer, committed an assault during a drug sale. Because of his father's imprisonment, his mother was forced to apply for Aid to Families with Dependent Children (AFDC), and at the same time, Antonio's behavior at preschool was noticed by his teachers and he was referred for special services.

Although the Martins had many problems, they also had some resources available both personally and in the community. Antonio was referred to a university-based multidisciplinary center for children with developmental problems. The center's program allows medical, psychological, speech-language, and social assessments to be carried out and a well-organized and transdisciplinary treatment plan developed. The center worked with the public school system to have appropriate educational services and curricula provided for Antonio. He did require speech-language therapy, which was provided by the school system. His mother received therapy from a social worker in a private agency to help her deal both with the immediate family crises and with her own history of abuse. In addition, child care for the younger children was arranged through a program that also provided job training and placement services. Antonio's emotional and behavior problems were addressed through family therapy with him and his mother, during which his mother learned how to discipline him effectively as well as how to work through his sadness about the loss of his father. Transportation for all these appointments was provided by Medicaid, which also paid for the medical and psychological services. A year after the initial evaluation, Mrs. Martin was able to take a secretarial job. Antonio's behavior problems were improved greatly, which appeared to be the result of both his improved ability to speak clearly as well as changes in his interactions with his mother. Mrs. Martin plans to move the family away from the projects as soon as she is able to save money for a deposit on an apartment in another section of the city. Although this family continues to be at risk, multi-level intervention and cooperation among professionals has led to a positive outcome. Given Mrs. Martin's personal resources, she has been able to use the help offered to provide for a better future for herself and her children.

Reprise: Clarissa Brown
Following the referral to child protective services (CPS), a service coordinator was assigned to monitor the home situation for the two sisters. Clarissa was referred to a local mental health agency for counseling services and participation in a support group for children of alcoholic families. The school's guidance counselor was identified as the person to maintain communication between CPS and the mental health center for ongoing service coordination with the local school. Sam's and Rebecca's divorce was finalized with the girls' father being awarded custody. Rebecca has re-entered treatment. Clarissa and Dawn are permitted to visit her in the program on a regular basis and participate in the family counseling group provided by the treatment agency. Sam is interviewed on a regular basis by the CPS coordinator and is being given parenting assistance to help him in his parent role.

SUMMARY

As families and their children are affected by substance abuse and addiction, a synergistic effect results that negatively affects not only the family's ability to function successfully but also the developmental tasks of the family's children that are important for school success. For interventions to be effective, a comprehensive view of the family and its issues must be taken, with multiple agency services being involved.

Families with multiple issues will not present typical characteristics. These families require a comprehensive assessment process as agencies collaborate on referral and service planning with the family. The family, with the help of professionals, must learn to prioritize their needs and obtain services important for their ability to function.

The needs of any vulnerable family are beyond the resources or the responsibilities of any single agency. The developmental needs of the family's children, the survival needs of the family unit, and the need for developing the family's ability to meet its own needs independently will require professionals to be flexible and innovative in how resources are matched with individual families. The more creative professionals can be in matching their own professional knowledge and skills with one another to work collaboratively with families, the better the odds are that the family will be helped to be successful.

Working with families and their children who present multiple issues is not an easy task. Frustration, burnout, lack of knowledge, and lack of resources can present formidable barriers to the most dedicated professional. Agencies must be cognizant of the issues that families and children may present to the service providers and provide appropriate resources to meet the needs of agency staffs. Support groups for service providers, "well-employee programs," organized recreational activities for staff, and ongoing opportunities for professional development are examples of ways in which agencies can help their staff address their own needs and in turn be more successful in working with clients.

REFERENCES

Beckman, L., & Amaro, H. (1986). Personal and social differences faced by females and males entering alcoholism treatment. *Journal of Studies on Alcohol, 47,* 135–145.

Beckwith, L. (1990). Adaptive and maladaptive parenting—Implications for intervention. In S.J. Meisels & J.P. Shonkoff (Eds.), *Handbook of early childhood intervention* (pp. 53–77). New York: Cambridge University Press.

Bowen, M. (1976). Theory in the practice of psychotherapy. In P. J. Guerin (Ed.), *Family therapy: Theory and practice* (pp. 42–90). New York: Gardner Press.

Brown, E.R. (1992). Program and staff characteristics in successful treatment. In M.M. Kilbey & K. Asghar (Eds.), *Methodological issues in epidemiological, prevention, and treatment research on drug-exposed women and their children, Research monograph #117.* Rockville, MD: U.S. Department of Health and Human Services; Public Health Services; Alcohol, Drug Abuse, and Mental Health Association; National Institute on Drug Abuse.

Bryant, D.M., & Ramey, C.T. (1987). An analysis of the effectiveness of early intervention programs for environmentally at-risk children. In M.J. Guralnick & F.C. Bennett (Eds.), *The effectiveness of early intervention for at-risk and handicapped children* (pp. 33–78). Orlando, FL: Academic Press.

Buddle, D., Rounsaville, B.J., & Bryant, K.J. (1992). Inpatient and outpatient cocaine abusers: Clinical comparisons at intake and one-year follow-up. *Journal of Substance Abuse Treatment, 9,* 337–342.

Charuvastra, V.C., Dalali, I.D., Cassuci, M., & Ling, W. (1992). Outcome study: Comparison of short-term vs. long-term treatment in a residential community. *The International Journal of the Addictions, 27,* 15–23.

Coles, C.D. (1992). How the environment affects research on prenatal drug exposure: The laboratory and the community. In M.M. Kilbey & K. Asghar (Eds.), *Methodological issues in epidemiological, prevention, and treatment research on drug-exposed women and their children, Research monograph #117.* Rockville, MD: U.S. Department of Health and Human Services; Public

Health Service; Alcohol, Drug Abuse, and Mental Health Association; National Institute on Drug Abuse.

Coles, C.D., & Finnegan, L.P. (1989). *Substance abuse in pregnancy: Reproductive and developmental risk.* (Available from the Human Genetics Laboratory, Department of Psychiatry, Emory University School of Medicine) Unpublished manuscript.

Craig, S.E. (1992, September). The educational needs of children living with violence. *Phi Delta Kappan,* pp. 67–71.

Creigs, B. (1989). Treatment issues for black, alcoholic clients. *Social Casework: The Journal of Contemporary Social Work, 70* (6), 370–374.

Culp, R.E., Watkins, R.V., Lawrence, H., Letts, D., Kelly, D.J., & Rice, M.L. (1991). Maltreated children's language and speech development: Abused, neglected and abused and neglected. *First Language, 11,* 377–389.

Cummings, N.A. (1991). Inpatient versus outpatient treatment of substance abuse: Recent developments in the controversy [Special issue]. *Contemporary Family Therapy: Addictions and the Family, 13,* 507–520.

Garbarino, J. (1990). The human ecology of early risk. In S.J. Meisels & J.P. Shankoff, (Eds.), *Handbook of early childhood intervention* (pp. 78–96). New York: Cambridge University Press.

Greenhough, W.T., Wallace, C.S., Alcantara, A.A., Anderson, B.J., Hawrylak, N., Sirevaag, A.M., Weiler, I.J., & Withers, G.S. (1993). Development of the brain: Experience affects the structure of neurons, glia, and blood vessels. In N.J. Anastasiow & S. Harel (Eds.) *At-risk infants: Interventions, families and research* (pp. 173–185). Baltimore: Paul H. Brookes Publishing Co.

Greenspan, S. (1990). Comprehensive clinical approaches to infants and their families: Psychodynamic and developmental perspectives. In S.J. Meisels & J.P. Shonkoff (Eds.), *Handbook of early childhood intervention* (pp. 150–172). New York: Cambridge University Press.

Halpern, R. (1993). Poverty and infant development. In C.H. Zeanah (Ed.), *Handbook of infant mental health* (pp. 73–86). New York: Guilford Press.

Hanson, B. (1985). Drug treatment effectiveness: The case of racial and ethnic minorities in America—Some research questions and proposals. *The International Journal of the Addictions, 20,* 99–137.

Harris, S.R. (1987). Early intervention for children with motor handicaps. In M.J. Guralnick & F.C. Bennett (Eds.), *The effectiveness of early intervention for at-risk and handicapped children* (pp. 175–212). Orlando, FL: Academic Press.

Imhof, J., Hirsch, R., & Terenzi, R.E. (1983). Countertransferential and attitudinal considerations in the treatment of drug abuse and addiction. *The International Journal of the Addictions, 18,* 491–510.

Individuals with Disabilities Education Act of 1990 (IDEA), PL 101-476. (October 30, 1990). Title 20. U.S.C. 1401 et seq. *U.S. Statutes at Large, 104,* 1103–1151.

Kurland, R., & Salmon, R. (1992). When problems seem overwhelming: Emphasis in teaching, supervision, and consultation. *Social Work, 37,* 240–244.

Lief, N.R. (1985). The drug user as a parent. *The International Journal of the Addictions, 20,* 63–97.

Maslach, C. (1982). *Burnout: The high cost of caring.* Englewood Cliffs, NJ: Prentice Hall.

McGee, R.A. (1989). Burnout and professional decision making: An analogue study. *Journal of Counseling Psychology, 36,* 345–351.

Ramey, C.T., & Ramey, S.L. (1992). Effective early intervention. *Mental Retardation, 6,* 337–345.

Reed, B.G. (1985). Drug misuse and dependency in women: The meaning and implications of being considered a special population or minority group. *The International Journal of the Addictions, 20* (1), 13–62.

Ryan, W. (1971). *Blaming the victim.* New York: Pantheon.

Smith, G.H. (1993). Intervention strategies for children vulnerable for school failure due to exposure to drugs and alcohol. *The International Journal of the Addictions, 28* (13), 1435–1470.

Staples, R. (1990). Substance abuse and the black family crisis: An overview. *The Western Journal of Black Studies, 14,* 196–204.

Stedman, D.J., & Eichorn, D.H. (1964). A comparison of the growth and development of institutionalized and home-reared mongoloids during infancy and early childhood. *American Journal of Mental Deficiency, 69,* 391–401.

Thom, V.A. (1994). Provider issues in work with early intervention clients and their families: Food for thought. *Infants and Young Children, 7,* v–viii.

U.S. Secretary of Health and Human Services. (1993). *Eighth special report to the U.S. Congress on alcohol and health.* Rockville, MD: U.S. Department of Health and Human Services, Public Health Service, National Institutes of Health, National Institute on Alcohol Abuse and Alcoholism.

Windom, C.S. (1993). Child abuse and alcohol use. In S.E. Martin (Ed.), National Institute on Alcohol Abuse and Alcoholism Research Monograph No. 22. *Alcohol and interpersonal violence: Fostering multidisciplinary perspectives.* Rockville, MD: U.S. Department of Health and Human Services, Public Health Service, National Institutes of Health [NIH PUB No 93–3496].

II

STRATEGIES FOR HELPING CHILDREN

4

Building Resilience
in Infants and Toddlers
at Risk

Marie Kanne Poulsen

The healthy infant born with sound developmental/neurodevelopmental functioning to an economically and socially stable parent, who is emotionally available and temperamentally matched, will thrive as a child. The child's inborn biological resilience, expanded by enhanced psychosocial and environmental circumstances, will allow for the development of the capacities needed to meet daily challenges and overcome adversity. Infants born to women who abuse alcohol and other drugs during pregnancy are at potential developmental risk as a result of the myriad of biological, psychosocial, and environmental circumstances that can influence the eventual outcome of the child. The single negative perinatal stressor of substance exposure alone does not predict the ultimate development of the child; however, an accumulation of negative pre- and postnatal circumstances can have devastating lasting results.

Nevertheless, the now-acknowledged continuum of potential resilience inherent in all children can serve to counterbalance the vulnerabilities seen in infants at risk (Murphy & Moriarty, 1976). If compensating resilience-building supports are provided for the infant and family, the child can surmount a number of biological, psychosocial, and environmental circumstances that place him or her in potential jeopardy.

95

RISK FACTORS INFLUENCING INFANT DEVELOPMENT

Many risk factors should be addressed in the development of a system designed to serve children exposed to substance abuse. Drug and alcohol abuse within a family can lead to such uncertainty and discord that a child's developmental, behavioral, and learning capabilities can become seriously compromised. When a child is exposed also to alcohol and other drugs in utero, the risks are increased exponentially. In particular, the biological repercussion of alcohol and other drugs can affect the child's central nervous system functioning, influencing the healthy development of social relationships, learning abilities, regulation of behavior, attention, and concentration (Griffith, 1992). The combination of prenatal and postnatal environmental exposure to familial substance abuse makes the growing child particularly susceptible for negative effects.

There is no one-to-one relationship between the type and the amount of alcohol and other drugs used during pregnancy and neonatal consequence. Infants born to mothers who use drugs and alcohol demonstrate a continuum of developmental outcomes ranging from children who have developmental disabilities, to those with milder dysfunction, to those who are healthy, robust children. Prenatal substance exposure should not be distinguished as a specific diagnosis, but rather as a marker of perinatal circumstance that may lead to possible central nervous system dysfunction. Although all drugs can affect the growth and development of the unborn child, the chronic use of alcohol during pregnancy remains the most lethal for a child's outcome (Bays, 1990).

Maternal Risk Factors

Impaired physical health, poor nutritional status, and a stressful lifestyle are significant prenatal maternal risk factors that influence birth weight, general health, and neurodevelopmental functions of the infant. Women who abuse drugs and who are intravenous drug users or who are involved with men who are needle users are at risk for human immunodeficiency virus (HIV) infections. Women who have multiple sex partners are at increased risk for all sexually transmitted diseases. Many of these women lack general good health and good health care. The lack of health care becomes more serious during pregnancy. Prenatal care could address maternal infections, poor nutrition, and the risks associated with substance abuse that influence neonatal status. As a result of a lack of sufficient public prenatal services and a disinclination by many to use available resources, it has been reported that pregnant women who use drugs and alcohol are up to four times less likely to receive prenatal care compared to other women (Chavkin, 1989).

In addition, the physical and mental stress effects of homelessness, spousal abuse, and social isolation on pregnant women can also lead to infants with lower birth weights and who are less healthy (Bennet, 1990). The physical and mental stress of these psychosocial circumstances can leave women emotionally drained and thus influence the quality of maternal caregiving after the birth of their child.

Risk for premature birth increases when pregnant women receive no prenatal care, or experience maternal infections and poor nutrition. Infants born to women who receive minimal or no prenatal care have significantly greater perinatal mortality and morbidity (Moore, Origel, Key, & Resnik, 1986). Some urban hospitals report that up to 80% of their new mothers who abuse substances receive minimal or no prenatal services. However, perinatal morbidity, associated with prenatal drug abuse, cannot be eliminated entirely by improved prenatal care (MacGregor, Keith, Bachicha, & Chasnoff, 1989).

Neonatal Medical Conditions

Neonatal medical conditions, such as intrauterine growth retardation (IUGR), failure to thrive, sexually transmitted diseases, HIV infections, fetal alcohol syndrome (FAS), and fetal alcohol effects (FAE), may affect learning, behavior, and development as the child grows.

Intrauterine Growth Retardation (IUGR) Intrauterine growth retardation refers to poor fetal growth. The fetus may be smaller than is expected for the gestational age, or fetal growth may have plateaued or slowed down, resulting in a newborn whose weight is below the tenth percentile for gestation on a standard intrauterine growth curve (Vohr, 1991). The prenatal use of heroin, cocaine, alcohol, and amphetamines has been associated with the increased incidence of IUGR (Fulroth, Phillips, & Durand, 1989; Oro & Dixon, 1987). IUGR is not a marker of disability, but nevertheless can be considered a marker of risk for later learning disability, attention-deficit/hyperactivity disorder, and behavior disorder (Allen, 1992).

Failure to Thrive Infants who have been prenatally exposed to drugs and alcohol are at increased risk for failure to thrive, indicating some significant growth delay that also may affect developmental progress and attachment (Singer & Fagan, 1984; Ward, Kessler, & Altman, 1992). An infant's failure to thrive may be the result of the compounding effect of increased gastrointestinal vulnerability, depressed interactive behaviors, and lack of maternal emotional availability.

Sexually Transmitted Diseases   The young woman, the poor woman, and the pregnant woman who abuses drugs are at increased risk for acquiring and passing sexually transmitted diseases to their offspring (Scott, 1989). Most sexually transmitted diseases (e.g., herpes) are acquired by the infant during the birth process. However, syphilis is transmitted across the placenta in utero. Untreated mothers may deliver infants who may manifest no clinical abnormality for weeks or months, and thus remain untreated themselves. Untreated infants may manifest general symptoms of fever, poor weight gain, and restlessness. Later, untreated congenital syphilis can result in visual or auditory impairment or neurological disease that can affect learning, behavior, and development (Williamson & Demmler, 1992). Studies have reported between 15% and 25% of infants born prenatally exposed to drugs and alcohol have a positive toxicological screen for syphilis (Burkett, Yasin, & Palow, 1990; Scott, 1989). Congenital syphilis could be contained or eliminated prior to birth through good prenatal care.

HIV Infections   The growing number of infants born with HIV antibodies is alarming. By spring 1992, almost 4,000 children infected with HIV had been reported to the Centers for Disease Control. The perinatal transmission of infection from mother to child accounts for the majority of new cases. Of women with acquired immunodeficiency syndrome (AIDS), 52% have a history of intravenous drug use (Wara, 1992).

Not all newborns who are HIV positive, however, get AIDS. Many infants passively carry the maternal antibody, which disappears as the infant matures. After 15 months of age, the presence of antibody to HIV is sufficient evidence of infection (Johnson, 1993). Once children become symptomatic, they may become progressively more neurologically dysfunctional leading to delayed motor milestones, delayed language and cognition, and increased motor weakness (Wayment, 1988). The combination of dealing with AIDS, issues surrounding drug recovery, and possibly a sick infant, places the parenting capacities of these women in extreme jeopardy. Because most children with HIV infections live for several years, they must be helped to cope with the challenges that come with a chronic illness and to deal with the social stigma that still accompanies this disease.

Fetal Alcohol Syndrome (FAS)   Fetal alcohol syndrome is the only established risk directly related to substance consumption. Prenatal alcohol exposure is one of the leading causes of birth defects and mental retardation in the United States (Bays, 1990). It is estimated that 1–3 per 1,000 children each year will be born with FAS. Alcohol-related abnormalities seen in FAS include growth retardation (e.g., small head size), central nervous system impairment, and facial malformations (e.g., small eyes, drooping eyelids, flat midface) (Streissguth, 1986). The cognitive abilities of children with FAS also can be seriously impaired. Studies have reported the average IQ of children with FAS to be 68 with a range from 6–105 (Larsson, 1982).

Fetal Alcohol Effects (FAE) Fetal alcohol effects, or alcohol-related birth defects (ARBD), are seen in an estimated 40,000 newborns each year (Cook, Petersen, & Moore, 1990). FAE and ARBD refer to less severe developmental sequelae than FAS that may influence a child's activity level, attention, intellectual abilities, speech, and behavior.

Neonatal Abstinence Syndrome In addition, the newborn may experience neonatal abstinence syndrome as a result of withdrawal from prenatal exposure to heroin and methadone. Withdrawal symptoms may appear up to 10 days after birth and last from 2–8 weeks. Central nervous system, gastrointestinal, respiratory, and autonomic signs and symptoms may include irritability, poor sleeping, mild tremors, high-pitched cries, increased muscle tone, poor feeding, diarrhea, frantic sucking of the fists, vomiting, dehydration, sweating, mottling, sensitivity to sounds, and respiratory distress (Zuckerman, 1991). Withdrawal signs and symptoms not only affect the weight gain and health status of the infant, but influence how the infant experiences the world and, most importantly, how the infant experiences and responds to the developing relationship with the parent.

Infant Neurodevelopmental Risk Factors

Healthy infants demonstrate certain important neurodevelopmental behaviors that help them relate effectively to the people, objects, and events in their world, leading to positive developmental outcome.

However, the repercussion of perinatal insult from prenatal exposure to drugs and alcohol, low birth weight, prematurity, small size for gestational age, and sexually transmitted diseases can result in neurodevelopmental behavioral vulnerabilities that may or may not be outgrown. The newborn and young infant may manifest low sensory threshold, increased muscle tone, poor regulation and organization of behavior, and depressed interactive behaviors (Deren, 1986). These neurodevelopmental immaturities not only affect how the child perceives and responds to the world, but, more importantly, may affect the manner in which caregiving is provided and received.

Feeding Patterns Feeding one's infant is a primary function of parenthood. Healthy newborns quickly learn to find and grasp the nipple, suck in an organized fashion, eat in a reasonable time, and retain food with very little prodding from the parent. Gradually, during the first few weeks of life, infants begin to develop regularity in their feeding schedules. The process of parents feeding their infants becomes a mutually satisfying situation with the parent acquiring a growing sense of parental efficacy and the infant learning to trust that the world is a predictable nurturing place.

When infants have difficulty grasping the nipple or have a weak suck, feeding can become an exhausting task. If the infant has difficulty retaining food, the process can be traumatic. When a mother or father has difficulty feeding a child, the parent's self-confidence and self-esteem can be placed in jeopardy. When the feeding situation becomes mutually anxiety-provoking, rather than mutually fulfilling, the quality of parent–child attachment can become imperiled.

Mother and infant will have a more positive feeding experience to the extent each is in a relaxed or calm state. Anticipating a feeding time before the infant is distressed can be helpful. A quiet, calm environment is soothing for both the mother and her infant. Modifying the amount of intake and burping the infant more frequently is helpful for some. Supporting the infant in a semi-flexed position and supporting the infant's chin or cheeks to help with sucking are handling techniques that also can enhance the feeding experience.

Sleeping Patterns Establishing a sleeping schedule indicates the infant is learning to regulate behavior. Newborns sleep 75% of the day. Most infants institute regular nap times and sleep through the night by 3 months of age. Infants with sensitive nervous systems or neurodevelopmental immaturities may have sleeping difficulties, such as trouble going to sleep and short sporadic periods of restless sleep. They may need assistance in becoming relaxed and calm before being put to bed. Sleep deprivation in infants may lead to increased fussiness, resulting in sleep deprivation for the adults and others in the household. The sleeping problems of an infant can create stress that can affect the development of infant behavior, the parent's self-esteem, and the quality of parent–child interactions.

Calming the infant before bedtime and providing quiet, darkened places to sleep can assist in the establishment of good sleeping patterns. Swaddling is soothing to the infant and providing soft music or a ticking clock has been helpful for some infants in falling asleep. When infants fuss before it is time for feeding, they can be offered a finger or pacifier for nonnutritive sucking.

States of Alertness An infant's capacity to control a level of consciousness and behavioral activity is another indication of neurological integrity and the capacity to regulate behavior. Healthy infants demonstrate a sequence of levels of alertness that include sound sleep, light sleep, drowsy wakefulness, calm focused alertness, fussiness, and crying. The newborn may experience an average of 3–5 minutes an hour in calm focused alertness. This important period of quiet alertness allows for mutual eye engagement by the parent and child and provides the foundation for parent–child bonding and relationship. When infants are unable to regulate or modulate their behavior, they may go from fussiness and crying to sleep after being fed. Valuable time for parent–infant engagement is lost and can jeopardize the quality of the relationship if the situation persists over time or if the parent interprets the behavior as a lack of desire or need for personalized intimate attention.

Infants prenatally exposed to phenocyclidine may demonstrate a hypervigilant state of alertness with long periods of alert wakefulness. However, during these periods the infants may constantly dart their eyes over their parents' faces and lack the calm focused attention that leads to mutual engagement.

Positioning can influence an infant's capacity to control a state of calm focused alertness. Infants who are held in an "en face" semi-upright flexed position, or who are held upright at the shoulder, or who are placed in a sidelying, flexed position find it easier to attain and maintain calm focused alertness. Shielding the infant's eyes from bright lights, tickling the infants' cheek to arouse, or swaying the infant gently are other ways to arouse the infant to a state of alertness.

Self-Consolation All infants cry. Healthy babies may cry up to 2–3 hours a day in the early months. Infants who can regulate their behavior frequently are able to control their whimpers and calm themselves to a more composed state without adult intervention. This allows them to spend more time in focused alertness to attend visually and auditorially and learn about the people, objects, and events in their world. Infants who have difficulty regulating their behavior may have all their whimpers escalate into full howls of distress for which comfort from others may be only marginally effective. Infants with immature nervous systems may cry for 6 hours or more a day. In addition, these infants with highly sensitive nervous systems may not respond to repositioning, patting, swaddling, stroking, cuddling, and pacifiers the way a more regulated infant might.

The sense of efficacy that is so important to both the parent and the infant can become imperiled when parent and child experience the inability to control the infant's distress effectively.

Anticipating infant distress and responding at the first whimpers can help prevent some prolonged crying episodes. Providing a finger or pacifier for nonnutritive sucking can help soothe some infants. Swaddling the infant in a flexed position also can help gain control over crying states. Handling strategies that have proved successful include placing one's hand firmly across the infant's chest, holding the infant's folded arms close to the infant's chest, and rocking the infant vertically and slowly. Some infants feel soothed by skin-to-skin contact. Massaging and bathing an infant in warm water may help calm the overwrought child.

Sensory Threshold Infants are born with certain internal physiological mechanisms that protect them from overstimulation. This process is called *habituation*. Newborns, who may become alert or startle when noise, bright lights, sudden touch, or movement first occur, physiologically "tune out" the stimuli when it is repeated if their nervous systems are intact. Gradually, as the infants mature, the process of habituation fades and infants become able to tolerate greater levels of stimulation without becoming overstressed. However, newborns with immature or highly sensitive nervous systems may not habituate, become overwhelmed with stimulation, and may dissolve quickly and easily into howling cries of distress. The overwhelmed newborn may withdraw, become rigid, or evidence signs of autonomic nervous system dysfunction (Gorski, Hale, Leonard, & Martin, 1983). If the nervous system remains hypersensitive, the child will remain overreactive to sensory stimuli.

The situation becomes compounded if the infant also has difficulty recovering from distress. A potential danger occurs if parents read or interpret the infant's distress response to be "leave me alone" cues rather than "protect me, I'm overwhelmed" signals. The infant needs help learning to be able to handle modicum amounts of stimulation.

Reducing the level and intensity of noise, light, movement, and/or commotion protects the hypersensitive infant from overload. The suddenness of unanticipated sound, movement, and bright light also can prove to be overpowering. Infants who can see and hear their mothers prior to being handled or moved are better prepared for the new situation. Hypersensitive infants need to be introduced to levels of stimulation gradually, starting with dim lights, quiet voices, and slow deliberate touch. This will help them learn to tolerate increasing levels of stimulation and build their sensory threshold.

Multiple sources of stimulation can prove to be overpowering for the sensitive infant. Maternal eye contact, touching, and voice can be too much for the infant to manage when all the stimulation occurs at once. Some infants who become overwhelmed when engaging in eye contact and listening to their mother's voice are able to handle the situation if at first humming, whispers, or a soft voice accompanies eye engagement. When infants are overcome by too much stimulation, they will avert their gaze from their mothers' eyes. Infants need to be allowed to rest rather than be pursued at these times.

Muscle Tone Neonates who experience perinatal stress may demonstrate flaccid or increased muscle tone. An increase or decrease in muscle tone is usually transient and levels as the infant matures (Als & Duffy, 1989). However, tone abnormalities may persist and interfere with function. Infants with persistent increased muscle tones may have difficulty nestling when their parents try to cuddle them. Inexperienced parents may interpret the infants' inability to cuddle easily to mean that they do not wish to be held. Parents can be taught new ways of handling and positioning their infants that make them easier to cuddle. Once positioned, most infants learn to enjoy nestling close to their parents' bodies. Also, infants who have unbalanced muscle tone may not be able to reach as easily for objects without assistance.

Positioning and handling strategies that encourage a balanced tone include placing the baby bed on a slight slant with the head at the higher end; placing a small pillow under the infant's head when diapering; carrying the infant in a bent forward sitting position or on a soft pillow; and placing the infant in a side-lying, flexed position. Some infants may need help in protracting their shoulders so opportunities for reaching and midline and exploratory play are increased.

Organization of Behavior Infants with maturation and experience are able to respond to the world in an increasingly more efficient, effective, and organized manner. They are able to incorporate social attention into their daily living activities without losing effectiveness. For example, a typical 1-month-old is able to seek eye contact in the process of nursing and the 2-month-old is able to stop nursing in order to smile to the caregiver's voice and be able to resume nursing in a smooth, efficient manner. The integration of social initiation and social responsivity into the activities of daily living provides a rich base for the enhancement of the relationship between parent and child.

An infant who is poorly organized may not be able to combine sequences of behaviors with efficiency. The disorganized 1-month-old will not be able to search for eye contact while in the process of nursing; and the 2-month-old may lose the nipple when smiling to mother's voice and may not be able to resume nursing with ease, resulting in a distressed crying baby, an anxious mother, and a stressful experience for both. The mother may learn not to relate to her infant during the feeding process, thus losing many important moments of potential meaningful engagement. The infant who is fed with an absence of social interaction does not have the opportunity to learn to integrate experience and organize behavior. Most immature infants can learn to organize their behavior better if the social interactions are introduced in a quiet less intrusive manner, such as with a soft voice, a hum, or a whisper.

Infants with low sensory thresholds or poor modulation of state also may demonstrate poor behavioral organization. When an infant is overly stimulated and unable to maintain calm focused attention, behavior becomes disjointed, disorganized, and ineffectual. Healthy 3-month-olds will see their mothers' faces, control their behavior to calm focused alertness, and be ready to initiate and respond to this typical situation of potential mutual engagement. Disorganized infants will see their mothers' faces, become inordinately excited, and instead of achieving a state of calm focused alertness with a readiness to engage, will begin to flail arms and legs in eager anticipation of an event that will not eventuate. These infants need parental intervention to help them attain a state of focused alertness and behavioral organization. Once parents intervene, the disorganized infants will be better able to initiate and respond in infant–parent interaction.

Infants are more able to organize behavior when they are protected from intense levels of noise, light, commotion and movement, and when they are introduced to increased levels of stimulation and different sources of stimulation gradually. Young infants can be helped to organize their eye engagement and following behaviors when they are swaddled and calmed prior to interactive contact.

Interactive Behaviors   Infants are born with behaviors that promote parent attention, interaction, and relationship. The infant's inborn propensity for eye contact, cuddliness, throaty sounds, smiling, and visually following love objects with the eyes sets up the infant for attachment to caregivers. When the parent recognizes, acknowledges, and responds to the infant's initiating behaviors, a mutual dialogue begins that manifests in increased mutual gazing, responsive smiling, vocal dialogue, and joint attention. Through mutual dialogue, the infant begins to develop a sense of self-efficacy and a sense of trust that the world is good and nurturing and the caregiver is loving, reliable, and predictable. Neurodevelopmental immaturities can result in fewer, less vigorous interactive behaviors on the part of the infant. It may be difficult for the mother to recognize her infant's more muted and sporadic attempts at social initiation. Infants who initiate less tend to receive less attention from caregivers, thus jeopardizing emotional, social, and cognitive development. Inexperienced, anxious, and overwhelmed mothers may need help in reading their infants' subtle social cues.

The most important interactive caregiving strategy is to recognize and respond to the infants subtle interactive cues. Immediate response to muted smiles, throaty vocalizations, and soft smiles helps the infant learn the world is a responsive, caring place. Infants should be positioned where eye contact between caregiver and infant is easily attained. Infants benefit when human interaction is incorporated into daily caregiving activities, such as feeding, bathing, diapering, and dressing.

CAREGIVING STRATEGIES FOR ENHANCING INFANT RESILIENCE

It is clear that the most serious repercussion of neonatal and infant neurodevelopmental vulnerability is the potential influence it may have on parent caregiving, the parent–infant bonding process, and the development of meaningful relationships between parent and child. Meaningful relationships are crucial to the healthy development of all children. They provide the "emotional fuel" children need to explore, discover, and learn. Meaningful relationships enhance the influence or power of adult modeling, guidance, and emotional support and provide children with a sense of self that enables them to persist in difficult tasks, pursue goals not immediately attainable, and handle internal frustrations and external stressors. Service providers need to determine which mother–infant dyads need added external supports or services in order for the family unit to thrive.

A group of highly sensitive newborns will "outgrow" their early difficult start due to the process of maturation and the inborn biological thrust toward health, development, and resilience (Rauh, Narcombe, Ruff, Jette, & Howell, 1982). If the neurodevelopmental vulnerabilities are mild or transient and the mother is experienced, emotionally available, and has a good support system, then positive outcome is fairly predictable and extra parenting support may not be necessary. Many experienced mothers with available "parent support systems" will be able to deal with their infant's neurodevelopmental vulnerabilities with no negative parent–child repercussions and minimal professional intervention.

However, when a parent is young, anxious, inexperienced, struggling with drug recovery, guilt, and depression, the care of even a healthy infant can be difficult and the development of a rich mother–child relationship could be imperiled.

When the infant's neurodevelopmental vulnerabilities are pervasive, prolonged, and significant, the parenting experience can be fraught with circumstances that affect the parent's sense of caregiving competence, the infant's sense of self-efficacy, and the quality of the relationship between parent and child. Without intervention that provides supports for parents and strategies to help the parents care for their infants more effectively, the vulnerable infants are at higher risk for negative developmental outcome.

Tasha

Tasha was born weighing 4 pounds. She was a wiry baby who had difficulty establishing both feeding and sleeping schedules. Tasha seemed to cry whenever she was awake, and cried harder when her mother, Holly, tried to soothe her. She slept for most of the time that she was not in acute distress. There were very few quiet moments between mother and child when Tasha was calmly alert. Tasha's constant crying was disturbing to Holly who said, "Tasha doesn't like me. She'd rather be left alone. She knows I took drugs."

Holly is a single mother with little emotional, social, or financial support. She also has three boys, ages 5, 7, and 8. Holly was overwhelmed with the care of the baby who did not respond to her the way she had expected.

Holly had used alcohol and crack throughout the first 7 months of her pregnancy when she obtained prenatal care. During her pregnancy, she tried several times to "quit drugs," but was unable to keep to her intentions. The clinic that provided Holly with prenatal care helped her enroll in a drug recovery program. Holly was clean at the time of Tasha's birth, but the effects of earlier substance abuse, inadequate nutrition, late prenatal care, and the emotional stressors were evident in Tasha's low birth weight and neurodevelopmental immaturities.

Holly was becoming more overwhelmed, agitated, and depressed. It became evident that this family needed additional community supports and services if it were to thrive.

Holly's drug treatment program was within a center that included child and family services for pregnant women abusing substances. Holly enrolled with Tasha in an early intervention "Mommy and Me" group and in a parent education group. The children were provided with needed counseling.

Holly learned different ways of approaching and handling her very sensitive baby. Tasha relaxed when she was swaddled in her blanket and was easier to feed. She was taught how to support Tasha's chin and cheeks in order to help her develop strong sucking patterns. Holly would gently nod her head and talk softly when Tasha's eyes met her own. She learned to wait patiently when Tasha had "enough" and would turn away. She learned how to soothe Tasha through vertical rocking and increase Tasha's periods of focused alertness by holding her in an upright position. Most importantly, Holly learned to notice Tasha's subtle smiles and muted throaty sounds as social cues, and the importance of responding to them.

Videotaping of mother–infant interactions were used extensively in the "Mommy and Me" group. Group leaders would "capture" good parenting on tape and use the examples in subsequent meetings. The videotapes proved to be an excellent vehicle for identifying parental strengths among all the women. Each mother was validated for her maternal caregiving. The sharing and discussion of the strengths not only provided good parenting models, but also were used to enhance parental self-esteem.

The group provided Holly with a "community of moms" that could offer support. The mothers formed their own informal support networks and some ended up sharing holidays.

Holly needed help in obtaining Women, Infant, and Children (WIC) vouchers and in finding a new place to live. In addition, she only could attend the center if transportation and child care were made available. With these comprehensive supports, Holly has managed to stay sober, keep her family together, and develop a relationship with her daughter. This remains a family with high needs. Continued supports are essential in order for this family to make it.

The key is to support the mother in the parenting process. There are several general caregiving guidelines that can provide direction for building and enhancing resilience in infants. Table 4.1 provides general principles of caregiving strategies for building resilience in infants.

Table 4.2 provides specific caregiving strategies that address infant neurodevelopmental vulnerabilities. The application of these strategies must match the particular need of the infant. Parents may need guidance, modeling, and support in interpreting and responding to muted infant social cues and to the application of positioning and handling strategies.

TODDLER DEVELOPMENTAL ADAPTABILITY AND RISK INDICATORS

Developmental resilience in the toddler will depend on several circumstances that include central nervous system functioning, constancy of primary caregivers, the quality of relationship with primary caregivers, the provision of developmental opportunity, stability and harmony of family life, and the availability of community supports and services to caregiver and child.

The degree to which prenatal drug exposure, prematurity, and intrauterine failure to thrive have contributed to the health of the

Table 4.1. Caregiving strategies for building resilience in infants

1. Availability of consistent emotionally responsive caregivers over time
2. Appropriate maternal responses contingent on infant-initiated signals
3. Protection from environmental overstimulation of noise, lights, people, touch, and commotion
4. Gradual introduction of small increments of environmental stimuli to build sensory threshold
5. Use of swaddling to help with toleration of sensory stimulation, to enhance organization of behavior, and to increase the calm focused alertness needed for environmental exploration and maternal engagement
6. Use of vestibular proprioceptive stimulation to reduce sensitivity to stimulation, to enhance visual alertness and social interaction, and to calm crying states
7. Use of handling and positioning to soothe, to improve muscle tone, to increase visual alertness and engagement, to encourage midline play, to support and maintain posture, to encourage movement, and to improve feeding
8. Gradual reduction of supportive techniques as infant matures or learns to compensate
9. Recognition of muted sporadic infant cues for social engagement or stress relief
10. Appropriate maternal interaction in terms of speed, intensity, and tempo
11. Appropriate responses to infant "over load signals" (e.g., yawning, gaze aversion, crying, sneezing, hiccoughing, color change)

From Poulsen, M.K. (1993). Strategies for building resilience in infants and young children at risk. *Infants and Young Children, 6*(2), 35; reprinted by permission.

central nervous system is significant when looking at toddler developmental status. There is great variability in the outcome of toddlers who as infants evidenced neurodevelopmental immaturities. Many children will outgrow their vulnerabilities and become healthy toddlers. However, a number of children prenatally exposed to drugs and alcohol will continue to evidence central nervous system vulnerabilities that affect attention, organization of behavior, and language development (Griffith, 1992; Rodning, Beckwith, & Howard, 1990). These effects influence how the vulnerable toddler responds to peer intractions, play situations, and adult expectations and, without intervention, may place the toddler's social and emotional development in jeopardy.

Toddlers who have not outgrown their neurodevelopmental immaturities may present as young children with low thresholds who are hyperreactive to sensory and emotional situations. These young children are sensitive to situations that would not bother their typically developing peers. As a result, they have difficulty dealing with what to them is experienced as an emotional or sensory overload. Their resulting behavior may remain immature and include overactivity, lack of focused attention, and the prolonged use of infantile means of conflict resolution that may include tantrums, hitting, and biting. Young children with low threshold need a protective environment to shield them from sensory and emotional overload. They need sensitive responsive guidance to help them learn to compensate for a poorly organized nervous system, and they need explicit instruction in the social expectations that nonvulnerable toddlers learn incidentally through family life experiences.

Helping Toddlers to Regulate Behavior

Resilient toddlers are able to handle the physical and emotional situations that are part of their daily living activities. Typically, toddlers are able to regulate their behavior and go with the flow of normal household commotion, irregular schedules, and somewhat inconsistent behavioral expectations. Toddlers are at risk when they remain hypersensitive to the physical and emotional world around them. For the children who have poorly organized nervous systems, such normal environmental changes may feel catastrophic and stress them beyond their ability to cope, resulting in chronic whining, crying, and acting out behavior.

These toddlers need to be protected from overstimulating situations or may need physical holding during times of sensory or emotional overload. Caregivers can help by verbally preparing toddlers for changes, by talking them through changes that occur, and by

Table 4.2. Developing neurodevelopmental competencies

	Neurodevelopmental vulnerabilities	Resilience-building strategies
Establishment of feeding patterns	Difficulty grasping the nipple Difficulty developing a strong suck Difficulty retaining food Difficulty establishing a feeding pattern	Provide a calm environment for mother and child Reduce amount of intake with more frequent feedings Position infant in semi-sitting flexed position Burp infant more frequently Support chin and cheeks to help with suck Provide frequent rest periods during feeding
Establishment of sleeping patterns	Restless sleep Irregular sleep patterns Night wakening Increased fussiness	Provide a quiet, darkened environment for sleep Swaddle the infant Calm the infant before bedtime Provide soft music or a ticking clock Offer finger or pacifier for non-nutritive sucking
Control over states of alertness	Minimal number of states of alertness Pervasive short duration of alertness Minimal eye engagement	Shield eyes from bright lights Hold infant in en face semi-upright cuddly position Swaddle infant with arms and knees in flexed position Sway infant gently to alert Tickle cheeks to arouse infant Hold infant upright at shoulder to alert Place infant in sidelying, flexed position before engagement
Capacity to recover from stress	Prolonged crying even with adult intervention Difficulty in recovering from distress Swift escalation from whimpers to howls	Respond at first whimpers Place hand firmly across infant's chest Swaddle infant in flexed position Provide finger or pacifier Bathe infant in warm water Hold infant's folded arms close to infant's chest Provide skin-to-skin contact Rock infant vertically and slowly
Balanced sensory threshold	Overreaction to movement, voice, and lights	Avoid overload to senses (i.e., reduce noise, movement, light touch and light movement, voice)

Table 4.2. *(continued)*

	Neurodevelopmental vulnerabilities	Resilience-building strategies
		Sing or speak softly at first
		Introduce stimuli gradually
		Allow infant to rest when infant averts gaze
		Approach the infant slowly with warning
		Avoid sudden movements when handling infant
Balanced muscle tone	Difficulty in cuddling Decreased reaching Decreased midline and exploratory play	Place baby bed on a slight slant with head on higher end Place a small pillow under infant's head when diapering Carry infant in a bent forward sitting position Position infant sidelying and flexed Avoid use of walkers Hold infant on a soft pillow Position shoulders forward to encourage reach and play
Organization of behavior	Difficulty combining sequences of actions	Swaddle agitated infant prior to eye engagement Protect from intense stimuli Introduce sensory stimuli incrementally Introduce multisensory stimuli gradually
Interactive behaviors	Fewer vocalizations Muted smiles Minimal cuddling Minimal initiation of social contact Diminished eye contact	Position parent's face close for infant touch Respond to muted infant smiles and glances Use eye engagement in close proximity Respond to all infant vocalizations Talk to infant during caregiving activities Massage and stroke infant with eye engagement or vocalizations Hold infant in a face-to-face position

remaining close to help them manage. Parents can help by building in quiet times and quiet places as part of the household agenda.

Helping Toddlers to Modulate Emotions

Resilient toddlers are able to regulate their behavior and recover from stress in a time that matches the level of stress experienced. Toddlers remain at risk when they have difficulty modulating emotions. Toddlers who are at risk may become increasingly active in response to overstimulating situations and have difficulty composing themselves, even with help. For toddlers at risk, conflict, anxiety, and disappointment may easily escalate to crying or aggressive acting out behavior.

These toddlers need someone to help them deal with feelings before they escalate out of control. Parents and caregivers need to learn to detect subtle cues of distress and be there to help their toddlers deal with it.

Helping Toddlers Accept Physical Contact

Resilient toddlers are able to relax easily and respond to caregiver's appropriate initiations of physical contact. Toddlers remain at risk if they avoid holding, rocking, and cuddling. Toddlers may appear not to enjoy holding, rocking, and cuddling because they have difficulty relaxing long enough to be responsive to caregiver's nurturance on the caregiver's terms. These toddlers may need help relaxing by parents joining them at their levels of energy and activity, and gradually calming the "frolic play" to the point where quiet encounters are possible.

Helping Toddlers to Organize Play
and Daily Living Activities Independently

Resilient toddlers learn to be self-dependent in age-appropriate activities. Toddlers remain at risk if they do not learn to organize play and daily living activities independently. When toddlers are very anxious or have poorly organized nervous systems, they may become easily overstimulated and have difficulty with focused play. They may be at a loss in a room filled with too many toys or objects or in the yard or park with large areas of unconfined space. Instead of focusing on a play activity, toddlers at risk may wander around and inattentively handle a variety of toys and materials. Close guidance by a caregiver can help toddlers learn to organize their own experiences. Language can be used to help toddlers decide how to focus and rehearse what to do and how to follow through. Fewer toys, reduced auditory and visual stimulation, and confined space also can help toddlers at risk organize play and daily living activities.

Helping Toddlers to Depend on Significant Adults

Resilient toddlers have developed the trust that adults are available to meet their needs. Toddlers remain at risk if they do not learn to look to significant adults to have needs met. Toddlers at risk who have experienced multiple caregivers or placements tend to show an overall decrease in the use of adults as sources of solace, play, and object attainment. Toddlers at risk frequently use fewer vocalizations, words, or gestures to indicate "lift me," "I want," "I need," and "come here." Toddlers who are not very attached to their caregivers may stand by the refrigerator and loudly cry out words to designate desire, rather than pointing. These children need a portion of each day carved out for individualized, personalized, child-directed interactions with a primary caregiver in order to develop the quality of relationship needed to engender trust and attachment.

Helping Toddlers to Respond to Verbal Guidance of Behavior

Resilient toddlers begin to learn adult expectations of behavior. Toddlers remain at risk if they do not learn to respond to verbal guidance of behavior. For some children, there is a significant lack of response to the usual verbal prohibitions and encouragements of behavior. By the time a child is a toddler, it is expected that the human voice is gaining in significance as a director of behavior. In fact, most 1-year-olds know the meaning of "the look."

For toddlers at risk, a more primary means of communication to elicit attention and response may be needed for a much longer time, including close proximity, touch, and direct eye contact before verbal guidance is given. This is very stressful to mothers, especially if they have other infants by the time their children are toddlers.

Helping Toddlers to Value Adult Recognition of Accomplishment

Resilient toddlers look to others for recognition for their achievements. Toddlers remain at risk if they do not learn to look to and value adult recognitioin of accomplishment, or if they do not learn to respond to verbal praise for behavior. Typically, toddlers demand attention to their accomplishments from the adults in their world and beam with pleasure when praise is forthcoming. Many toddlers at risk merely look at their "masterpieces" and make no attempt to use nearby adults to recognize their accomplishments. Many such children ignore volunteered praise, unless it too is accompanied by close proximity, direct touch, and eye contact before praise is given. Then a soft smile might be seen to come across the toddler's face, as if to say, "oh, you must mean me."

It is hypothesized that toddlers at risk either did not get enough of the cuddling, stroking, eye contact, and talking from a consistent caregiver in the early months, or that because of an immature nervous system, they were not able to incorporate all the early nurturing actions that give the human voice later significance. Thus, the early disorganization of experience can have a detrimental effect on the development of attachment, which in turn negatively affects the development of a sense of self-esteem. The infant at risk thus has remained at risk as a toddler who lacks the internal resources needed to cope with the developmental and behavior demands.

There are several general caregiving strategies that can provide direction for building and enhancing resilience in toddlers. Table 4.3 provides a list of strategies for caregivers.

Table 4.3. Caregiving strategies for building resilience in toddlers and young children

1. Use of proximal behaviors in caregiver–child interaction, including call to attention, eye contact, and touch before verbal directions, prohibitions, information, and praise are given
2. Protection from overfatigue by establishment of personalized bedtime rituals and routines
3. Protection from overstimulation of too many children, adults, transitions, noise, light, commotion, and emotional distress
4. Use of rituals for hellos, goodbyes, and daily transitions so child can predict behavior
5. Modeling, encouragement, acknowledgment, labeling, and responding to child's expression of feeling while setting limits on harmful behavior
6. Encouragement of autonomy and decision making by providing limited choice, whenever possible
7. Teaching and guidance of social behavior and provision of language and process for peer conflict resolution
8. Encouragement of self-dependence that matches child's functional level
9. Modeling and provision of relaxing time, relaxing place, and relaxing activities for child
10. Modeling and encouragement of representational play to express feeling and re-create significant events
11. Observation of child's behavior and intervention before behavior is out of control
12. Timely response to toddler's or young child's needs and initiation of social interaction
13. Teaching the at-risk child to learn cause and effect in relationship by providing words that relate effect to action (e.g., "You grabbed his toy. That makes him upset. Use your words and tell him it's your turn next.")
14. Personalized, one-to-one child centered time spent daily to build relationship

From Poulsen, M.K. (1993). Strategies for building resilience in infants and young children at risk. *Infants and Young Children, 6*(2), 36; reprinted by permission.

EARLY INTERVENTION

A critical factor for positive toddler development is the capacity of the child to build an attachment and relationship with the caregiver that is dependent upon:

- Constancy of mothering figure over time
- Emotional availability of mother or caregiver
- Match between maternal parenting and child temperament
- Provision of opportunity for expression of self, decision making, and self-dependence

Children of mothers who are substance abusers tend to have more people taking care of them and more changes in placements than other children. Children in out-of-home placement are particularly vulnerable in this regard. Children who do not participate in trusting relationships over time are subject to developing poor attachments to others and are at increased risk for later social and emotional problems and behavioral difficulties (Kronstadt, 1991).

Frankie
Frankie was 4 years old when his mother went to the hospital to have a baby, but his mother did not return home with his new sister. Instead two strangers came to the babysitter's apartment and took him to a stranger's house, leaving his teddy bear behind. His 5-year-old brother was sent somewhere else.

Frankie's new sister had a positive screen for cocaine and was removed from her mother's care once it was determined that it would be unsafe for her to go home. Frankie's mother went to a residential drug treatment program. Frankie and his brother were placed in separate foster homes. Although she used drugs during all three pregnancies, this is the first time drug treatment had been offered to her.

Frankie did not adjust well to his new placement. He would not go to bed at night and frequently wet his pants. Frankie was one of four foster children. He seemed to fight with them constantly. His foster mother saw him as a problem child and wondered whether to keep him.

Several elements of this situation have placed the social-emotional health of Frankie in jeopardy. His behavior in the new placement should be interpreted in light of his recent separation and loss. Frankie had no opportunity to say good-bye to his mother or his brother, or to be reassured of their impending return. He was removed from his babysitter with no familiar objects, clothes, or toys. No one had found out about his favorite foods, his fears, or his bedtime rituals. His daily living activities (e.g., preparing for bedtime, toileting) and his behaviors can be expected to regress under these circumstances.

An emotional care plan should be developed for Frankie that addresses plans for contact (e.g., telephone calls, photographs, postcards, or personal contact) with his mother and brother, Frankie's fears, daily living activities, bedtime rituals and favorite toys and foods, and opportunities for personalized one-to-one interaction with his new foster mother in order to develop a relationship. The foster family will need added child care support to give Frankie the extra attention he needs.

Although it is important not to stereotype pregnant and parenting women who abuse drugs and alcohol, it is equally important to understand how life experiences can influence parenting styles, skills, and expectations.

A profile of pregnant and parenting women in publicly funded drug treatment programs reveals a picture of parental vulnerability and underscores the need for parent support services (Ambrose & Poulsen, 1990; Kronstadt, 1989; Peluso & Peluso, 1988). Life experiences that may hinder a woman's parental knowledge, skills, and capacity for mother–child relationship include:

- Single parenthood without financial and social supports
- History of physical abuse or sexual exploitation
- Absence of good parenting models and functional family memories
- Social isolation
- Unresolved issues of depression, guilt, separation, and loss
- Struggles with becoming and remaining drug free

These life experiences clearly influence a woman's parental ability to cope, parental self-esteem, emotional availability, and capacity for responsive caregiving (Anthony & Cohler, 1987; Escalona, 1984). The lack of parenting models in a woman's life may mean that extra help is needed in learning how to appreciate her infant's unique temperament and behavior, read her infant's subtle social initiation cues and readiness for mother–child interaction, notice her infant's distress cues and need for comfort, and broaden her repertoire of caregiving strategies that match her infant's developmental level and temperamental needs. Women who have not experienced "good mothering" themselves need added counseling and support.

The critical issues of early intervention for infants and toddlers prenatally exposed to drugs and alcohol focus on the enhancement of the capacity of the mothers and fathers to parent their children. The critical issues are

1. The sobriety of parenting figures and all family members
2. The establishment of quality parent–child relationships
3. The provision of supports, services, and strategies required to support the infrastructure of the family
4. The amelioration of infant–toddler psychosocial and neurobehavioral risk indicators
5. The physical, emotional, and social well-being of the infant and toddler and all family members

The collaboration of community programs is essential in order to meet the needs of the infant, toddler, and family in a comprehensive, coordinated manner. This will call for interagency service coordination that may include the following services: drug recovery, mental and physical health, infant early intervention and prevention, social welfare (e.g., housing, Food Stamps, job training), and parent education and support. Federal and state infant health and development programs include Women, Infant, and Children (WIC) programs, Part H Infant Early Intervention programs, Head Start Parent Child Centers, Maternal Child Health High Risk Infant Follow-up Programs, and the Early and Periodic Screening, Diagnosis, and Treatment (EPSDT) programs. In addition, many families will need the instrumental supports of transportation and child care.

SUMMARY

In order to meet the varying needs of young children and families who have been affected by substance abuse, communities need to offer an available and accessible continuum of community-based services and supports. Child and parent resources and priorities must be assessed by health, development, mental health, and social service professionals. An integrated comprehensive child and family service coordination plan must be formulated and implemented within the context of family sociocultural and religious values.

REFERENCES

Allen, C. (1992). Developmental implications of intrauterine growth retardation. *Infants and Young Children, 5*(2), 13–28.

Als, H., & Duffy, F.H. (1989). Neurobehavioral assessment in the newborn period: Opportunity for early detection of later learning disabilities and for early intervention. *Birth Defects, 25,* 127–152.

Ambrose, S., & Poulsen, M. (1990). *Substance abusing mothers whose children are in out-of-home placement* (Preliminary Report). Los Angeles: Children's Institute International.

Anthony, E.J., & Cohler, B.J. (Eds.). (1987). *The invulnerable child.* New York: Guilford Press.

Bays, J. (1990). Substance abuse and child abuse. *Pediatric Clinics of North America, 37*(4), 881–904.

Belman, A.L., Diamond, G., Dickson, D., Horoupian, D., Llena, J., Lantos, G., & Rubenstein, A. (1988). Calcification of the basal ganglia in infants and young children with acquired immunodeficiency syndrome (AIDS). *American Journal of Diseases of Children, 36,* 1192–1199.

Bennet, F.C. (1990). Recent advances in developmental intervention for biologically vulnerable infants. *Infants and Young Children, 3*(1), 33–40.

Burkett, S., Yasin, S., & Palow, D. (1990). Perinatal implications of cocaine exposure. *Journal of Reproductive Medicine, 35*(1), 35–42.

Chavkin, W. (1989, July 15). Help, don't jail, addicted mothers. *New York Times,* p. 21.

Cook, P.S., Petersen, R.C., & Moore, D.T. (1990). *Alcohol, tobacco and other drugs may harm the unborn.* Rockville, MD: U.S. Department of Health and Human Services.

Deren, S. (1986). Children of substance abusers: A review of the literature. *Journal of Substance Abuse Treatment, 3,* 77–94.

Escalona, S. (1984). Social and other environmental influences on the cognitive and personality development of low birth weight infants. *American Journal of Mental Deficiency, 88,* 508–512.

Fulroth, R., Phillips, B., & Durand, D. (1989). Perinatal outcome of infants exposed to cocaine and/or heroin in utero. *American Journal of Diseases of Children, 143,* 905–910.

Gorski, P.A., Hale, W.T., Leonard, C.H., & Martin, J.A. (1983). Direct computer recording of premature infant and nursery care: Distress following two interventions. *Pediatrics, 72,* 198–202.

Griffith, D. (August, 1992). *Three year outcome of poly-drug exposed children.* Paper presented at the meeting of the American Psychological Association, Washington, DC.

Johnson, C. (1993). Developmental issues: Children infected with the human immunodeficiency virus. *Infants and Young Children, 6*(1), 1–10.

Kronstadt, D. (1989). *Pregnancy and cocaine addiction: An overview of impact and treatment.* Sausalito, CA: Far West Laboratory for Education, Research, and Development.

Kronstadt, D. (1991). Complex developmental issues of prenatal drug exposure. *The Future of Children: Drug Exposed Infants, 1*(1), 36–49.

Larsson, G. (1982). Prevention of fetal alcohol effects. *Acta Obstetricaet Gynecologica Scandanavia, 62,* 171.

MacGregor, S., Keith, L., Bachicha, J., & Chasnoff, I.J. (1989). Cocaine use during pregnancy: Correlation between prenatal care and perinatal outcome. *Obstetrics and Gynecology, 74,* 882–885.

Moore, T.R., Origel, W., Key, T., & Resnik, R. (1986). The perinatal and economic impact of prenatal care in a low socioeconomic population. *American Journal of Obstetrics and Gynecology, 154,* 129–133.

Murphy, L.B., & Moriarty, A.E. (1976). *Vulnerability, coping and growth.* New Haven, CT: Yale University Press.

Oro, A., & Dixon, S. (1987). Fetal and neonatal medicine: Perinatal cocaine and methamphetamine exposure. *Journal of Pediatrics, 111,* 571–578.

Peluso, E., & Peluso, L.S. (1988). *Women and drugs: Getting hooked, getting clean.* Minneapolis, MN: CompCare Publishers.

Poulsen, M.K. (1993). Strategies for building resilience in infants and young children at risk. *Infants and Young Children, 6*(2), 29–40.

Rauh, V., Narcombe, B., Ruff, P., Jette, A., & Howell, D. (1982). The Vermont infant studies project: The rationale for a mother–infant transition program. In L.A. Bond & J.M. Joffe (Eds.), *Facilitating infant and early childhood development* (pp. 258–280). Hanover, NH: University Press of New England.

Rodning, C., Beckwith, L., & Howard, J. (1990) Attachment in play in prenatal drug exposure. *Development and Psychopathology, 1,* 277–289.

Scott, J. (1989, September 26). Young, poor suffer silent epidemic. *Los Angeles Times,* p. 1, 21.

Singer, L.T., & Fagan, J.F. (1984). Cognitive development in the failure-to-thrive: A three year longitudinal study. *Journal of Pediatric Psychology, 9,* 363–383.

Streissguth, A.P. (1986). The behavioral teratology of alcohol: Performance, behavior and intellectual deficits in prenatally exposed children. In J. West (Ed.), *Alcohol and brain development* (pp. 3–44). New York: Oxford University Press.

Vohr, B. (1991). Preterm cognitive development: Biologic and environmental influences. *Infant and Young Children, 3*(3), 20–29.

Wara, D. (1992, May). *Perinatal AIDS and HIV diagnoses and treatment update.* Paper presented at the Advances and Controversies in Clinical Pediatrics meeting, San Francisco, CA.

Ward, M.J., Kessler, D.B., & Altman, S.C. (1992). *Infant–mother attachment in children with failure to thrive.* Unpublished manuscript.

Wayment, H.A. (1988). Infants with AIDS: Implications for development. *Early Child Development and Care, 41,* 39–47.

Williamson, W.D., & Demmler, G.J. (1992). Congenital infections: Clinical outcome and educational implications. *Infants and Young Children, 4,* 1–10.

Zuckerman, B. (1991). Drug-exposed infants: Understanding the medical risk. *The future of children: Drug exposed infants, 1*(1), 26–35.

Zuckerman, B., Frank, B., Hingson, R., Amaro, H., Levenson, S., et al. (1989). Effects of maternal marijuana and cocaine on fetal growth. *New England Journal of Medicine, 320*(12), 762–768.

5

Classroom Interventions for Young Children at Risk

Carol K. Cole

Across the United States, educators are concerned with the increasing numbers of children coming to school who are not ready to learn, children who are highly distractible and have short attention spans, children who display poor social skills, children with difficulty in the areas of speech and language or short-term memory, and children from dysfunctional families and communities. The idea that the increase in mothers who use drugs during pregnancy can be directly correlative to the increases in children's problems seen in classrooms is too simplistic. This conclusion was perpetuated, however, when newscasts routinely displayed premature, sickly infants as the "innocent victims" of their mothers' drug abuse. It was against the backdrop of headlines that declared "Educators at New Frontier" (Stone, 1990, p. 1), or "Crack Babies Turn 5 and Schools Brace" (Chira, 1990, p. A1), or pronounced that "these children . . . are like automatons" (Hopkins, 1990, p. 66) that real fear and concern swept classrooms and school boards across the country.

In 1990, the National Institute of Drugs and Alcohol estimated that more than 5 million women of child-bearing age were using illegal substances (Office of the Inspector General, 1990). The National Institute of Alcohol Abuse and Alcoholism estimated that in a preschool classroom of 15 children, 3 children have parents who are alcoholics (Robinson, 1990).

Educators are concerned over the increase in the number of children exposed to drugs and alcohol. In *Exceptional Children,* Jeptha Greer wrote, "perhaps most frightening of all is that doctors and other health care professionals can only speculate about what we may be facing" (1990, p. 382). Educators also were told that "afflicted youngsters . . . will leave your resources depleted and your compassion tested" (Risk, 1990, p. 19). The same year, "Crack Babies: Ready or Not, Here They Come" was the lead article in *American Teacher,* the official publication of the American Federation of Teachers (Laderman, 1990). The article stated the concern of some educators that, "urban schools would be pressed to the limit trying to teach the flood of children born to mothers who used crack." But it also noted that many educators found a range of competency within this population, with many children functioning within the normal range cognitively and some children identified as being gifted.

Prenatal drug exposure does not automatically determine developmental outcome (Center for Substance Abuse Prevention [CSAP] National Resource Center, 1993). Children exposed to alcohol, tobacco, and other drugs (ATOD) may be at risk for impaired cognitive, behavioral, and social development. They may display a range of delays and uneven patterns of learning. Language, memory, coordination, and organizational abilities may be impaired (Cole & Jones, 1990). However, there is no typical developmental profile for children with a history of prenatal drug exposure. Outcome and behaviors seen in individual preschoolers must be viewed in relationship to other factors (Griffith, Azuma, & Chasnoff, 1994). Stressors such as exposure to poverty, violence, and poor health care; early insecure attachment patterns; multiple placements; abuse, neglect, and possible neurological damage can undermine a child's resilience. Coping with these stressors can all affect the child's ability to cope with the expectations of the classroom. It is not always possible to predict how an individual child will react to stressors, which child will be affected, when, and in what ways. However, understanding how to best serve vulnerable children has implications for program planning in education, personnel preparation, and interagency collaboration.

The purpose of this chapter is to discuss the qualities of early childhood programs that can best serve young children exposed to drugs and alcohol. The focus is the classroom milieu and how protective factors and facilitative approaches (Cole et al., 1989) can support social, emotional, and therefore, cognitive development. When implemented, these strategies can support a process to help counteract the negative influences of prenatal and postnatal exposure to drugs and alcohol.

PROFILE OF DRUG EXPOSURE

There is no consistent pattern emerging in children prenatally exposed to drugs. To date, very little research exists that fully addresses the complexity of issues raised in the variations of outcomes seen in children exposed to drugs (CSAP, 1993). In a review of 46 experimental studies, significant adverse developmental outcomes associated with prenatal drug exposure occurred in only half of the outcomes. The majority of these studies indicated adverse outcomes primarily for infants in the first week of life and in the neurodevelopmental domain (Carta et al., 1994). A wide variety of characteristics has been observed in children with a history of prenatal drug exposure and teachers have reported that it is hard to distinguish children exposed to drugs from other children at risk (Cole et al., 1989, Laderman, 1990; Weston, Ivins, Zuckerman, Jones, & Lopez, 1989). Although there is some evidence that there is an increase of poor outcomes for a small number of older children (Carta et al., 1994), it is not clear if this is because testing as the child gets older can assess performance more easily or if, as the child gets older, the variables in the environment have greater impact. In studying preschool children, Cohen and Erwin report (1994) a wide diversity of characteristics found in 50% of the children with a history of prenatal drug exposure. Although another 25% of the children displayed increased aggression, poor attachments, and unoccupied behavior, "the behavioral differences could not be attributed to the effects of drug exposure per se" (p. 248). The resilience and plasticity of individual children, the complexity of maternal child interaction, as well as the variety of caregiving environments involved, underscore why there is no typical profile of a child prenatally exposed to drugs.

Toddlers

Developmental outcome is the result of an interaction between the biological mandate and the caregiving environment. Neurodevelopmental vulnerabilities may be the result of a premature birth, drug exposure, or low birth weight. In the caregiving environment, multiple placements, untrained caregivers, and ongoing instability can negatively influence outcome, while consistent, responsive care and supportive family-centered intervention will support potential.

Young Children

As the young child enters a prechool setting, behavior, learning style, and development must be viewed as the result of a constellation of factors. Assumptions that prenatal exposure to drugs results in a significant rise in problematic behaviors for children are not necessarily supported by research (Cohen & Erwin, 1994). In a follow-up study of 3-year-old children exposed to multiple drugs, a majority were found to be cognitively and behaviorally functioning within normal patterns. Approximately one third of the children displayed delays in language development (Griffith, 1992). Carta reports that one half of the children showed adverse outcomes in the language and social domains combined (1994). As a group, the performance for children prenatally exposed to drugs is more hopeful than has been reported in the media. However, within the continuum of outcomes, individual children obviously are affected by exposure to drugs.

For some children, the problems, such as disorganization and behavioral unpredictability (Cole et al., 1989), low threshold for over stimulation (Griffith, 1992), and loss of boundaries (Cohen & Erwin, 1994), reported in infancy continue into preschool. For such children, transitions within the classroom schedule can be particularly stressful (Cohen & Erwin, 1994; Cole et al., 1989; Wilkes, 1993).

The staff must consider each child's general health, particular temperament, stages of development, neurological competency, quality of relationships with caregivers, and past experiences to design and implement an educational program that best meets the child's needs (Chasnoff, Griffith, Frier, Murray, 1992; Kronstadt, 1991; Poulsen, 1992).

Families

Just as there is no typical profile of a child prenatally exposed to drugs, there is no typical profile of a family involved in substance abuse. Some children prenatally exposed to drugs are removed from their parent's custody at birth. Others are removed during the first or second year. It is common for many children prenatally exposed to drugs to experience multiple placements. Many reside with grandparents and extended families; others reside with single parents. Some parents continue to abuse drugs, and some do not.

It is well understood that substance abuse occurs across the socioeconomic spectrum; however, there are no published studies involving middle and upper-class families. Most of the information about families who abuse drugs is gathered about families of low socioeconomic status using public treatment facilities, and therefore the studies may be biased (Myers, Olson, & Kaltenbach, 1992; Vincent, Poulsen, Cole, Woodruff, & Griffith, 1991). Although socioeconomic status is correlated strongly to social-emotional competency in children (Werner & Smith, 1982), it is but one factor. In families where children are experiencing multiple risk factors, over time, developmental outcomes will be less than optimal (Dunst, 1993; Rutter, 1983). A study of 215 4-year-old children concluded that it was not the socioeconomic level, but the number of risk factors within each socioeconomic level that determined functional outcome of the family (Sameroff & Fiese, 1990).

INTERVENTION STRATEGIES

Outcomes for children with a history of drug exposure are dependent on biological and environmental risk factors combined with opportunities and protective factors that support resilience (Garbarino, 1990). Educational practice that attempts to provide interventions by separating the characteristics that can be attributed solely to organic influences (prenatal drug exposure) or, conversely, solely to the result of environmental experiences (the postnatal caregiving) are simplistic and ineffective. Children being raised in households where substance abuse occurs are often exposed to multiple risk factors (e.g., dysfunctional parenting, violence, depression). Implementing educational strategies without understanding family dynamics in the context of addiction and recovery will be less than optimal. Additionally, a child who is constitutionally more sensitive, temperamentally difficult, premature, and in other ways biologically compromised is at increased vulnerability when raised in families who face multiple risk factors (Poulsen, 1992; Werner, 1990).

Reviews of literature done by Honig (1986) and by Dunst (1993) point to parental education, income, job and marital stability, health, mental health, and styles of coping and parenting as examples of the variables that contribute to positive child outcome. To be truly successful, intervention strategies for children must recognize the levels of stress experienced by families and must include opportunities (e.g., housing, health care, stable employment) in which families can participate in providing positive outcomes for themselves and their children.

Classroom Intervention

Successful classroom educational strategies must be child specific and incorporate a flexibility in planning strategies that combine facilitative and directive approaches. Although biology may set the stage for the child's development, it is the responsive caregiving that will determine ultimate outcome. (Sameroff & Fiese, 1990; Schorr & Schorr, 1988). The classroom must be acknowledged as a potentially powerful caregiving environment, a place that can mitigate or exacerbate a child's ability to cope with factors that place him or her at risk. A nurturing classroom can be a place that promotes resilience, a place that buffers against stress. The classroom climate can affect whether children will be trustful or be fearful, cooperate or compete, respect or ridicule, or solve problems through communication or by aggression and avoidance (Ford, Davern, & Schnorr, 1992). When classrooms support a child's natural curiosity to learn, self-esteem, skill acquisition, and social competence are increased. Classrooms that uphold such experiences for children in early childhood programs have been shown to decrease the risk status (Rutter, 1990; Werner, 1990) and increase the possibilities of long-term positive academic and behavioral outcomes (Schorr & Schorr, 1988).

Responsive Relationships

Relationships are essential building blocks for all learning—cognitive, emotional, and behavioral. It is only in the context of a good relationship that a child's true potential will be known. Socially appropriate behavior, achievement of intellectual potential, and evolving self-esteem begin with early experiences in which adult expectations are presented in a predictable and safe manner that ensures the child's developmental success. Children who have secure and trusting relationships with caregivers are more independent, actively explore their environment, and are more willing to follow directions in the social setting (Phillips & Howes, 1987). Responsive relationships incorporate acceptance, reciprocity, and communication (Brazelton, 1992; Curry & Johnson, 1990; Greenspan, 1990).

Acceptance

The evolution of self involves experiences of trust and mistrust (Erikson, 1963; Maslow, 1962). Long before an infant can talk or think abstractly, the experience of having physiological needs met predictably and consistently within a reasonable time promotes a belief that the world is safe and persons in that world are trustworthy. This permits learning, and extends simple experiences into the more complex realm of cause and effect, time and space, abstract thinking, and social competence (Cook & Tessier, 1992; DeVries & Kohlberg, 1987; Erikson, 1963; Greenspan, 1990).

Because issues of trust and mistrust are so basic to growth and development, strategies to ensure acceptance must be a cornerstone in program planning. Relationships that value and support children and provide clearly defined expectations provide the safety required to take risks, to explore the environment, and to experience social interaction. From this basis, children become autonomous and learn to develop a capacity for nurturing, empathizing, and being responsible. Children who have experienced emotional deprivation, inconsistent care, multiple placements, or prolonged separations may lack the experience of feeling accepted. They may not have the skills required to engage others effectively in getting simple needs and wants met. Relationships may need remediation before a child can risk trusting (Robinson, 1990).

Reciprocity

The philosophical underpinnings of working with children and families must include respectful reciprocal relationships. This means actively supporting a partnership of growth and development (i.e., listening without judgment, taking an interest in other's activities spending time with the child and family, acknowledging feelings, valuing individual and cultural differences). Reciprocity means give and take. Observe behavior in oneself as well as in the children. Spend time learning to read the cues of individual children that signal distress, fear, or over stimulation (Lally, 1990). Make adaptations to the environment and your interaction with the child that accommodates the child's changing needs. This responsive reciprocity builds resilience (Poulsen, 1993). The responsive classroom builds resilience in children when it nurtures independence through the safety of appropriate expectations, the predictability of events and schedules, the availability of suitable materials and activities, plus ample opportunity to make choices and have control.

Communication

Language can be a powerful tool by which to share information, report events, clarify observations, and convey expectations, feelings, and attitudes. Language can provide the connection among feelings, thoughts, and behavior. For some children, disruptions in early social interactions can adversely affect the ability to acquire language and thereby affect the ability to communicate adequately. Following the child's lead in a conversation, repeating and rephrasing speech, and mapping language onto the child's experience can be effective strategies in talking to young children at risk (Curry & Johnson, 1990).

Because cultural and linguistic diversity may affect styles of communication between staff members and with children, adults working together with children in the preschool setting must develop communication strategies that promote an atmosphere in which feelings and individual coping styles are respected.

IMPLEMENTING RESPONSIVE RELATIONSHIPS IN THE CLASSROOM

Key to the implementation of responsive relationships in the classroom is using interventions that support acceptance, reciprocity, and communication. Through acknowledging actions and feelings, building bridges and boundaries, and creating a classroom community with choice and cooperation, children are supported in their growth and development and willingness to adapt to program structure.

Adam

Adam came to the attention of the authorities at the time of his younger sister's birth. She was premature and born with severe deformities. At the hospital his mother had tested positive for cocaine and alcohol. Adam, who was 17 months old, was taken into custody by protective services. At the time, he was living with his biological mother and one other sibling, although he frequently had been cared for by his paternal grandmother since his birth.

Subsequent caregiving arrangements included living in an emergency shelter for 1 month (17–18 months of age), being placed with the paternal grandmother for 3 months (19–23 months of age), returning to live with his mother for 6 months (2–2.6 years of age), then being placed in a group home facility with 4 other children under the age of 5 for 6 months (2½–3 years of age), and finally, at age 3.2 years, being placed out of the county with a biological aunt.

Adam had been living with his biological aunt for 6 weeks when he was enrolled in the preschool program. Although Adam had been a full-term healthy baby, Adam's aunt confirmed that his mother had used drugs during her pregnancy. He had ongoing problems with otitis media, but otherwise was in good health.

His preschool program was a child care setting that was open from 6 A.M. to 6 P.M. He started his day at 8:00 A.M. and was picked up by 5:00 P.M. Twenty other preschool children were in his room. There were five full-time staff plus parent volunteers in the room at all times. However, because of scheduling constraints there was much rotation among staff. The teacher who greeted him in the morning left at 10:00 A.M. The teacher who said good-bye to him in the evening started her day at 2:00 P.M.

When Adam started the program, staff commented on his appearance, abilities, and behavior. He excelled in the area of self-help, was well-behaved at the lunch table, knew his colors and shapes, and recognized numbers to 5. He was a stocky, well-built child. He was initially very quiet. There was a monotone quality to his voice and a slackness to his jaw. He made very little eye contact and had an almost vacant, immobile quality to his movements. He did not explore toys or materials. During outside time in the yard, Adam did not play. He looked confused, and would stand in one place, drooling or blowing spit bubbles.

By the end of the first month, Adam had started to test limits in the classroom. He refused to participate in group activities. He interacted with no other children. He would not make choices and did not like prompting. His language was full of three- and four-word expletives. He was described by staff as bright but moody, impulsive, defiant, and manipulative. He had poor receptive language and began to throw toys and hit and hurt other children.

Every part of the day became potentially volatile. Adam's reactions to transitions or unnecessary changes in routines were predictably unpredictable. Some days he would be clingy, and some days he would throw himself on the floor crying when asked to change activities, but most often he refused to participate. Staff found his behavior perplexing and his sporadic mastery of their expectations frustrating.

Staff members met to design an intervention plan. The discussion involved opinions and concerns from staff. Some wondered if the behavior problems could be the result of difficulty hearing because of ongoing ear infections. Another pointed out he only had been in the program a short time and had gone through a "rough beginning." Another member was concerned that he was a dangerous "drug baby" and perhaps should be placed in a more restrictive environment. Only one staff member talked about how the staff's schedule might impair Adam's ability to cope with expectations.

It was agreed that Adam might benefit from increased individualized attention. This was accomplished by assigning a teacher to spend additional personalized time with Adam.

The teacher selected to do this was decided upon by the staff together and was a teacher who expressed a fondness of Adam and he for her. With staff agreement, administration rearranged the hours of two teachers so that Adam would have 30 minutes of one-to-one time with this teacher. This teacher also would be the one to share experiences and strategies directly with Adam's aunt.

After 6 weeks, staff members reported positive changes in Adam. His play was less aggressive and he seemed happier. He was beginning to join activities without help and follow a teacher's directions. He was beginning to play. Inside, he was beginning to engage in dramatic play, while outside, he was beginning to ride a tricycle. The time spent with the selected teacher seemed to be working. His aunt reported his behavior was improving at home as well.

Intervention: In the beginning, this individualized time was very structured. The routine did not deviate. The greeting each time was the same, the opening activity was the same, the next activity was played at the same table, and the teacher sat in the same chair. After the activity was over, the toy was stored on the same shelf. Also, the words used to prepare Adam to make transitions back into the larger group were the same. The teacher explained she had to share her time with the other children now, but during lunch time he would sit by her in his special chair.

Within a week, Adam asked for another activity. Slowly, the choices and structure of this time were expanded. The teacher took her cues from Adam, at times imposing more structure and clearer expectations and at other times letting Adam have control and direct her role. She modeled how Adam could say, "I need help," if he wanted or needed her to do something. They practiced this. Reciprocity developed.

Within a month, Adam was seen incorporating some of this teacher's behavior in his play in the larger group. He was seen reading a story to two other children, imitating the way this teacher held the book. On another occasion, he was heard to tell peers, "It's inside time," using the same inflection in his voice the teacher used. A particularly important milestone for Adam occurred when he risked asking to get his needs and wants met. It happened when several children and the teacher were on the rug playing with the farm animals. Adam was watching from under a table across the room. In a somewhat quiet voice, Adam was heard to say, "I need help."

——————————

Acknowledging Actions and Feelings

Essential prerequisites for successful learning include trusting in oneself and others, learning when and when not to persist and take risks, and knowing when to incorporate autonomous and cooperative problem-solving skills. Children behave and misbehave for a reason; their behavior is communication that must be understood in the context of individual development, temperament, and experience. Only when children encounter different responses to their behavior will they come to view the world differently and therefore behave differently. When an adult acknowledges the child's reality and engages in appropriate nurturing, the child will learn to interact with others with care and empathy. When the adult fosters high expectations and balances challenges with support, the child will experience mastery and confidence.

Reality Acknowledging a child's reality by spending time observing, listening, asking questions, and engaging the child in problem-solving dialogues can enhance the child's feelings of acceptance. Having an understanding of what the child has experienced helps frame the interpretation of behavior (Johnson & Cole, 1992; Vincent et al., 1991).

Children at risk often have difficulty with novel classroom experiences (e.g., a zoo trip, different bus driver, new food). When the behavioral responses to such events are exaggerated for some children, teachers must make plans to accommodate individual differences. For example, in preparing for a trip to the zoo, a child who was recently bitten by a dog may need reassurance that the animals will not come out of the cage and bite. Another child may need a hand held throughout the trip to provide physical contact necessary to support the child from becoming overwhelmed by all the novel stimuli. Still another child may need time to talk about her fears about being left in the zoo because she remembers being lost in a shopping mall. Feelings and actions need to be acknowledged and interventions individualized. Doing so will provide the child with a sense of belonging and acceptance. This will assist the child in being able to cope with the expectations of the event with more appropriate behavior.

Vulnerable children may fluctuate in the way they respond to stressors or stimulation on a daily or even hourly basis as they are

learning new behavioral responses. What staff perceive as maladaptive behavior (e.g., acting out, withdrawal or passive-aggressive), in
fact may be adaptive coping when seen from the child's perspective.
For example, after an initial "honeymoon" of appropriate classroom
behavior, a child, such as Adam, who has experienced multiple
placements, may begin to test limits (e.g., running out of the room,
throwing puzzles on the floor). This testing of the limits is provoca-
tive; it may happen for a variety of reasons, but quite possibly is a
way for the child to re-create past events in order to attempt to gain
control. The goal of this child's misbehavior then is to provoke the
adult to act. If the child believes he has caused the adult to put him
in time out, send him to the office, or remove him permanently from
the classroom, the child has created an event that reinforces the effect the behavior has had in the past. If the behavior is viewed as
simply inappropriate, without the context of the child's experience
considered, then the intervention will be misdirected.

Mark

The day the school psychologist came into the room to assess
4½-year-old Mark, he was climbing up on the sink, wielding
a plastic knife at children and teachers, vehemently refus-
ing to participate in activities, and attempting to run out of
the yard (certainly not appropriate classroom behavior, but
not necessarily severely disturbed behavior). Three days before, Mark had been "turned over" to protective services by
his stepfather, literally left on the office steps. This was his
first day back at school and he was very angry. He was living
with his aunt again. Mark had never lived with the same
family members or in the same house for longer than 6
months.

Intervention: The staff knew Mark did not like to be
touched when he was upset so there was no attempt to contain or hold him. The primary teacher used simple concrete
phrases as she recounted Mark's experience to the class and
other staff. She spoke openly and without judgment about
what happened. The staff asked Mark open-ended questions
(e.g., if he wanted to talk about where he was staying now,
what he did when he was left on the steps of the building).
Because the staff knew Mark had difficulty expressing himself, they assured him they would stay with him until he was
finished telling his story. They provided him with choices of
activities, suggesting he could paint or dictate a story or play

alone with the toy cars. Only after the reality of his situation was acknowledged and validated by teachers were classroom expectations reiterated and a compromise for appropriate behavior negotiated with him. Intervention of Mark's behavior took into consideration the reality of this crisis, the instability in his past experiences, his developmental competencies, and his current style of coping.

Antonio

Antonio was a hypervigilant child. He had a remarkable memory. If something had been misplaced, Antonio could tell you where to find it. He was very quiet, cautiously watching what was expected of him before entering an activity. He avoided trouble by carefully following the rules. He lived with his mother and younger brother. His mother was single, well-educated, and very concerned about her boys, but his maternal grandmother abused drugs. Sometimes she used Antonio and his brother as decoys or lookouts at the mall while she stole merchandise she could later sell to support her drug habit.

Intervention: In this program the classroom routines were predictable, and a consistent staff encouraged discussion of feelings and experiences. A goal for Antonio was to become more spontaneous in play and take more risks in new situations. During the course of the year he became more comfortable. Over time he began to feel safe enough to engage in typical exploratory behavior, actively engaging in his environment. The constant hyperalert "looking over his shoulder" behavior seemed to subside. Occasionally he wouldn't know where he left something. He began to risk being silly and getting loud. When staff made "mistakes" (e.g., spilling food, forgetting supplies, singing the wrong words), humor, acceptance, and lack of negative consequences were modeled. When Antonio "forgot" the rules or began to test limits, the staff perceived the behavior in the context of Antonio's development and allowed his new behavior and levels of acceptance.

Helping Children Be Successful There are guidelines staff can follow to help children exposed to drugs and alcohol be more successful; the following suggestions are often helpful.

Observe Child Behavior in Context Accept that behavior happens for a reason. Get as much information as you can about why a behavior is happening. Make a hypothesis, keep a behavioral log, and ask questions. Is the child new to the setting? Is the behavior chronic, new, or different? How does the child go about getting needs and wants met? What do you know about the child's culture; the family's childrearing beliefs? What and who are the supports in the child's life? How would you describe the child's temperament, stages of development, and experiences? How do classroom expectations, structure, and personnel support or undermine the developmental need for security as well as independence?

Focus on Support and Acceptance of Individual Differences Development occurs in a general, predictable way, but with a wide range of individual variation. Keep in mind the child's strengths, potential, and motivation. When in doubt, assume differences, not deficits, and accept those differences.

Allow Flexibility within the Framework of Classroom Structure Sufficient time should be given to complete tasks, practice new skills, and make transitions. Provide opportunities for children to make choices and have control. Open-ended materials (e.g., blocks, paint, clay) permit unique outcomes. Year-end activities should reflect the expanding and increasingly complex skills learned over the year. Novelty and variety will gradually replace sameness and repetition.

Help Establish Acceptable Methods of Self-Regulation Establish acceptable methods of self-regulation for children. Rules that are established must be kept to a minimum and stated clearly. However, children will not learn to cope with classroom expectation, recover from stressful circumstances, or become self-regulated simply by being told what to do and what not to do. Negotiations of acceptable behavior must be individualized and include dialogue, trial and error, and ongoing adaptations. Using headphones, pacing in the back of the room, going for a walk around the yard, or holding certain objects during transitions may work for one child, but not another or may be possible in one setting, but not another. Initially, broader limits of acceptable behavior may need to be tolerated while getting to know the child. Help to organize the child's experience by reflecting back on what has occurred and what was said; be empathic, be authentic.

Role Model Children learn by imitation of role models. For example, when Adam was beginning to learn expectations in the classroom, he employed some of his teacher's behavior. He echoed her words and mimicked her storytelling style. Incorporating her affect and organization was a way of rehearsing control and learning to master his own behavior. Mark's teachers engaged him in reflective problem solving to come up with a mutually acceptable way to cope with the tremendously stressful situation of being abandoned. Antonio's hypervigilant behavior was a concern because it interfered with his growth and development. Teachers modeling "acceptance" in the face of making "mistakes" (e.g., safe nurturing when stress was manageable) reduced the need for his overly cautious behavior.

A positive educational experience for children at risk clearly cannot guarantee permanent positive outcomes. However, studies of resilience underscore the importance of a supportive relationship in sustaining human growth and influencing potential outcome (Beckman & Lieber, 1992; Frailberg, Shapiro, & Cherniss, 1980; Rutter, 1990; Werner & Smith, 1982). In one study on the importance of supportive relationships, 24 children were placed in a therapeutic school after being removed from Nazi concentration camps. As adults, they attributed their "affirmation of life" to the warmth and nurturing of the nursery school teacher who taught them "to behave compassionately" (Werner, 1990).

Children will learn from teachers who

Avoid judgment   Everyone has opinions, values, and biases. Self-examination and knowledge can clarify interactions with children. Know what behaviors in children trigger what behaviors in you. Are you inadvertently passing along personal stereotypes? Where and how were they acquired? For what reason? Avoid comparisons and the use of "good" and "bad" judgments.

Show the ability to relate   Children are more responsive and trusting when they believe their teacher is "human." If you do not want children to lie, do not tell stories. If you do not know the answer, admit it. When asked your opinion, give it honestly and simply. Explain your actions and feelings, and share your humor. If you made a mistake, acknowledge it and apologize.

Show interest   Find the time to spend with them. Have conversations, ask questions, and listen to their answers. Engage children in reciprocal play, and help them make sense of expectations and classroom organization. Support perseverance, and facilitate lessons and activities rather than instruct.

Reflection   Teachers as well as children come to the classroom with their own particular temperaments, stages of professional development, and unique experiences. Teachers come with their own stressors and coping styles. Jersild writes ". . . a teacher cannot make much headway in understanding others unless he is endeavoring to understand himself" (1955, p. 5). Working with young children and their families can evoke strong, ongoing feelings and even call to mind our own childhood experiences.

> *Teachers come from all over the district to visit my program. It is known for being well organized and arranged to give the kids many options and choices during the day. It is so important for me to provide children with choices. To do that well, things need to be well organized, in good working order, accessible, and the expectations made clear. I'm good at it, but it wasn't until today's workshop that I realized my passion for providing this kind of environment probably comes from my childhood. We were that stereotypic dysfunctional family. So much of my life was unpredictable and out of my control then. It is so important to find ways to give children choices and the control I never experienced as a child.*

These feelings, memories, and values lead to interpretations about behavior, development, and learning style seen in the classroom. Interpretation of behavior often determines intervention. For example, providing Adam with additional adult support was interpreted as "spoiling" him by staff who had been successfully raised in a more restrictive and authoritarian environment (Baldwin, Baldwin, & Cole, 1990). Other staff members saw the additional support as a necessity, a precursor to learning, a way to counteract the experiences of inconsistency in his prior caregiving environments. By intentionally promoting a relationship in which Adam could trust that his basic needs would be met, his demands acknowledged, and his wants validated and supported, he would expand his behavioral and cognitive competencies. The possibility of a hearing loss (because of frequent and ongoing ear infections) expanded the interpretation of Adam's behavior from simply the result of being a "drug baby."

Program planning must have time incorporated for teachers to do the following:

Define, refine, and implement philosophical approaches The degree to which teachers participate in ongoing personal and professional dialogues determines in part the degree of success programs have in serving children and families. Inservice training, coaching, mentorship, on-site demonstrations, and supervision all can be used by staff to sort out complex reactions and emotions felt when working with young children and their families and to help realize the range and influence they have and do not have on children. Opportunities to become reflective professionals must be seen as a necessity. Such practices must be ongoing and must balance a core knowledge of the profession with a process that recognizes it takes time to make a change (Weikart, 1994; Wolfe, 1994).

Expand knowledge of children and families affected by substance abuse Attending inservices and workshops or having speakers address the complex issues of working with children exposed to substance abuse can increase understanding. For example, although most educators will agree that drug addiction is a disease, many hold the belief that parents could just stop if they would only try harder. Many children at risk are involved in service delivery systems (e.g., court system, protective services, foster care) besides education; however, teaching staff has little knowledge about these systems, how to gain access to them, or what a child's experience with them may be like. Additionally, early childhood staff may know a great deal about child development, but very little about the field of addiction. Recovery from substance abuse is a complicated process. That relapse is an expected part of recovery is important for staff to know. It may help staff reframe the behavior seen in a parent such as withdrawal, guilt, and acting out, and be a cue to provide additional support to the child during this time. Establishing interagency collaborations can provide reciprocal services, coordinate interventions, and maximize outcomes that can serve parent and child together (Zuckerman & Brown, 1993).

Safely acknowledge personal reactions, biases, limitations, and strengths in working with families affected by substance abuse Parents of children enrolled in the classroom still may be using drugs, and may, in fact, be more involved in the disease of addiction than in the care of their child. Interactions with these families may be frustrating and sporadic. Staff reactions, feelings, and opinions are legitimate. Time must be designated and supervision provided that facilitate a teacher's ability to cope with these realities and face overt behavior, which may adversely affect the child and caregiver, while continuing to nurture the child.

Building Bridges and Boundaries

The regularity of rules, routines, reinforcements, and role modeling are traditional ways in which to build bridges and establish boundaries necessary in meeting the academic and emotional needs of young vulnerable children. Children at risk may fluctuate in the way they respond, on a daily or even hourly basis, to classroom events as they are learning new behavior patterns. It is important that the staff perceive behavior from the child's point of view and plan for the latitude of behavior that may be observed during the time the child is experimenting with new and more acceptable behavior. A child's autonomy, self-initiative, and mastery are encouraged when teaching staff focus on support and acceptance.

Children can begin to feel physiologically and psychologically safe in programs that are predictable. When the classroom milieu is consistent, children have more time to pursue self-regulation, construct knowledge, and practice social interaction. When the staff explain to children what will happen in the classroom, why it will happen, and what is expected, children begin to trust in their ability to make sense of the world around them and to internalize and master expectations. Clearly defined boundaries that help organize child behavior and support processes that bridge a child's ability to cope with classroom expectations can be found in an appropriate curriculum, classroom environment, routines, rules, observation and assessment, staff resources, and parent partnerships.

An Appropriate Curriculum   Educators help to build bridges for children when the curriculum regularly reflects an understanding of child development in general and individual development in particular. Curriculum, as defined by the National Association for the Education of Young Children (NAEYC), is "an organized framework that delineates the content children are to learn, the processes through which children are to achieve the identified curricular goals, and the context in which teaching and learning can occur" (National Association for Education of Young Children, 1990, p. 19). Specific developmental objectives can be taught, but they must not be at the expense of the child's intrinsic motivation and healthy strivings for mastery. Successful program planning incorporates effective strategies for teaching children with specific special needs and adaptations that will provide the acquisition of effective communication, adaptive skills, social interaction, motor development, and cognitive skills (Wolery, Strain, & Bailey, 1992).

Children learn about the world around them, learn how to deal with feelings, and become symbolic thinkers through play. Children who engage in active exploration (e.g., moving, connecting, taking apart, sorting, comparing, reorganizing objects) develop cognitively and emotionally (Piaget, 1973). Adults who encourage play provide props and participate in the activities that validate its importance.

> *During time outside for the first 3 months George's play consisted of riding the tricycle. Some staff members felt it was time to suggest that George experiment with other things such as the easel, the sand*

box, or an art activity. Other staff members talked about how competent George was at riding and what pleasure he took in this activity. Because he was living in an upstairs apartment with 12 people, there was no space to engage in gross motor activities. The staff decided to wait another month before insisting George change activities. They brought out traffic signs and the gas station play kit to extend the tricycle activities. Before the end of the month, George got off the bike and began to explore other activities on his own.

The staff's decision to support George's tricycle riding considered his behavior in the context of his experiences and respected his basic competencies and his need of time for mastery. As with Adam, the staff considered George's stage of development, his attention span, and his need for comfort and safety. When both boys came to trust the predictability of expectations, the security of structure, and the availability of nurturing adults, they could take more risks and initiate more options in their play. Adding props to George's tricycle play provided novelty and complexity. With Adam, expanding the structure of interaction matched his growing competency to make choices, follow directions, and experience pleasure.

Classroom Environment All children need a classroom that is predictable. Living with the stressors of a chaotic home or neighborhood environment requires a classroom that is particularly sensitive to the need for structure and respects the need for private time and personal space. Including children in problem solving and decision making when changes in the classroom are necessary will reduce problem behaviors and promote success for children who have a low threshold for inconsistency, disorganization, or overstimulation. Activities that are repetitive (as were planned with Adam) and happen at the same time, at the same table, and with the same materials can be soothing to children who have little control in their lives. Making sure art projects and work samples are safe and protected is a concrete way of promoting trust and demonstrating that you value the child. Permitting children to have some experiences in which they do not have to share toys and materials with each other acknowledges the egocentric perspective of this age and allows children to be more generous in sharing at other requested times. Successful classrooms will provide space in which

- Inviting textures and colors are used.
- Play areas are easily supervised.
- Traffic patterns are clear.
- Light and ventilation is sufficient.

- Closed areas are provided for being quiet or alone.
- Open areas are provided for cooperative play.
- Play areas are well defined.

Successful classrooms will provide materials that are

- Sufficient and available.
- Open-ended to accommodate a range of development.
- Introduced and explained to children about possible use.
- Sometimes shared and sometimes not shared.
- Sometimes accessible and sometimes inaccessible.
- Organized and clearly stored.
- Safe.

Successful classrooms will provide equipment that is

- Clean.
- In good repair.
- Appropriate in size (e.g., chairs, tables, cupboards).
- Added, covered or closed, or taken away to monitor stimulation.

Routines The rhythm of daily classroom routines helps children experience the sequence of events. Routines give the classroom environment predictability in which to practice self-regulation safely, learn to cope with feelings, and maintain an equilibrium in the face of classroom expectations. Routines can protect children from overstimulation and lay the foundation for a sense of order—this permits learning. On days when there are changes in the routine (i.e., special assemblies, fire drills, new materials, or substitute teachers), the staff should expect that children with poor ability to self-regulate or a history of nonsupportive caregiving may not do well. Providing additional time for preparation and offering reassurance and confidence can help children cope during such times of high stress.

———

May
May's classroom was well designed. The physical space was arranged to provide activity centers, places for quiet time, cooperative learning, and group gatherings. The staff were well trained, nurturing, and experienced. Materials and activities supported child choice. Considerations were given to individual differences, and adaptations were made to accommodate special needs. The schedule was consistent and routines were predictable. In the beginning, May was content to play on the rug with the Legos. She could play uninterrupted for quite

some time, building her structures facing the wall. She had good fine motor coordination. At age 4, her creations were quite involved, mixing detail and invention that implied thoughtful planning. During circle time, she sat on the other side of the bookshelf, out of sight of her classmates, quietly singing to herself. Outside, she would climb the bars and ride the tricycle. She seemed to prefer the solitary activities. When few demands were placed on May or when she was given ample opportunity to organize herself, she presented herself as very capable cognitively. However, if there were disruptions in the routine, or if the activities were not ready or if changes were not adequately explained, you could count on May becoming more difficult to control. Her activity level would increase and there would be much flitting around the room. When offered adult support she would become increasingly difficult to control. She was bright enough to eventually find ways of removing herself or getting removed (placed in time out) from the situation. You could count on May's behavior to be the room barometer for too much noise, too much stimulation, too much unpredictability, too many glitches in the routine, too many activities not set up and ready, or too little teacher attention directed at children.

Intervention: The goal for May was to engage in play with other children and learn to cope appropriately with the demands of an active, stimulating, and therefore often unpredictable preschool setting. To that end, and over a period of time the teacher found ways to acknowledge and support May's need to spend time alone. Gradually, as she grew in her ability to read May's cues, she knew when to increase demands for group participation and peer interaction. She provided additional support during particularly over-stimulating stressful group times (e.g., Halloween parade, community walks) so May could participate successfully. Slowly, May's tolerance for novel events increased and she was able to adapt successfully to most classroom expectations. With continued support and encouragement, May began to play along side of and eventually with other children in the block corner or in the dramatic play corner.

Classroom routines are a necessity for children like May who have a low threshold for overstimulation (Griffith, 1992). Although routines are necessary, they alone are not sufficient. May's success was facilitated by the reciprocity of a respectful relationship with the teacher. Their interaction involved ongoing evaluation, deciphering of cues, and experimenting with when to increase demands or when teacher expectation needed to be decreased. There was frustration and repeated trial and error. It was a process, one in which the child participated in the authorship of growth and development. The ongoing relationship provided the support necessary for the child to learn to trust, take risks, and practice the skills necessary in mastering and internalizing the coping strategies necessary to be successful in this classroom.

Within 6 months, May could tolerate staying through both circle and group music time with little adult support. On hard days she needed to bring her stuffed dog. The dog had its own chair and May reminded it of the rules. Sometimes she would give the stuffed animal something to hold "to help him be quiet."

Successful routines in the classroom will accommodate children's physical needs, provide time to practice novel experiences, and be facilitated by visual and verbal cues.

Accommodate Children's Physical Needs Children's physical needs must be accommodated; for example, it is inappropriate for young children to sit for long periods. To accommodate their needs,

- Balance teacher-directed and child-initiated activities.
- Provide periods of activity and quiet time.
- Alternate the length of time spent at activities within groups or working alone.
- Help children through times of the day that are difficult for them.
- Become aware of cues of hunger, illness, or not having enough sleep.
- Help children develop strategies to cope with stressful situations.
- Learn to self-soothe, as it enhances self-esteem, autonomy, and responsibility.

Provide Time to Practice Novel Experiences Carefully providing time and support to practice new experiences enhances a child's confidence and mastery, which in turn fosters the risk taking necessary for learning. To provide time to practice novel experiences,

- Explain what is to happen.
- Act as if you were having the experience for the first time too.

- Ask questions and listen to concerns.
- Remind children that mastery comes with repetition.
- Provide ample time so children will not be hurried in this process.
- Respect individual temperaments, cognitive abilities, caregiving experiences, and learning style.

Make Associations Using Visual and Verbal Cues   Make associations with activities by using concrete visual and verbal cues. To make associations with visual and verbal cues,

- Use the same name (e.g., music time, outside time) to label activities. This helps children make associations.
- Ask questions such as "Then what happens?" or "After music we . . . ?" This promotes an ability to sequence and problem solve.
- Pay attention to responses. They can alert difficulties the child may be having in processing, language, or adaptive skills.

Transitions are a part of classroom routines. Transitions can be extremely stressful for young children because they involve ending one thing and beginning another. Stopping and starting, coming and going, and loss and change are familiar experiences for children who come from substance-abusing environments and have experienced abrupt changes in residence or caregivers (e.g., the child who is removed in the middle of lunch from his foster parents of 18 months by the mother who has regained custody; the child who is taken out of the state by relatives because the mother has been incarcerated for shoplifting; the child who spends time each week rotating between his aunt, grandmother, foster mother, biological mother, and babysitter until final custody is awarded). Children's concern about these changes and losses are reflected in their questions and play. Adults need to be able to address those concerns with empathy and honesty.

Transitions from home to school or between activities or areas in the classroom can become trigger events for unwanted behaviors because of the memories of past experiences they evoke in the child. For example, when a child suddenly "disappears" (e.g., moves, is adopted) from the classroom, other children in the classroom will be affected. There may be an egocentric concern that they were somehow responsible. They may worry that they too may "disappear." When no acknowledgment is made of the departure, it reinforces prior experiences that relationships are insignificant and transitory.

Making transitions a successful part of the classroom routine entails limiting the number that occur, explaining what changes are occurring, designing a plan, and using daily experiences.

Limit the Number of Transitions   Limit the number of changes. Look at the schedule. Count how many times children have to make changes during the day. Can this number be reduced or streamlined?

Explain What Changes are Occurring and Why They Occur Explanations of changes taking place and why can be as concrete as 5-minute warnings or can be used to clarify how the day will be different. Sometimes explaining the what and why of transitions may necessitate suspending the planned activity. For example, planned activities may need to be postponed to address Mark's experience of being left on the steps of the protective service building and answer questions such as "Why did the mother make him go away?"

Design a Transition Plan   Recognize that transition is a process that has a beginning, a middle, and an end. In the beginning, signals (e.g., warnings, blinking the light, ringing a bell, raising an arm) are key components in helping children prepare and cope with transition. The middle time often includes waiting. Having small interim activities (e.g., stories, finger plays) makes this time more successful. The end will go more smoothly if the materials are ready for children to use when they get to the next activity.

Use Daily Experiences   Transitions evoke feelings. Using current events to help children practice and learn to cope with change always will be more effective than prescribed lessons about affect or feelings. Intentionally develop relationships that support the emotional process of transition. Reassure children that adults will be there to provide support. Make greetings affirming and sincere and plan good-bye rituals carefully. Have children draw pictures, or send the child off with a photo album to remember the experience. When relationships end, help children to understand that they will be missed and they will miss others.

Rules   Often there is a disparity between what is appropriate behavior in the home or neighborhood and expected behavior in the school setting. For example, the rule that all children are to use the bathroom only at certain prescribed times at school may seem absurd to children who have the skills and experience to use a bathroom independently at home. When teachers can comfortably acknowledge the incongruity of some of the classroom expectations and open up a discussion about feelings, children will be more apt to accept the rules and cooperate.

This may mean that, initially, the staff needs to allow broader behavioral limits in order to observe and understand a child's needs. The staff needed to accept Antonio's hypervigilant behavior as an adaptive necessity that kept him safe before they could develop an intervention plan that would help him become more spontaneous and take pleasure in the classroom. Allowing May to participate in circle time from the other side of the block cabinet provided allowances for her low tolerance for stimulation. Providing flexibility in established rules also promotes understanding of individual differences and provides support for individual growth in the context of the classroom cohesion.

> *Visiting the child care center for the first time, the consultant noted that all the children were working in small groups. The materials were varied and the children were involved with the activities, all of the children that is except one, a 3-year-old in the doll corner. She was alone rearranging play dishes on the small table and pretending to cook. She seemed not to notice the other children. The consultant continued to observe the young girl. As she did, a large, robust 5-year-old left his activity and announced, "She is new," as if to say she does not have to follow the rules yet and it is okay.*

When establishing procedures by which the classroom will operate,

- Have high expectations.
- Remember admiration promotes confidence.
- Limit the number of rules, keep them simple, and state them in a positive way.
- Provide time for making choices and decision making.
- Explore cause-and-effect relationships.
- Engage children in problem solving and alternatives for conflict resolution.

Observation and Assessment Child behavior exists in context and must be viewed as communication that provides clues for what the child needs. The extremes in behavior observed in the classroom are often in response to external and internal stressors, such as the disrupted equilibrium experienced by the child. Becoming aware of patterns of behavior through careful observation in the classroom during these times is one part of the intervention process. When planning intervention, keeping anecdotal records and work samples is a way to facilitate understanding. Descriptions of the targeted behavior, when it occurs, what signals the child is giving preceding losing control, the events that trigger the behavior, and the adult's response will be helpful when included in a behavioral log (Griffith, 1992). Becoming familiar with a time line of the child's experiential history may help in understanding the child's feelings and behavior.

Disruptions are more critical at certain stages of development. How the changes were prepared for, facilitated, and integrated also are important in supporting or undermining a child's coping skills. As with Adam, Mark, and Antonio, it is important to know if the child experienced any of the following instances:

- Multiple caregivers and, if so, at what age and for how long
- Abrupt moves from one household to another and, if so, at what age
- Prolonged separations and, if so, at what age
- Quality and consistency in care
- Caregivers affected by few or many stressors
- Caregivers with good or minimal support systems
- Caregivers with appropriate coping strategies

Staff Resources   It is important that programs have sufficient staff to ensure responsive interactions. However, too many adults to relate to (e.g., Adam's story) can be ineffective for children who first need to experience consistency. Children who experience a series of separations and losses may indiscriminately seek out adults to get needs and wants met. Other children avoid contact as a way of self-protection.

Relationship-based planning acknowledges that primary attachments in the school setting are of a child's own choosing and often cross professional titles. The primary relationship may be with the assistant teacher, bus driver, custodian, speech-language specialist, or another student. These connections can be powerful and productive and can enhance intervention because the child participates in choosing the relationship. Programs that promote attachment and value the importance of significant relationships accept that staff are not interchangeable in the eyes of children.

In order to nurture positive attachment between staff and children,

- Changes should be made in staff assignment only when necessary.
- Volunteers should be chosen based on longevity of commitment.
- Care should be taken in selecting the same substitute staff.
- Staff should be hired that are well trained and demonstrate the capacity for empathy.

Parent Partnership   Viewing parents as valued members of the educational team is the initial step to developing collaboration between parent and teacher. When the teaching staff are willing to share general information (e.g., how children differ in coping with separation, suggestions to facilitate transitions or cope with sibling rivalry), parents begin to trust professional expertise as helpful. However, professionals must acknowledge the wealth of specific parental expertise (e.g., the child's likes and dislikes, temperament, assessment of concerns) if there is to be the reciprocal partnership necessary for successful teaching.

To enhance the collaboration with parents it is understood that cultural and linguistic differences must be valued, communication must be ongoing, and drug abuse must not negate parental love for a child (Smith, 1992).

Cultural and Linguistic Differences Must Be Valued Cultural and linguistic differences must be valued by the parents and teacher. Invite parents to volunteer in the classroom to share traditions, and ask parents to teach words and rituals from each other's culture. Incorporate pictures, foods, stories, and music in an ongoing way that support cultural differences. It is helpful to find supportive adults who can translate and share information between teaching staff and parents.

Communication Must Be Ongoing Communication must be ongoing between parents and the staff. Information should be shared in a clear, honest, and logical way without using jargon. Take time to reflect on what is being discussed and accentuate the positive. Establish a consistent style of communication by telephone, notes, or ongoing classroom visitations. Most important, always remember to listen to the other person, especially in discussions about a child.

Drug Abuse Must Not Negate Parental Love for a Child A parent's drug abuse does not make the love for a child disappear. However, parents who use drugs may engage in childrearing practices that are less than optimal. Understanding the stressors that families are experiencing and providing supports (e.g., resources, education) that address these concerns may influence parenting style. Workshops, films, and speakers can be used to address discipline, parental coping strategies, and ways to gain access to community resources. When parental concerns are the starting point of such parent education, attendance and positive outcomes will be enhanced.

Create Community Through Choice and Cooperation

Creating a sense of belonging in a classroom community may be a critical protective factor for young children in helping to ameliorate the adverse effects of exposure to drugs. Initially, because of irritability or unresponsiveness, or because of caregiver inability or unavailability, children exposed to drugs and alcohol may have experienced compromised attachments. The quality of early attachment relationship is linked with the child's social competence and, in turn, social competence (e.g., being liked, cooperating, successfully interacting) predicts later adjustment in adolescence (Beckman & Lieber, 1992, Kemple, 1991). Likewise, being raised in a chaotic, dysfunctional environment does not afford children appropriate role models or adequately prepare them for the demands of preschool. (Crittenden, 1989; Oyemade & Washington, 1989; Robinson, 1990).

To facilitate a classroom community, children need ongoing opportunities to develop competence in social skills (Curry & Johnson, 1990; Haring, 1992; McEvoy, Odom, & McConnell, 1992). Children learn to make choices, develop friendships, reconcile needs, negotiate solutions, practice reciprocity, and delay gratification by interacting with each other in play situations, group experiences, and day-to-day experiences. They learn to take other perspectives and understand the causes and effects of their actions and the consequences of their choices.

Children come to respect individual differences when those differences are acknowledged and accepted as part of the classroom community. When Adam's teacher explained that Adam needed to sit by her during lunch time she included his peers in the discussion of why. Some of them made sure that no one else sat in his special chair. Mark's behavior also was explained openly and with empathy, thus modeling understanding and inclusion.

Teachers can enhance social interaction within the classroom when they structure activities, implement rituals and ceremonies that enhance classroom cohesion, respect individuality, and practice conflict resolutions.

Structure Activities Provide physically and emotionally safe activities for children to participate in and work together. Either during activities or between activities, allow ample time for free play to encourage interaction and cooperation. Design activities with props, roles, and rules to structure interaction when necessary.

Implement Rituals and Ceremonies that Enhance Classroom Cohesion Implement rituals and ceremonies for activities that enhance classroom cohesion. Special name tags used only for field trips, a specific song to start an activity, individualized hellos, and regular rituals to say good-bye can encourage a sense of community within the classroom. Celebrating special occasions in a prescribed way, for example, a birthday child gets to choose the color of the napkins used or the color of the frosting on the cake baked in class, becomes part of the classroom culture also. Children can anticipate, practice waiting for, and make choices about these events. Such activities can be the precursor to perseverance, delaying gratification, and making long-term goals.

Respect Individuality Staff members should respect the individuality of all children, and that means recognizing and appreciating diversity. Being fair does not mean treating everyone equally. Try to model encouragement and acceptance for children to learn.

Practice Conflict Resolutions Develop a common language for the classroom community to practice conflict resolutions. Using daily experiences to practice problem solving also is helpful. Brainstorming, having meetings, asking open ended questions, and recording discussions will help in difficult situations.

> *As Terry and Sasha approached the teacher it was obvious there was a conflict over something on the Play-Doh table. The teacher said rather abruptly, "I don't want to hear about it. If you two have something to discuss, go to the bench, sit down, and talk. Tell me when you are ready or need help." The two children walked over to the bench and sat down. The teacher explained that these 4-year-olds had been in her classroom almost 2 years. During the better part of those years there had been ongoing practice about resolving conflicts. In the beginning of the first year of the program, sometimes the routines would be delayed so that enough time could be spent on talking about conflicts, problem solving, and negotiating solutions. In the beginning, she said her role was as an active mediator, verbalizing positions and encouraging dialogue, but now she did not need to be so involved. The children had developed their own skills.*
>
> *A few minutes later, Terry and Sasha were on the bench laughing. Terry called out, "We're ready." The teacher went over and asked each of them if the discussion was over and if it went okay. They both nodded, got up, and went back to the Play-Doh table together.*

SUMMARY

Children prenatally or environmentally exposed to drugs and alcohol are children first. There is a range of presenting behavioral and cognitive delays associated with, but not solely attributed to, drug and alcohol exposure. Labeling children from families affected by substance abuse should be avoided. Behavior, learning style, and development seen in the classroom setting is not static, but rather the result of interactions and adaptations between biology and environment. The classroom can be designed to promote resiliency and offer a process of experiences that counteract risk factors. Supporting the development of responsive relationships is a key component in this effort. Acknowledging feelings and responding to a child's behavior in context of temperament, experience, and development nurtures trust. Building bridges and boundaries in the classroom ensures the structure and support children need to take risks, practice new skills, and become autonomous. Given choices, children learn consequence and communication. They learn to take initiative, to problem solve, and to cooperate with others in the community within classroom.

REFERENCES

Baldwin, A.L., Baldwin, C., & Cole, R.E. (1990). Stress-resistant families and stress-resistant children. In J. Rolf, A.S. Masten, D. Cicchetti, K.H. Nuechterlein, & S. Weintraub (Eds.), *Risk and protective factors in the development of psychopathology* (pp. 257–280). New York: Cambridge University Press.

Beckman, P.J., & Lieber, J. (1992). Parent–child social relationships and peer social competence of preschool children with disabilities. In S.L. Odom, S.R. McConnell, & M.A. McEvoy (Eds.), *Social competence of young children with disabilities: Issues and strategies for intervention* (pp. 65–92). Baltimore: Paul H. Brookes Publishing Co.

Brazelton, T.B. (1992). *Touchpoints: Your child's emotional and behavioral development*. Reading, MA: Addison-Wesley.

Carta, J.J., Sideridis, G., Rinkel, P., Guimaraes, S., Greenwood, C., Baggett, K., Peterson, P., Atwater, J., McEvoy, M., & McConnell, S. (1994). Behavioral outcomes of young children prenatally exposed to illicit drugs: Review and analysis of experimental literature. *Topics in Early Childhood Special Education, 14*(2), 184–216.

Center for Substance Abuse Prevention (CSAP), National Resource Center for the Prevention of Alcohol and Other Drugs. (1993) *Annual report on the state of the field: The prevention of perinatal abuse of alcohol and other drugs*. Fairfax, VA: Author.

Chasnoff, I.J., Griffith, D.R., Frier, M.C., & Murray, J. (1992). Cocaine/polydrug use in pregnancy: Two year follow-up. *Pediatrics, 89*(2), 284–289.

Chira, S. (1990, May 25). Crack babies turn 5 and schools brace. *New York Times*, p. A1.

Cohen, S., & Erwin, E. (1994). Characteristics of children with prenatal drug exposure being served in preschool special education programs in New York City. *Topics in Early Childhood Special Education, 14*(2), 232–253.

Cole, C.K., Ferrara, V., Johnson, D., Jones, M., Poulsen, M.K., Schoenbaum, M., Tyler, R., & Wallace, V. (1989). *Today's challenge: Teaching strategies for working with young children prenatally exposed to drugs/alcohol*. Los Angeles: Unified School District, Division of Special Education, Los Angeles.

Cole, C.K., & Jones, M. (1990). Working with children at risk due to prenatal substance exposure. *Prise Reporter, 21*(5), 1–5.

Cook, R., & Tessier, A. (1992). *Adapting early childhood curricula for children with special needs*. New York: Macmillan.

Crittenden, P.M. (1989). Teaching maltreated children in the preschool. *Topics in Early Childhood Special Education, 9*(2), 16–32.

Curry, N.E., & Johnson, C.N. (1990). *Beyond self-esteem: Developing a genuine sense of human value.* Washington, DC: National Association for the Education of Young Children.

DeVries, R., & Kohlberg, L. (1987). *Constructivist early education: Overview and comparison with other programs.* Washington, DC: National Association for the Education of Young Children.

Dunst, C.J. (1993). Implications of risk and opportunity factors for assessment and intervention practices. *Topics in Early Childhood Special Education, 13*(2), 143–153.

Erikson, E.H. (1963). *Childhood and society.* New York: Norton.

Ford, A., Davern, L., & Schnorr, R. (1992). Inclusive education: "Making sense" of the curriculum. In S. Stainback & W. Stainback (Eds.), *Curriculum considerations in inclusive classrooms: Facilitating learning for all students* (pp. 37–61). Baltimore: Paul H. Brookes Publishing Co.

Frailberg, S., Shapiro, V., & Cherniss, D.S. (1980). Treatment modalities. In S. Frailberg (Ed.), *Clinical studies in infant mental health* (pp. 49–77). New York: Basic Books.

Garbarino, J. (1990). The human ecology of early risk. In S.J. Meisels & J.P. Shonkoff (Eds.), *Handbook of early childhood intervention* (pp. 78–95). New York: Cambridge University Press.

Greenspan, S. (1990). Comprehensive clinical approaches to infants and their families: Psychodynamic and developmental perspectives. In S.J. Meisels & J.P. Shonkoff (Eds.), *Handbook of early childhood intervention* (pp. 119–145). New York: Cambridge University Press.

Greer, J.V. (1990). The drug babies. *Exceptional Children.* Reston, VA: Council for Exceptional Children.

Griffith, D.R. (1992). Developmental/educational prognosis for children exposed to cocaine and other drugs prenatally. *Phi Delta Kappan, 74*(1), 30–34.

Griffith, D.R., Azuma, S.A., & Chasnoff, I.J. (1994). Three year outcome of children exposed to drugs. *Journal of American Academy of Child and Adolescent Psychiatry, 33*(1), 20–27.

Haring, T.G. (1992). The context of social competence: Relations, relationships, and generalization. In S.L. Odom, S.R. McConnell, & M.A. McEvoy (Eds.), *Social competence of young children with disabilities: Issues and strategies for intervention* (pp. 307–320). Baltimore: Paul H. Brookes Publishing Co.

Honig, A.S. (1986). Stress and coping in children. In J.B. McCracken (Ed.), *Reducing stress in young children's lives* (pp. 142–167). Washington, DC: National Association for the Education of Young Children.

Hopkins, E. (1990, October). Childhood's end. *Rolling Stone, 589,* 66–72, 108–110.

Jersild, A.T. (1955). *When teachers face themselves.* New York: Teachers College Press.

Johnson, D.J., & Cole, C.K. (1992). Extraordinary care for extraordinary children. In R.D. Stephens (Ed.), *School safety* (pp. 7–9). Westlake Village, CA: National School Safety Center.

Kemple, K.M. (1991). Preschool children's peer acceptance and social interaction. *Young Children, 46*(5), 47–54.

Kronstadt, D. (1991). Complex developmental issues of prenatal drug exposure. *The Future of Children, 7,* 36–49.

Laderman, D.A. (1990). Crack, babies: Ready or not, here they come. *American Teacher, 75*(3), 10, 11, 16.

Lally, J.R. (1990). Creating nurturing relationships with infants and toddlers. In J.R. Lally (Ed.), *A guide to social emotional growth and socialization* (pp. 40–46). Sacramento, CA: Department of Education, Sacramento.

Maslow, A.H. (1962). *Toward a psychology of being.* New York: Van Nostrand Co.

McEvoy, M.A, Odom, S.L., & McConnell, S.R. (1992). Peer social competence intervention for young children with disabilities. In S.L. Odom, S.R. McConnell, & M.A. McEvoy (Eds.), *Social competence of young children with disabilities: Issues and strategies for intervention* (pp. 113–133). Baltimore: Paul H. Brookes Publishing Co.

Myers, B.J., Olson, H.C., & Kaltenbach, K. (1992). Cocaine-exposed infants: Myths and misunderstandings. *Zero to Three, 13*(1), 1–5.

National Association for Education of Young Children. (1992). Guidelines for appropriate curriculum content and assessment in programs ages 3–8. A position statement of the National Association for the Education of Young Children and National Association of Early Childhood Specialists in State Department of Education. Adopted November 1990. In S. Bredekamp & T. Rosegrant (Eds.), *Reaching potential: Appropriate curriculum and assessment for young children* (pp. 9–27). Washington, DC: Author.

Office of the Inspector General, U.S. Department of Health and Human Services. (1990). *Crack babies.* Washington, DC: Author.

Oyemade, U.J., & Washington, V. (1989). Drug abuse prevention begins in early childhood: And is much more than a matter of instructing young children about drugs! *Young Children, 44*(5), 6–12.

Phillips, D.A., & Howes, C. (1987). Indicators of quality child care: Review of research. In D.A. Phillips (Ed.), *Quality in child care: What does the research tell us?* (pp. 1–19). Washington, DC: National Association for the Education of Young Children.

Piaget, J. (1973). *The child and reality.* New York: Viking Press.

Poulsen, M.K. (1992). *Schools meet the challenge: Educational needs of children at risk due to prenatal substance exposure.* Sacramento, CA: California Department of Education, Special Education Division.

Poulsen, M.K. (1993). Strategies for building resilience in infants and young children at risk. *Infants and Young Children, 6*(2) 29–40.

Risk, M.C. (1990). The shadow children. *The American School Board Journal, 177*(1), 19–24.

Robinson, B.E. (1990, May). The teacher's role in working with children of alcoholic parents. *Young Children, 45*(4), 68–73.

Rutter, M. (1983). Stress, coping, and development: Some issues and questions. In N. Garmezy & M. Rutter (Eds.), *Stress, coping and development in children.* New York: McGraw-Hill.

Rutter, M. (1990). Psychosocial resilience and protective mechanisms. In J. Rolf, A.S. Masten, D. Cicchetti, K.H. Nuechterlein, & S. Weintraub, (Eds.), *Risk and protective factors in the development of psychopathology* (pp. 181–214). New York: Cambridge University Press.

Sameroff, A.J., & Fiese, B.H. (1990). Transactional regulation and early intervention. In S.J. Meisels & J.P. Shonkoff (Eds.), *Handbook of early childhood intervention* (pp. 119–145). New York: Cambridge University Press.

Schorr, L.B., & Schorr, D. (1988). *Within our reach: Breaking the cycle of disadvantage*. New York: Doubleday.

Smith, I.E. (1992). An ecological perspective: The impact of culture and social environment on drug-exposed children. *OSAP Prevention Monograph, 11*, 93–108.

Stone, A. (1990, March 9–11). First wave of crack kids hits school. *USA Today*, p. 1.

Vincent, L.J., Poulsen, M.K., Cole, C.K., Woodruff, G., & Griffith, D.R. (1991). *Born substance exposed, educationally vulnerable*. Reston, VA: Council for Exceptional Children.

Weikart, D. (1994). The research shows. In J. Johnson & J.B. McCracken (Eds.), *The early childhood career lattice: Perspectives of professional development* (pp. 96–99). Washington, DC: National Association for the Education of Young Children.

Werner, E.E. (1990). Protective factors and individual resilience. In S.J. Meisels, & J.P. Shonkoff (Eds.), *Handbook of early childhood intervention* (pp. 97–116) New York: Cambridge University Press.

Werner, E.E., & Smith, R.S. (1982). *Vulnerable but invincible: A longitudinal study of resilient children and youth*. New York: McGraw-Hill.

Weston, D., Ivins, B., Zuckerman, B., Jones, C., & Lopez, R. (1989). Drug exposed babies research and clinical issues. *Zero to Three, 9*(5), 1–24.

Wilkes, D. (1993). *Hot topics: Children exposed to drugs: Meeting their needs*. Greensboro, NC: Southeastern Regional Vision for Education.

Wolery, M., Strain, P.S., & Bailey, D.B. (1992). Reaching potentials of children with special needs. In S. Bredekamp & T. Rosegrant (Eds.), *Reaching potential: Appropriate curriculum and assessment for young children* (pp. 92–111). Washington, DC: National Association for the Education of Young Children.

Wolfe, B.L. (1994). Effective practices in staff development: Head start experiences. In J. Johnson & J.B. McCracken (Eds.), *The early childhood career lattice: Perspectives of professional development* (pp. 111–114). Washington, DC: National Association for the Education of Young Children.

Zuckerman, B., & Brown, E.R. (1993). Maternal substance abuse and infant development. In C.H. Zeanah (Ed.), *Handbook of infant mental health* (pp. 143–158). New York: Guilford Press.

6

Classroom Strategies for Children and Adolescents

G. Harold Smith

Not all children arrive at school prepared for success. Success in school is contingent upon a variety of factors to which schools must respond if children affected by substance abuse in their families are to be successful.

Every child is a product of 1) his or her own developmental processes, 2) genetic inheritances from parents, 3) the deleterious or positive influence of the environment, and 4) potentially damaging effects of prenatal exposure to a variety of teratogenic substances including drugs and alcohol. There is no consistent, standard outcome nor is there a standard solution to determine how children exposed to substance abuse will demonstrate their needs and what schools can and should do to help children be successful. It is difficult to understand the extent to which an individual child's dysfunctional learning and behavior result from prenatal exposure to substances.

The commitment to the achievement of all students must begin at the district level with the board of education and superintendent accepting responsibility for each student's achievement. The local school is the critical point at which the district fulfills its mission. School boards need to work with the expectation that each child can learn and will learn given an appropriate educational setting. With these expectations, the district and schools will be better able to meet their responsibility to provide an environment, curriculum, and instructional model that will meet the special educational needs of the child and meet the district's obligation and mission to prepare each student to function in his or her community.

Children whose families abuse drugs and alcohol and are exposed to similar environments demonstrate a continuum of vulnerabilities resulting from an accumulation of risk factors (Aylward, 1992; Bays, 1990). Every student learns in a unique way whether exposed to substance abuse or not. The educational needs of students who have been prenatally exposed to drugs and alcohol and who are growing up in a home with substance abuse reflect the synergistic effects of clinical and environmental issues that come from the home, neighborhood, and school.

Children whose mothers abuse alcohol or other drugs during pregnancy or who are growing up in a home where these substances are abused share many of the risks for failure demonstrated by children from problematic social environments. However, because of the potentially damaging results of fetal exposure to teratogenic substances and the sometimes tragic effect that the substance abuse has on families, these children have increased vulnerability to failure.

Alvin

Alvin is in the second grade and is 8 years old. He has been enrolled in his current school for the last 3 months. Prior to this he had been in five different schools for his first and second grades. Alvin's 24-year-old mom is a single parent who has visited the school for a parent–teacher conference in a drunken state. The last time, the teacher reported, she had a black eye, cut lip, and was drunk again. His father is unknown, and there are no other family members available. The family receives public welfare.

Typically, Alvin arrives at school late and usually asks staff for something to eat. The school social worker has made several attempts to get his mother to sign the required application forms to qualify for the school's breakfast and lunch programs. To date the last set of forms has not been returned. A home visit is planned for next week.

This morning Alvin arrived at school visibly upset. His teacher asked the school's guidance counselor to talk with Alvin. At first he was reluctant to go with the counselor and even more reluctant to begin talking. Finally, like a dam bursting, he began sobbing and telling the counselor about a "new daddy," Craig, who had moved into the home.

Last night the "new daddy" hit his mom and forced her to leave the home to "go out and make some money." According to Alvin, she was crying when she arrived home, and he thought she had been hurt. She was asleep this morning when Alvin left for school. Alvin shared with the counselor that he was afraid to go home, but he also was afraid to leave his mother alone with this man.

The counselor took Alvin to the cafeteria for a sandwich and milk. A call was made by the school's principal to the area child protective services office who will initiate an immediate follow-up. Alvin will remain at school until the service coordinator contacts the principal.

His teacher, Ms. Cunningham, was told about the home situation. Ms. Cunningham will remain very close to Alvin throughout the school day and will escort him back to the counselor's office if he becomes upset again.

CHARACTERISTICS AND NEEDS OF STUDENTS AFFECTED BY SUBSTANCE ABUSE

Substance abuse in a student's family will affect students' behaviors and may result in a variety of psychological needs (Bays, 1990). Clinical damages that may result from prenatal exposure to drugs and alcohol may be compounded by postnatal environmental issues arising from further substance abuse by the child's caregiver (Chasnoff, Griffith, Frier, & Murray, 1992; Griffith, 1991, 1992; Schutter & Brinker, 1992), including exposure of the child to violence (Levoy, Rivinus, Matzko, & McGuire, 1991), trauma, inadequate parenting, stress of dysfunctional homes, and lack of developmental readiness opportunities that are essential for school success.

Psychological and Emotional Needs

The psychological and emotional development of children is related directly to the care they receive and the environment in which they are reared (Aylward, 1992; Garbarino & Gilliam, 1980; Garmezy & Rutter, 1980). All children need a caring and protective environment, which most children receive by growing up in families that are equipped to meet their physical and emotional needs. Children growing up in dysfunctional homes affected by substance abuse are at high risk for not receiving adequate care and protection to support their development. These children are vulnerable for psychological and behavior problems (Besharov, 1990).

Students coming to school from dysfunctional or traumatized home environments may have developed a repertoire of coping strategies and behaviors that are supportive to their functioning in these settings but that are not appropriate in the school setting (Murphy, 1984). Maladaptive student behavior resulting from dysfunctional family networks may be an attempt by the child to 1) accept responsibility for the family's dysfunctions, 2) act as mediator for family conflicts and other issues, and 3) to withdraw from perceived danger and threat. These responses may affect school behavior, particularly if the student perceives that the same threat factors are present at school as in the home, or if the student is unable to develop alternative coping behaviors more appropriate to the school setting and necessary for success in this environment.

Attachment Between Child and Adults Children with an inappropriate attachment to a significant caregiver may demonstrate developmental delays in a number of areas that are important for school success, including social and emotional skills, self-concept and self-esteem, language delays, and possibly cognitive dysfunctions (Bowlby, 1988; Karen, 1990). The attachment process between a child and the primary caregiver may be affected by inadequate parenting skills, conflicting priorities between care for the child and drug dependency, issues arising from dual diagnoses of the principal caregiver, physical abuse of the child, and exposure to family violence and trauma (Garbarino, Kostelny, & Dubrow, 1992; Jones & Houts, 1992; Jones & McCurdy, 1992; Kashani, Anasseril, Alison, & Holcomb, 1992; Terr, 1991).

Although school personnel—as well as the student—cannot influence home conditions, careful planning and commitment from the school and its staff may be able to offset or ameliorate many of the dysfunctional behaviors the vulnerable student brings from the home and family. The school should be established as a "secure base" (Bowlby, 1988) for the child. This can be done through consistency and structure within the school's organization of the instructional day and through allocation of staff resources.

The need for a consistent child and adult relationship emphasizes the importance of schools providing consistency of staff who work with the students. Unfortunately, this is more easily said than done in light of the common problems with staff turnover in schools and communities that are viewed as "difficult."

Children from dysfunctional families may have little positive experiences with their caregivers. For these youngsters it is critical that teachers and staff respond to children in a consistent manner to support the child being able to build trust in adults and peers through appropriate adult role modeling (Robinson, 1990). Teachers will need to assume responsibility for demonstrating healthy adult and child relationships, be appropriate adult role models, help the child to learn that adults will meet his or her needs for safety and security, lend appropriate emotional support, and provide structure and consistency within the classroom and other learning environments.

The issue of environmental and clinical influences on behavior has significant implications for teacher training in helping teachers learn how to be careful observers of children's behaviors and understand the multiple dynamics and issues in a dysfunctional family environment that may be affecting behavior. Although traditional behavior management strategies may be very helpful, a key factor in helping children succeed in the classroom is the teacher's ability to maintain a relationship with the individual child and consistently respond to behavior in an appropriate and supportive manner rather than with punitive and negative responses.

Feelings have a powerful influence on behavior. Schools will need to provide learning experiences including discussion groups, individual counseling, and immediate interventions for the child in crisis to help him or her get in touch with personal emotions and learn how to use these as tools for success rather than failure. Students may need to be helped in learning how a particular response "feels" and in learning to use this experience to determine whether or not that strategy is likely to be successful in a given setting.

Exposure to Violence and Trauma Children and youth in homes where substances are abused have an increased risk of exposure to physical abuse, sexual abuse, and severe violence and trauma arising from this environment. It has been estimated that 14 of every 100 children ages 3–17 years will experience family violence. These students are particularly vulnerable for being observers of violence in their home and community and for being the recipient of life-threatening violence (Craig, 1992).

Family violence, child abuse, or spousal abuse sometimes is dealt with in the same manner in which the family attempts to deal with substance abuse by one or more family members—namely, hiding this fact and insisting that family members not discuss this with others. The family's energies become focused on survival and secrecy within its immediate structure, placing additional burdens on the family's children and often preventing the parents or adult caregivers from obtaining needed community services.

Students exposed to violence or abuse present a continuum of behavioral and psychological needs that present vulnerability for school and personal failure as a child and as an adequate and functioning adult. Although some students exposed to abuse and violence are recognized and reported, a significant number are not recognized and their maladaptive behaviors are blamed on other factors. Behaviors such as hyperarousal, hypervigilance, and impulsivity are common among students who are abused (van der Kolk, 1987). Children diagnosed with attention-deficit/hyperactivity disorders have many symptoms in common with the behaviors of students who have been the victims of abuse or exposed to violence and trauma in their environments.

Research on children and youth coming to school from violent environments is beginning to address the issue of disassociation for students who are responding to severe stress and trauma in their environment. Research by Craig (1992), Putnam (1993), and Terr (1991) indicate that children who are exposed to severe stress resulting from personal exposure to abuse or violence may demonstrate significantly lower developmental levels, inability to focus on a given task, repetitive play symbolizing the original trauma, dysfunctional learning processes and cognition, and dysfunctional socialization skills.

Traumatized students will use a variety of survival strategies that may be misinterpreted by teachers who are not aware of the issues in the child's home. These students may become hypervigilant to environmental cues, may remove themselves emotionally and cognitively from the immediate environment because of triggering stimuli, and perhaps may be unable to demonstrate concepts or skills that were taught during a period in which the student had mentally "tuned out" the activities in the classroom even though every indication was that the child was paying attention. The reader is referred to Craig (1992); Garbarino, Kostelny, and Dubrow (1991); and van der Kolk (1987) for additional reporting on this issue with implications for classroom organization and management of learning.

The school has an important role in supporting a community's response to children who are abused. However, in most cases state laws designed to protect confidentiality of children and their families may prevent effective interagency cooperation that can be beneficial to all. Interventions for traumatized students will require careful consideration of the child's psychological needs that may go far beyond the typical resources of the school. Although school personnel have important roles in identifying students with numerous needs as well as serving as a critical link between the student and community, child protective and mental health agencies, teachers, and other support staff must be very attentive to professional boundaries in addressing clinical needs of the family and child.

Classroom teachers and administrators need to be careful observers for behaviors that may indicate abuse and exposure to violence in the home and need to recognize children's reports of home incidents. Teachers may not be aware that an incident being reported by a child is actually a recounting of abuse that has occurred. Teachers may not be comfortable with or know how to respond to a student's report or questions about family issues, particularly when death, violence, sexual abuse, and physical abuse are the issues.

Staff development programs for teachers and support for reporting abuse and neglect are now required in many states. Additional resources for teachers, including an effective liaison with school social workers, adequate counseling resources, and service liaison agreements with community social service and protective services agencies, are essential.

Special Health Concerns

HIV and AIDS Infection with the human immunodeficiency virus (HIV) and resulting diagnosis of acquired immunodeficiency syndrome (AIDS) are related to substance abuse (Crocker, Cohen, & Kastner, 1992; Siegel, 1988). Children whose parents are affected by substance use are at risk for difficulties arising from HIV and AIDS in a variety of ways.

- Transmission of the AIDS virus from the infected pregnant woman to her child in utero or following birth (Caldwell & Rogers, 1991)
- Loss of the primary caregiver through death
- Removal of the child from the home with placement into foster care
- Being blamed for the illness or death of the parent and subject to potential abuse and neglect
- Abandonment

Children who are diagnosed HIV positive or with AIDS or whose parents may be infected will present special educational issues for school planning (Chanock, 1992; Seidel, 1992; Simonds & Rogers, 1992). Children whose parents are infected will require close social and emotional support from the school and community resources (Rosen & Granger, 1992).

Children who are themselves HIV positive will evidence a range of developmental needs as the disease progresses. Collaborative team planning involving school personnel, physical and mental health service providers, social service and foster care agencies, service coordination agencies specializing in AIDS services, volunteer organizations, and other community resources should be initiated early for these children and their families.

Medication Issues Schools usually are able to assist children with learning problems. However, when a child's behavior becomes disruptive to the classroom and school environments, educators have limited resources to address these issues. Teachers report that a major issue for children and youth suspected of being affected by substances that interfere with school performance is that their behavior may be unpredictable (C.D. Coles, personal communication, April 11, 1992).

For some teachers and medical practitioners, medication may be seen as the easiest and quickest way to deal with children's maladaptive behaviors. Medication prescribed for controlling a child's behavioral and learning dysfunctions raise special concerns that should be discussed by all who are concerned. The use of medication to help a child control maladaptive behavior or learning problems is not a panacea. Whether or not medication is appropriate for a particular child is dependent upon the etiology or cause of the child's learning or behavior problem and a determination by a transdisciplinary intervention team as being appropriate to meet the child's needs (Levy, Harper, & Winberg, 1992). This team should include the child's primary medical care provider(s), psychologists, classroom teacher(s), parent(s), and other professional staff who may be working with the family. School-based team members have important roles to play in working with the medical practitioners to make the decision to prescribe medication, monitoring the effects of various dosages, and determining when medications should be changed or discontinued.

Administration of medication may be a major concern for students who live in a home in which structure and organization are absent. Careful assessment must be made of potential etiologies, and consideration should be given to the use of less intrusive behavior management strategies as an alternative intervention for children's behavioral and learning needs. Parents who are unable to organize a daily routine may be incapable of administering medication according to the prescribed dosage; therefore, supplementary resources may be required. Failure to recognize that a family may be unable to administer medication properly can result in children being undermedicated as well as being at risk for being overmedicated. There is also the possibility that parents may administer medication to their other children or to themselves that can result in a dangerous situation.

ADOLESCENTS

The use of substances by a child whose parents are substance abusers is cyclical in nature. Children who are affected by inadequate parenting and observe the use of substances by their parent(s) to relieve depression or other emotional needs may then begin experimenting with drugs and alcohol as a form of escape or self-medication for depression (Kanel, Yamaguchi, & Chen, 1992).

Adolescence is a critical developmental period for all children, especially for children in families affected by substance abuse (Kumpfer, 1989). In the developmental process of adolescence, students address a variety of issues including a need to achieve a higher level of independence in making decisions about peer networks, the importance of school and community activities, and their role within the family. A dysfunctional family environment will present an increased vulnerability for failure of the youth to achieve critical developmental skills for adult life. They also may be at risk for the development of coping strategies that may interfere with typical developmental outcomes of the adolescent period and other dysfunctional behaviors that may be demonstrated during this period or as adults.

Normal developmental needs of adolescents may be counter to issues of control and authority that have been established in a substance-misusing home in order to maintain some semblance of organization and order. The need for adolescents to achieve their own independence, the natural developmental process of questioning authorities and parents, and the need for peer group support may place students in direct opposition to their parents' need for isolation and dependence on physical discipline to control the younger members of the family (Emshoff, 1990). When the adolescent challenges parental authority in the home, he or she is potentially at high risk for physical abuse (Garbarino & Gilliam, 1980).

Schellenbach and Guerney (1987) identify the following factors that may contribute to physical abuse of adolescents:

1. Family communication patterns involving excessive authority or excessive permissiveness
2. High level of conflict within the family
3. Behavioral challenges presented to parents by adolescents
4. Adolescents who are themselves experiencing stressful events including drug and alcohol abuse

5. Parents responding with higher levels of discipline and lower levels of support for their children

The adolescent may attempt to deal with the dysfunctions in the family by isolating him- or herself from peers, adding further risk to typical development by eliminating or limiting the peer group that is so important during this period. For these students, a priority should be placed on helping the youth establish an appropriate peer network for social activities, personal support in crisis situations, and for developing appropriate recreational and leisure time activities.

Adolescents who live in homes affected by substance abuse may show a high level of depression, anxiety, and anger resulting from suppressed or expressed family conflict or violence among family members. If the student perceives that these emotions can be relieved by the use of drugs and alcohol, a risk for continued intergenerational substance abuse is presented. Emshoff (1990) identifies the following factors that support effective school-based interventions for students who come from families affected by substance abuse: The school provides accessibility to a broad population of adolescents. Adolescents, especially those with alcoholic parents, have limited mobility for attending out-of-school programs. Also, adolescents may find it difficult or embarrassing to initiate contact with an outside agency. The school setting gives recognition to the fact that a parent's alcoholism may have implications for academic performance and fits with the concept of the school as being concerned with the total functioning and development of children.

Effective counseling and support programs for children and adolescents exposed to substance abuse in their families will help them begin to understand that they are not responsible for the substance abuse, that they can make their own choices, as well as provide support to break the cycle of intergenerational use of drugs and alcohol (Robinson, 1990).

Student support groups similar to those sponsored by the Children of Alcoholics and Children of Drug Abuse movements are a valuable resource to schools and can help students identify alternatives to address personal needs. Participating in value clarification activities, learning how to make appropriate choices, developing appropriate peer networks, and understanding the dynamics of the family that may affect a student's behaviors and choices are examples of strategies and activities that can be provided in these programs.

These peer support groups provide education on substance abuse and assistance in developing appropriate coping skills to address family issues, decision making, and peer relationships (Ackerman, 1983; Morehouse, 1989). Groups may be organized to support liaison with social service and health agencies for the student and family, help to maintain close communication with foster care service providers who may be involved with the student, and encourage access to substance rehabilitation and treatment on behalf of these students (Jones, McCullough, & Dewoody, 1992).

Student Assistance Programs (SAP) are another resource for teenagers who are either using substances or are at high risk for substance abuse because of personal or family issues (Anderson, 1988; Carpenter, 1990). The SAP is a mutual assistance support group designed to support self-referral and identification by peers who are recognized as leaders of students at high risk. Peers act as leaders to the group and offer resources to understand personal needs, obtain community resources, and help to identify other youth who are at risk for substance abuse. Students may be referred to the SAP by other students, faculty, or by self-referral. In student support programs, students may share information about their families with peer or adult leaders that requires referral to child protective agencies. In these situations, students may require support in participating in the decision to refer to community agencies and will need continued assurance of their own personal integrity and value. The extent to which a teacher or other school staff member is able to provide support to students for family issues can become a very sensitive issue. If the child's parent(s) or caregiver(s) perceive that the school is intruding on family matters, the reaction can be catastrophic for school and family relations and for the child.

A student who reports abuse or neglect may be at high risk for retribution by a parent or other family member. Reporting by the school may result in extreme stress on the relationship between the school and family. However, the priority concern of the school is the physical and emotional well-being of the student. Close collaboration with other community agencies, especially legal and law enforcement agencies, is required.

The school has a responsibility to protect the child within the mandates of applicable state laws and regulations. The more subtle issues require careful consideration of how the school can support the child in separating school and home issues and providing information to students to assist in coping with family needs.

LOCAL SCHOOL ORGANIZATION

School improvement is dependent upon principal leadership and the ability of the school's leadership team to build and foster a sense of school and community partnership, consensus for school priorities and goals, and maximum utilization of all available resources within the community. Principals have the responsibility to provide leadership and direction for the organization of the school's resources for effective management of learning as well as addressing the needs of staff members. Although a number of leadership skills are necessary to achieve these goals, several are especially critical.

- Team building within the school and between the school and community
- Communication skills to help school staff and community understand each other
- Established strategies for involvement in setting priorities and the development of needed resources
- Planned support of a variety of activities that result in meaningful involvement by staff and community in identifying needs of vulnerable children and their families, setting realistic goals, monitoring of resource utilization, and assessing student, staff, and community outcomes

A clear statement of expectations and accountability should be provided from the district leadership to guide local school staff in the identification of local priorities. Local schools are responsible for the development and implementation of programs and services for children, staff, and families of vulnerable children in response to the district's expectations and mission.

Early identification of vulnerable students is a critical priority. Procedures are needed that will encourage teachers to identify students manifesting learning or behavioral difficulties. In-school student support teams provide support to the classroom teacher in assessing the student's needs, identifying appropriate learning resources and strategies, and determining whether additional interventions are appropriate. It is the responsibility of the school-based leadership team to give direction and support to put the support team in place, allocate authority and responsibility for its operation, and provide ongoing review and assessment of services.

CLASSROOM ORGANIZATION

Children who arrive at school vulnerable for failure because of either biological or environmental issues or both require

1. A school environment that is responsive to their learning and emotional needs

2. A developmentally appropriate curriculum
3. Instructional activities that are sensitive to the individual child's psychoneurological processes and developmental levels
4. School staff who are willing to develop meaningful relationships with the individual child

Because of potential damage resulting from prenatal exposure, as well as the child's response to environmental stress, developmental expectations may require modifications varying from flexibility within the school week or day to major revisions reflecting long-term developmental issues for the child.

Individualization of curriculum is critical for these students to make learning a successful experience, to serve as a tool to help the student learn self-worth, that the environment can be responsive to personal needs, and how to manage challenges and opportunities to contribute to personal success.

Classroom organization with consistent and predictable behavioral intervention strategies will be a key resource for children and their teachers. Children under stress will require consistency in classroom management and behavioral interventions that are designed to identify early signs of stress, and interventions that help the child to retire from stressful settings in the classroom. In some cases, the child may be successfully redirected to other tasks to relieve the stress. Other more serious situations may be addressed by helping the child move to a quiet area in the classroom or outside of the room, depending on the degree of intervention required to stabilize the behavior.

Teachers will need to be sensitive to the ability of students to cope, which may vary within the school week depending on the family's circumstances at different times during the week. For example, if the family has serious encounters with drugs or alcohol beginning on Friday and extending through Sunday, Monday will not be a good day for the child. He or she may arrive at school disheveled, hungry, and perhaps evidencing abuse. As the home situation becomes more stable during the week, the child may begin to show a higher capability of functioning in the classroom as stress levels in the home are reduced. Then toward the end of the school week, a higher level of anxiety may develop in the child as the weekend approaches.

This type of response by the child to home and family issues requires the teacher to plan for sometimes significant shifts in teaching strategies and expectations for student performance. Shifts in teaching styles to take advantage of the student's preferred learning modalities absolutely will be required if the student is to have any chance of success.

The classroom instructional system will need to provide for regular and systematic assessments of student needs. This can be accomplished through both formal and informal observations focusing on behavior and learning with appropriate shifts in strategies as necessary. Daily logs documenting behavior, interventions, and assessment of the success of the intervention are invaluable.

Students affected by substance abuse may come to school responding to inappropriate adult behavior in their families and home and be unable to make the necessary shifts to more appropriate school behavior. The student's behavior at school often is reflective of home and family issues the student is attempting to resolve or survive.

The model that teachers establish for students is absolutely essential in order to help the student understand that adults vary in their behavior and that certain behaviors are required for success in different environments. This perspective takes the burden off the child who may have developed adequate coping strategies within a dysfunctional family and is now faced with the need to develop a second pattern of behaviors for the school setting.

Alvin Reprise:
Alvin's school has established an educational support team (EST) made up of the school's instructional lead teacher, assigned psychologist and school social worker, special education teacher, and regular classroom teachers. The team accepts referrals from other teachers to assist them in meeting the educational needs of students who are experiencing academic or emotional and behavior problems. The team working with the principal has the authority to develop recommended modifications, to assign school resources, and to monitor implementation and results of the interventions toward resolving the student's problems.

Alvin's teacher worked with the guidance counselor to prepare a referral to the EST that was submitted as a "priority." The teacher's referral provided current achievement data, mental abilities testing, and a behavioral checklist. The team agreed with the teacher that although Alvin has the cognitive ability to achieve on his grade level, his achievement scores from group tests indicate a significant discrepancy between anticipated and actual achievements. The referral noted that Alvin was off task for a significant part of the day and appeared to be day dreaming. Alvin is able to refocus his attention when his name is called, but this only lasts for a very brief period of time before he is off task again. Alvin did not demonstrate any behaviors typically associated with absence seizures. Further assessment by the psychologist indicates that although Alvin shows indications of a neurological processing difficulty, a far bigger issue for him is dealing with the stress in his home. As the psychologist put it, "Alvin has so much on his mind with his mother that he has very little energy left to spend on academic instruction."

The team's first decision was to continue support for Alvin from the counselor. The instructional lead teacher was assigned to Alvin's class to work with him and three other students in a small group setting. The purpose of this instructional support was to identify specific areas in reading and arithmetic requiring remediation and to assist the teacher in developing an effective teaching style to be used with Alvin. A progress report was to be provided at the end of 4 weeks by the classroom teacher and the instructional lead teacher.

The progress/monitoring report submitted by the teacher showed that Alvin was doing significantly better in participating in group activities and some gains had been noted in the areas of reading and arithmetic. He excelled in the small group setting using a combination of orally and visually presented materials.

The team is moving forward to discuss a short-term placement for Alvin in a special education program at his school where he can receive resource services and remain in his regular classroom. The special education teacher will come to his classroom to work with Alvin and two other students. The team felt very strongly that it would not be to Alvin's advantage to make any major moves for him at this time. He needs to remain in as stable a situation as possible at school.

The school social worker is responsible for sharing this information with Alvin's mother and will seek her agreement that the school's efforts can be shared with the community team working with the family. Alvin's mother also will be

encouraged to take him for a thorough medical assessment
through the area public health clinic.

Classroom Environment

All children require consistency and predictability in the school environment. However, students who come to school from dysfunctional
and inconsistent home environments require that schools systemati-
cally organize classrooms and procedures and routines that 1) minimize disturbances and interruptions during the school day, 2) support consistency of responses by staff to children, 3) implement
procedures that support orderly transitions within the classroom and
between the classroom and other parts of the building, and 4) offer
emotional and physical support to children who are stressed either
by activities at home and school or by difficulties inherent in trying
to cope with the requirements of two different environments (Delapena, 1991; Poulsen, 1991). Classroom organization and structure
begin with school-level organization and structure under the direction of the principal.

Students have a higher likelihood of being able to function successfully in the classroom if schools are able to establish clear expectations for student behavior with consistent support, maintain established routines and schedules, and avoid interruption and changes
to daily activities to the maximum extent possible. Consistency and
predictability within the classroom is critical for students at all levels
whether or not the student is dealing with substance abuse or other
problematic family issues, or is from a family without these problems. The class schedule presents both a potential resource and
teaching tool to help students understand how the school day is organized, their responsibilities within this environment, and strategies
to help them adapt to changing tasks and activities.

As students grow older there is typically less control by the
teacher to provide consistent and predictable classroom environment. This is an issue that must be addressed at the administrative
level for the entire school. Interruptions by intercom systems during
class discussions, fire drills, changes in schedules by support staff,
and conflicts for planned class activities all present potentially crucial
barriers for children to function successfully. For example, intercom
systems have the potential to be the bane of teachers' and students'
existence and instead become a convenience for administrators to
the detriment of the classroom environment. The following considerations should be addressed in order to meet the needs of students

requiring consistent, predictable, and structured classroom environments:

- Consistent schedules for announcements and set times for interruptions should be established.
- Volume of the intercom system should be reviewed carefully and adjusted to the minimal level necessary for teachers and students to hear the information being provided.
- Emergency messages (e.g., "Your mother will pick you up after school") for a child should be delayed until the predetermined time for interruptions, or an office staff person should be sent to the classroom to provide this to the teacher to be relayed appropriately to the child.
- Routines and rituals are particularly important at critical points of the day especially at the beginning and end of each day, when the student may be at high risk for failure.
- Fire and emergency drills announced in advance relieve students who may be anxious about the school day. Consistent practice in drills until they are learned and demonstrated by the students also relieves anxiety. Alternative evacuation procedures to assist children in moving from the classroom may be necessary.

   A strategy that can be used to move children in an orderly and fairly rapid manner from one area of the building to another is the "lifeline." The lifeline is a coiled rope that is stored near the entrance/exit of the classroom. Teacher and students practice uncoiling this rope and grabbing the rope to move from the room. All of the students maintain their hold on the rope until they are safely moved to designated areas.
- Careful planning and confirmation with all necessary individuals in advance of planned activities, with alternative plans also in place, is important. For example, if Plan A for the field trip doesn't work, what is Plan B and is a Plan C necessary?
- Alternative arrangements must be planned for potential absence of support or resource personnel. For example, what are the provisions if the librarian or speech-language therapists are ill? Who maintains these services?
- A commitment must be made by school administrative and leadership staff that school-wide procedures and schedules are absolutely sacred and will not be changed without adequate notice to the maximum extent possible. When changes are necessary, students should be given a full explanation of why and what will be provided in place of the planned activity.

Curriculum

Both formal and informal assessments of students, including sensitive and systematic teacher observations, are powerful tools to support appropriate curriculum development and implementation. Repetitive learning is necessary for students whose learning processes may be affected by prenatal exposure or environment issues to which the student is being forced to respond both within and outside of the school. For example, a student previously may have been taught a concept or skills and because of various factors this learning may not be consistent, or previously learned information may not be available to the student when asked to demonstrate concepts that were evidenced earlier (Craig, 1992).

Curriculum is a body of knowledge organized according to presumed developmental levels of the students that schools are responsible for teaching. Curriculum is the concepts, values, and facts that a district or state have identified as being necessary for students to function independently in their immediate environments and in the adult world as participating and contributing citizens. Curriculum is a major concern for students who have been exposed to substance abuse. The school's primary mission continues to be one of preparing students to be participating and contributing citizens of their community. However, for students who are affected by substance abuse in their homes, an additional goal is required—namely, to interfere with a potential vulnerability to drugs and alcohol abuse by the student.

Curriculum development and structure can address the learning needs of children affected by substance abuse. Some of these learning needs may be outside the traditional responsibilities of the local education system. For example, teaching a child alternatives that may be used in responding to an alcoholic parent have typically not been the responsibility of classroom teachers nor school staff but is essential in order for the child to survive in the immediate environment and have the necessary emotional responses to respond to the challenges of the school environment. Curriculum for students who have been prenatally exposed to drugs and alcohol that resulted in cognitive dysfunctions will have to be carefully structured to address long-term functional life skills including vocational preparation, adaptive behaviors, decision making, and social relationships (Streissguth, Clarren, & Jones, 1985).

Students diagnosed with FAS or fetal alcohol effects (FAE) present unique issues for education because of limitations in the learning processes and lower cognitive functioning levels (Brown et al., 1991; Burgess & Streissguth, 1992; Clarren, 1986; Coles et al., 1991;

Conry, 1990; Sampson, Streissguth, Barr, & Bookstein, 1989). Life-long supportive services may be required and should be addressed early within the educational planning process for the individual student (Dorris, 1989; Streissguth et al., 1991). Special curricula and individualized instructional strategies may be required to meet the needs of these students. Instruction may have to provide for repetition of teaching, systematic application of learned skills in a variety of settings, and continued assessments of student progress to support modification of strategies and content (Kleinfeld, 1991). These students will require a curriculum with major emphasis on adaptive behaviors and survival skills beyond those typically included for students with cognitive limitations resulting from other etiologies.

Teaching Transference Skills Teaching students prenatally exposed to drugs and alcohol to apply learned strategies in more than one setting independently is a major challenge because of the specific neurological damage caused by ethanol exposure. It often is difficult for students to learn how to transfer concepts from school to the home and community. This is a curriculum and classroom management concern. Educational programs need to focus on real life experiences (Malbin & Rathbun, 1991) and provide extensive experiences in various settings for students to apply learned skills. This requires that schools teach specific survival and vocational skills in the community and in home-based settings.

Instructional Activities

Students who may be coming to school from stressful environments may demonstrate difficulties in making transitions from one instructional activity to another and possibly from one area of the classroom or school to another.

School-age children who have difficulties making transitions within the classroom and from the classroom to other areas of the school may have had difficulties moving from one activity to another or from one setting to another in preschool experiences. Although the dynamics influencing this difficulty are not confirmed, there is the assumption that children may be responding to psychoneurological issues as well as fear about what may be encountered in the new setting; that is, the fear of the unknown is greater than the current activity or setting.

The ability of the child to focus and attend to tasks without being distracted by environmental stimuli is an issue that arises for students demonstrating an inability to complete tasks and an inability to remain focused on a given task. It is the responsibility of the teacher to manipulate the classroom environment and learning activities for the student. Potential neurological damage and high levels of stress affect the child's ability to function within a traditional classroom emphasizing color, action, creativity, and other resources that may help a room to appear attractive and fun but that spell disaster for some students.

Task analysis of the learning task and control of environmental stimulus must be addressed for students affected by prenatal exposure to drugs and alcohol and environmental factors affecting learning and behavior (Villarreal, McKinney, & Quackenbush, 1992). How a teacher organizes a task for the student can be a major determinant of success or a major stumbling block setting the student and teacher up for failure. Any task that is assigned to the student should be structured clearly with a clear beginning and ending to respond to the student's learning style and attention span. Helping the student organize the work area using masking tape or colored paper to define spaces for pencils and paper is often helpful.

When a teacher notes that a student is unable to complete a task or begin work within an anticipated time frame it may very well be that the child does not understand what it is that is being asked of him or her. Asking the student the following questions can clarify very quickly and easily if this is an issue:

1. What is your task; what are you supposed to do?
2. When will you know it is completed?
3. How will you know it is correct?

Strategies appropriate for students with attention-deficit/hyperactivity disorders, learning disabilities, and behavioral and emotional impairments will be successful in working with students affected by substance abuse who also may evidence short attention spans, organizational dysfunctions, self-regulation difficulties, and social-emotional relationship problems due to neurological and/or environmental issues arising from maladaptive home environments (Gold & Sherry, 1984; Vincent, Poulsen, Cole, Woodruff, & Griffith, 1991).

Socialization

Socialization skills are important for everyone to be successful in their daily lives. Our concept of ourselves as important and worthwhile individuals is reflected in how others respond to us. The student's ability to respond appropriately and successfully to others results from learned experiences throughout the child's day. Some of these skills are learned incidentally, others are learned through structured experiences. For example, appropriate table manners are learned through observing other people and being taught what is deemed to be acceptable and what is not acceptable. Knowing when and how to remove oneself from a potentially conflicting situation is sometimes learned incidentally by experience and observation. For other children, these and other basic socialization and adaptive skills must be taught as an integral part of the school's instructional day.

For students whose environment is not supportive of incidental learning or who have learned inappropriate coping strategies, the school will have to respond with appropriate learning experiences, careful monitoring of behavior, and interventions that do not negatively affect the child's perception of him- or herself as a valued and worthwhile individual who is capable of managing environmental demands successfully.

Schools should help students learn a variety of coping strategies appropriate to the developmental needs of the child that can be applied in home and school settings. The student may be required to utilize two or more different decision-making criteria in order to identify which strategy is appropriate; for example, the behavior strategy learned at school may be a disaster and potentially dangerous to the student in the home. This is particularly critical for young children. Teachers must be sensitive to the survival demands of the child in a dysfunctional family and recognize that the child may be developmentally unable to use dual systems of response and coping. The priority in these situations is to focus on basic survival strategies—both physical and emotional. Children should be helped to be aware that they cannot affect family behavior and must instead focus on their own needs.

Teacher–Student Relationships   The relationship that a teacher establishes with the vulnerable student will support the student's more adequate sense of self and ability to build affective and social skills important for relationships with peers and adults. Teachers help the student learn that adults will be responsive to students' needs, helping to build the student's sense of security and ability to function. These are skills that are typically learned by children at a very early age. However, for vulnerable children the classroom must be structured to provide those things typically provided by a family and home not affected by substance abuse.

Spending time alone with the vulnerable student, and talking at eye level and with a sound level so that no one else can understand what is being said, will help the youngster to understand that he or she is special and deserving of the care and attention of an important adult. One of the major needs of children and youth from dysfunctional families is a lack of relationships with appropriate and adequate adults. A very brief 1-to 2-minute period spent daily with the student may very well make a major difference in the student's ability to function in the school environment and later serve as a resource to deal with adult issues.

Teachers must demonstrate a respect for the student's space and work areas on the same basis that the teacher expects for his or her desk or other personal areas in the classroom. Just as the teacher would expect the student to stay out of the teacher's desk, a teacher should intrude on the student only after asking the student's approval. For example, the teacher would ask, "John, may I see your work?" or, "John, may I help you with that problem?" This may appear demeaning to the teacher's presumed authority to see or do anything he or she pleases; however, this attitude and approach is another way of sending the message to the student that he or she is deserving of respect, has control of the immediate environment, and, through the teacher's modeling appropriate behavior, learns an important skill in how to respond to others successfully, all of which may be absent in the child's home setting.

Responding to Students   Class rules provide an opportunity for the student to observe predictability and consistency of the teacher's response to behavior, which may be lacking in the home or family. An expectation that teachers will respond to a student's request for assistance in a timely and appropriate manner is reasonable. Students should be ensured that when they use appropriate means to signal a need for assistance, the teacher or assistant will respond promptly and appropriately. This is accomplished by the teacher immediately moving to the student or assuring the student that his or her appropriate sign is recognized. This is also an important tool in helping the student to be aware of his or her worth and importance. For example, a teacher saying, "Amy, I see your hand. I will be with you in 45 seconds," begins to teach concepts of time that the child may not have incorporated because of home environments. Initially, some students can delay an anticipated response from the teacher for 30 seconds or less. When the desired response is not forthcoming, other strategies that usually are not appropriate will be used—which will get the response of the teacher.

Changing Student Behavior   Sometimes a student's behavior is so intrusive that a decision must be made to address the need for changing or eliminating the behavior. Asking a student to change his or her behavior is at least as challenging as asking an adult to lose weight or stop smoking. It may not be easy for the child nor the adults supporting this change to identify ready signs of progress toward the desired goal nor to put in place contingencies for managing the behavior.

Targeting the behavior to be addressed is the first step, followed by documentation of the situations in which the behavior is demonstrated and when it is not demonstrated; identifying stressors that may trigger the behavior and rewards or consequences appropriate to the child will require very careful planning.

Students coming to schools from inconsistent home environments will present particular issues for behavior management strategies. Consistency of teacher and staff response will be the major factor in determining if the student will be successful in making desired changes in how he or she responds to factors within the classroom environment.

Adaptive Skills Schools expect that their students will come to school capable of taking care of their personal needs including toileting, feeding, self-entertaining, and carrying out appropriate social-emotional relationships, which are a result of parental teaching, developmental processes, and incidental learning. Students who come to school with inadequate parenting may require daily life skills training as a part of the individual student's daily curriculum. Such areas as care of clothing, simple food preparation, leisure time activities, and personal care (e.g., tooth brushing, washing, hair combing) are not typically included in the curriculum of general education classrooms. These needs should be assessed and appropriate supportive instruction provided if necessary.

Communication Skills Children and youth may require support in developing vocabulary that they can use to communicate their own needs and feelings so that others understand the issues they are addressing. An expanded and accurate vocabulary provides tools in developing appropriate and supportive relationships with others, both peers and adults. Giving students information and vocabulary about drug and alcohol abuse provides a way for students to talk about concerns and issues. Helping students understand they are not responsible for the family's drug and alcohol abuses, that they cannot control how the family functions, and that they are not the only child with families in distress can be very supportive of children's development. A number of resource materials have been developed dealing with children from families of substance abuse that provide support in this area.

Most students come to school having learned already that certain behaviors will have an effect on their environment; sometimes this may be positive, sometimes not. However, children whose learning has been restricted because of parenting or other environmental issues or who have learned that their behaviors do not have a consistent response may require support in the school for cause–effect concepts and skills.

Helping students learn that their actions will have an effect on others—peers and adults—is a developmental task that should be addressed within the instructional program. Role playing is extremely valuable for students. It gives them an opportunity to practice a variety of responses that may occur at school and home. Practice with appropriate responses is an important component.

SUMMARY

Students of school age who have been prenatally exposed to drugs or who are growing up in a home in which substances are abused will present many different educational needs. Issues affecting school organization, allocation of resources, curriculum development, and teaching strategies may result from clinical and environmental factors.

The school has a responsibility to meet the educational needs of all of its students. In order to meet this mission for students successfully, the school needs a comprehensive perspective of the needs of the student and the family. In all likelihood, these will exceed the resources available in most school districts.

REFERENCES

Ackerman, R.J. (1983). *Children of alcoholics: A guide for parents, educators and therapists.* New York: Simon & Schuster.

Anderson, G.L. (1988). *The student assistance program model.* Greenfield, WI: Community Recovery Press.

Aylward, G.P. (1992). The relationship between environmental risk and developmental outcome. *Developmental Behavioral Pediatrics, 13*(3), 222–229.

Bays, J. (1990). Substance abuse and student abuse: Impact of addiction on the student. *Pediatric Clinics of North America, 37*(4), 881–904.

Besharov, D.J. (1990, July/August). Crack children in foster care. *Children Today,* pp. 21–25, 35.

Bowlby, J. (1988). *A secure base: Parent–child attachment and healthy human development.* New York: Basic Books.

Brown, R.T., Coles, C.D., Smith, I.E., Platzman, K.A., Silverstein, J., Erickson, S., & Falek, A. (1991). Effects of prenatal alcohol exposure at school age. II. Attention and behavior. *Neurotoxicology and Teratology, 13,* 369–376.

Burgess, D.M., & Streissguth, A.P. (1992). Fetal alcohol syndrome and fetal alcohol effects: Principles for educators. *Phi Delta Kappan, 74*(1), 24–28.

Caldwell, M.B., & Rogers, M.F. (1991). Epidemiology of pediatric HIV infection. *Pediatric Clinics of North America, 38,* 1–17.

Carpenter, M.R. (1990). *Making the right moves in student assistance programs.* Atlanta: Georgia Department of Human Resources and Georgia Department of Education.

Chanock, S. (1992). Transmission of HIV infection: Implications for policy.

In A.C. Crocker, H.J. Cohen, & T.A. Kastner (Eds.), *HIV infection and developmental disabilities: A resource for service providers* (pp. 215–222). Baltimore: Paul H. Brookes Publishing Co.

Chasnoff, I.J., Griffith, D.R., Frier, C., & Murray, J. (1992). Cocaine/polydrug use in pregnancy: Two-year follow-up. *Pediatrics, 89*(2), 284–289.

Clarren, S.K. (1986). Neuropathology in fetal alcohol syndrome. In J.R. West (Ed.), *Alcohol and brain development* (pp. 158–166). New York: Oxford University.

Coles, C.D., Brown, R.T., Smith, I.E., Platzman, K.A., Erickson, S., & Falek, A. (1991). Effects of prenatal alcohol exposure at school age. I. Physical and cognitive development. *Neurotoxicology and Teratology, 13*, 357–367.

Conry, J. (1990). Neuropsychological deficits in fetal alcohol syndrome and fetal alcohol effects. *Alcohol Clinical Experimental Research, 14*(5), 650–655.

Craig, S.E. (1992). The educational needs of children living with violence. *Phi Delta Kappan, 74*(1), 67–71.

Crocker, A.C., Cohen, H.J., & Kastner, T.A. (Eds.). (1992). *HIV infection and developmental disabilities: A resource for service providers.* Baltimore: Paul H. Brookes Publishing Co.

Delapena, L. (1991). *Strategies for teaching young children prenatally exposed to drugs.* Chicago, IL: National Association for Perinatal, Addiction, Research and Education UPDATE.

Dorris, M. (1989). *The broken cord.* New York: Harper Perennial.

Emshoff, J.G. (1990). *A preventative intervention with students of alcoholics in protecting the student.* New York: Hawthorn Press.

Garbarino, J., Dubrow, N., Kostelny, K., & Pardo, C. (1992). *Students in danger: Coping with the consequences of community violence.* San Francisco: Jossey-Bass.

Garbarino, J., & Gilliam, G. (1980). *Understanding abusive families.* Lexington, MA: Lexington Books.

Garbarino, J., Kostelny, K., & Dubrow, N. (1991). What students can tell us about living in danger. *American Psychologist, 46*(4), 376–383.

Garmezy, N., & Rutter, M. (Eds.). (1980). *Stress, coping, and development in children.* Baltimore: Johns Hopkins University Press.

Gold, S., & Sherry, L. (1984). Hyperactivity, learning disabilities and alcohol. *Journal of Learning Disabilities, 17*(1), 3–6.

Griffith, D.R. (1991). *Intervention needs of children prenatally exposed to drugs.* Congressional testimony before the House Select Committee on Special Education.

Griffith, D.R. (1992). Prenatal exposure to cocaine and other drugs: Developmental and educational prognoses. *Phi Delta Kappan, 74*(1), 30–34.

Jones, D.C., & Houts, R. (1992). Parental drinking, parent–student communication, and social skills in young adults. *Journal of Studies on Alcohol, 53*(1), 438–456.

Jones, E.D., & McCurdy, K. (1992). The links between types of maltreatment and demographic characteristics of children. *Child Abuse and Negligence, 16*, 201–215.

Jones, R., McCullough, C., & Dewoody, M. (1992, Winter). Responding to obscure needs. *School Safety*, pp. 20–24.

Kanel, D.B., Yamaguchi, K., & Chen, K. (1992). Stages of progression in drug involvement from adolescence to adulthood: Further evidence for the gateway theory. *Journal of Studies on Alcohol, 53*(5), 447–457.

Karen, R. (1990, February). Becoming attached. *Atlantic Monthly*, pp. 35–50, 63–70.

Kashani, J.H., Anasseril, E.D., Alison, C.D., & Holcomb, W.R. (1992). Family violence: Impact on children. *Journal of the American Academy of Child and Adolescent Psychiatry, 62*(1), 22–34.

Kleinfeld, J. (1991). *Fetal alcohol syndrome in Alaska: What the schools can do.* Unpublished manuscript, Alaska Department of Education, Northern Studies Program, University of Alaska, Fairbanks.

Kumpfer, K.L. (1989, October 13). *Children, adolescents, and substance abuse: Review of prevention strategies.* Paper presented at the meeting of the American Academy of Child and Adolescent Psychiatry Institute on Substance Abuse, New York.

Levoy, D., Rivinus, T.M., Matzko, M., & McGuire, J. (1991). Children in search of a diagnosis: Chronic trauma disorder of childhood. In T.M. Rivinus (Ed.), *Children of chemically dependent parents* (pp. 153–170). New York: Brunner-Mazel.

Levy, H.B., Harper, C.R., & Winberg, W.A. (1992). A practical approach to children failing in school in pediatric neurology. *Pediatric Clinics of North America, 39*(4), 895–928.

Malbin, D.B., & Rathbun, A. (1991, December). *Preliminary findings: Perceptual shifts and proactive strategies in families with FAS/FAE.* Presented at the National Association for Perinatal Addiction Research and Education National Training Forum, Chicago, IL.

Morehouse, E.R. (1989). *It's elementary: Meeting the needs of high-risk youth in the school setting.* South Laguna, CA: National Association for Children of Alcoholics.

Murphy, J.P. (1984, May). Substance abuse and the family. *Journal for Specialists in Group Work*, pp. 106–112.

Poulsen, M.K. (1991). *Schools meet the challenge: Educational needs of children at risk due to prenatal substance exposure.* Sacramento, CA: Resources in Special Education.

Putnam, F.W. (1993). Disassociative disorders in children: Behavioral profiles and problems. *Child Abuse and Neglect, 17*, 39–45.

Robinson, B.E. (1990, May). The teacher's role in working with children of alcoholic parents. *Young Children*, pp. 68–73.

Rosen, S., & Granger, M. (1992). Early intervention and school programs. In A.C. Crocker, H.J. Cohen, & T.A. Kastner (Eds.), *HIV infection and developmental disabilities: A resource for service providers* (pp. 75–84). Baltimore: Paul H. Brookes Publishing Co.

Sampson, P.D., Streissguth, A.P., Burr, H.M., & Bookstein, F.L. (1989). Neurobehavioral effects of prenatal alcohol: Part II. Partial least squares analysis. *Neurotoxicology and Teratology, 11*, 477–491.

Schellenbach, C.J., & Guerney, L.F. (1987). Identification of adolescent abuse and future intervention prospects. *Journal of Adolescents, 10*, 1–12.

Schutter, L.S., & Brinker, R.P. (1992). Conjuring a new category of disability from prenatal cocaine exposure: Are the infants unique biological or caretaking casualties? *TECSE, 11*(4), 84–111.

Seidel, J.F. (1992). Children with HIV-related developmental disabilities. *Phi Delta Kappan, 74*(1), 38–42, 56.

Siegel, L. (1988). *AIDS and substance abuse.* New York: Harrington Park Press.

Simonds, R.J., & Rogers, M.F. (1992). Epidemiology of HIV infection in children and other populations. In A.C. Crocker, H.J. Cohen, & T.A. Kastner (Eds.), *HIV infection and developmental disabilities: A resource for service providers* (pp. 3–14). Baltimore: Paul H. Brookes Publishing Co.

Streissguth, A.P., Aase, J.M., Clarren, S.K., Randels, S.P., LaDue, R.A., & Smith, D.F. (1991). Fetal alcohol syndrome in adolescents and adults. *Journal of the American Medical Association, 265*(15), 1961–1967.

Streissguth, A.P., Clarren, S.K., & Jones, K.L. (1985). Natural history of the fetal alcohol syndrome: A 10-year follow-up of eleven patients. *Lancet,* 85–90.

Terr, L. (1990). *Too scared to cry: How trauma affects students . . . and ultimately us all.* New York: Basic Books.

Terr, L.C. (1991). Childhood traumas: An outline and overview. *American Journal of Psychiatry 148*(1), 10–20.

van der Kolk, B. (Ed.). (1987). *Psychological trauma.* Washington, DC: American Psychiatric Press.

Villarreal, S.F., McKinney, L.E., & Quackenbush, M. (1992). *Handle with care: Helping children prenatally exposed to drugs and alcohol.* Santa Cruz, CA: ETR Associates.

Vincent, L.J., Poulsen, M.K., Cole, C.K., Woodruff, G., & Griffith, D.R. (1991). *Born substance exposed, educationally vulnerable.* Reston, VA: Council for Exceptional Children.

III

DEVELOPING COMMUNITY-BASED MODELS OF SERVICE

III

7

Children at Risk in Out-of-Home Placement

Marie Kanne Poulsen

The escalation of drug and alcohol abuse, in combination with the increased homelessness, poverty, and domestic violence of the 1980s and 1990s, has given rise to increased numbers of children whose well-being has been determined to be endangered to the extent that removal from their families is deemed necessary. Drug and alcohol abuse are among the most commonly named factors contributing to the increase in child maltreatment (Herskowitz, Seck, & Fogg, 1989). Approximately 50% of the states in America report that substance abuse is the dominant characteristic in child protective services caseloads (Gall, 1990). It has been reported that up to 80% of the children in out-of-home care are there for drug-related reasons (Digre, 1992). Included are the newborns of thousands of women who have lost custody because positive toxicology screenings for illegal drugs are viewed, in many communities, as predictors of future abuse and neglect.

Child protective services (CPS) is the component of the child welfare system that is legally mandated to protect children from the abuse and neglect that may jeopardize their well-being. When a report of suspected abuse or neglect is made, CPS is required to investigate. PL 96-272, the Adoption Assistance and Child Welfare Act of 1980, provides the legal framework for a comprehensive response to children at risk and their families. State child welfare agencies must make "reasonable efforts" to preserve the family unit through the provision of support services in the community. However, the overwhelming number of child abuse and neglect reports combined with the lack of available community support services has resulted in yearly increases in the numbers of children requiring out-of-home placement. The average number of children in foster care increased 53% in 5 years from 280,000 children in 1986 to 429,000 children in 1991 (General Accounting Office, 1994).

IMPACT OF PRENATAL SUBSTANCE ABUSE

The exact number of children in out-of-home placement who have been prenatally exposed to drugs and alcohol is unknown. Many infants who are in foster care were not tested at time of birth. However, the significant increase in out-of-home placements is generally attributed to the increased use of illegal substances during pregnancy and the lack of publicly funded drug recovery programs and other community support services that would preserve the family unit (Klerman, 1991). Since the mid-1980s, most of the increase in foster care placements has been experienced in communities hardest hit by crack cocaine (Besharov, 1990b). In 1991, 55% of the very young children (birth to 3 years) placed in foster care were estimated to have been prenatally exposed to cocaine or cocaine derivatives. An additional 11% were estimated to have been prenatally exposed to alcohol and other drugs (General Accounting Office, 1994).

In some communities, referrals to child protective services have contributed to a 3,000% increase in the number of drug dependency-related petitions filed in a 5-year span (National Court Appointed Special Advocates [CASA] Association, 1989). During that time, public hospitals were noting increased numbers of infants born to mothers addicted to drugs, and several community hospitals began developing protocols to test newborns suspected of prenatal drug exposure. Those tested were infants born to mothers with a history or indications of drug abuse, or infants of mothers who had a precipitous delivery or no prenatal care. Some hospitals have a policy to report all children with a positive toxicological screening to child protective services, which has inundated the foster care system in many urban areas. However, reporting as *required by law* varies among the states (English, 1990).

Not all states include infants prenatally exposed in their child abuse—reporting statutes. Those states with existing statutes either directly require professionals to report infants who have been prenatally exposed to drugs to child welfare or include drug exposure in their child abuse and neglect definitions. Florida, Massachusetts,

Oklahoma, and Utah mandate that drug dependence or physical addiction are reasons to report newborns to child protective services. Minnesota's law requires hospitals to administer toxicology screens to all pregnant women suspected of taking drugs or infants suspected of being exposed, and to report positive screens to protective services. Illinois mandates reporting newborns whose blood or urine contains any amount of a controlled substance or metabolite thereof, except when a positive screen is a result of medical treatment. In contrast, California's and Iowa's laws state that a positive toxicological screening alone is not sufficient basis for reporting a child to protective services. This is based on the belief that a positive toxicology test alone is not presumptive of future abuse or neglect and should not be the sole basis for dependency jurisdiction. Parental adequacy and the effect of their behavior on child health and safety must be considered. There also must be a reasonable suspicion that the infant is at risk for future abuse and neglect. California's hospitals have been given the added responsibility of determining family risk, although no state standards have been established to accomplish this.

Federal law dictates that unnecessary separation of parent and child must be avoided. However, allowing a mother who abuses drugs to leave the hospital with her infant remains controversial. Many hospitals feel ill-equipped to make the determination of family risk. In spite of the 1991 California state law, the numbers of infants with positive toxicology screens who were reported to Los Angeles County child protective services increased in 1992.

OUT-OF-HOME PLACEMENT

It has been estimated that 30%–50% of infants identified at birth as prenatally exposed to drugs go into the foster care system (Office of the Inspector General, 1990). Placement options within the foster care system include kinship care, foster family care, and congregate care.

Kinship Care

For generations, extended families have formed informal helping networks in raising the children if birth parents are unable or unwilling to take responsibility. Currently 1.3 million children live with relatives in the United States (National Council of Juvenile and Family Court Judges, 1991)—grandparents make up two thirds of those relatives. These families do not come to the attention of child protective services. However, there is another group of children being raised by relatives because they were reported to child protective services for abuse or neglect.

If services to children within their birth families are not adequate enough to avoid separation of parent(s) and child, services out of their home but within their own extended families is considered to be the most desirable option (Child Welfare League of America, 1992). In some jurisdictions, it is mandated as the placement of choice. Children benefit when kinship, cultural, and community ties are maintained. By placing children with family members, the trauma of separation is lessened (although never removed). Currently, there are no specific national policies regarding the care of children in kinship placements.

Kinship care involves the legal and informal placement of the child with relatives or other members of the kinship network, including godparents. Many children are placed with kin to avoid Dependency Court action. Over 100,000 children are currently living with relatives or members of the kinship network (Curtis, 1992). Approximately 50% of infants who are identified as prenatally exposed at birth are currently placed with relatives (Office of the Inspector General, 1990). Children placed in kinship care have more stable placements. They tend to stay in one place longer than those in placement with nonrelatives (Child Welfare League of America, 1992). Critics of kinship care for children born to parents addicted to drugs or alcohol address the intergenerational nature of substance abuse and stress the need for a thorough evaluation and monitoring of relative placement. Critics also fear that relatives will return children to parents without informing child protective services (Besharov, 1990a).

Communities differ on the extent to which the kinship placement is evaluated and monitored. Extended family members still may be rearing their own children and experiencing limited finances and resources. The addition of more children in the household may prove overwhelming and not in the children's best interests. Many times children are placed with relatives with no assessment of the receiving family's ability to meet the child's emotional and social special needs that arise from the experiences of separation and loss. All placement options should be evaluated in terms of available resources, the presence of familial conflicts, and the need for financial assistance.

Reimbursement for kinship care placement, however, remains controversial. Not all relatives are being supported currently, and the amount of reimbursement may vary. Some relatives become state-approved licensed family foster care providers and receive foster care reimbursements; others receive Aid to Families with Dependent Children (AFDC), but this may apply only to "blood relatives," leaving godparents and other members of the kinship network unsupported. Illinois and New York pay nonfederally eligible kinship care providers; California does not (Children's Research Institute of California, 1992). The Ninth United States Circuit Court of Appeals recently upheld an Oregon law denying state benefits to relatives providing foster care. Nationally, most relatives receive no reimbursement (Hailey, 1990).

If a lack of financial support means a burden to the relatives and added stress to that family unit, the best interests of the children involved cannot be served.

The group in greatest need for respite, child care, and financial support services are the grandparents who are assuming the full responsibility for raising another generation of children. In some neighborhoods affected by substance abuse, up to 70% of day care and after day care children are being reared by grandparents (Gross, 1989).

The Department of Children's Services in Los Angeles County (1988) has identified important characteristics of family functioning and resources that must be evaluated before children are placed in the care of relatives. Assessment of characteristics include the following:

- Drug and alcohol abuse
- Physical, intellectual, and emotional status
- Willingness to work with child protective services
- Willingness to provide for child's special medical and physical needs
- Parenting skills
- Responsiveness to the emotional needs of the child
- Capacity to protect the child from violence
- Ability to provide a clean, safe, and healthy environment

Kinship care is a realistic option only if the child's needs will be met.

Family Foster Care

The crisis in foster care stems not only from the increase in children being removed from parental custody, but also because of the decrease in the numbers of relatives and foster parents available. There was a 30% decrease in the number of available family foster placements between 1984 and 1991 (Child Welfare League of America, 1991). There are several reasons for the shortage; they include the following:

1. Many women who would be foster mothers have joined the work force.
2. Payments to foster parents have not kept pace with inflation.
3. Reimbursement rates do not always cover the cost of care.
4. Children in placement are younger and require more care.
5. More children have special needs, and foster parents are feeling overwhelmed, untrained, and unsupported.
6. Services such as respite care, child care, and mental health programs are not available or accessible in many communities.

Several other factors contribute to the crisis, including over representation of minority children, an increase in the numbers of infants and young children, the incidence of multiple placements in the system, and the increase of children with special needs.

It has been determined that children of color are overrepresented in the child welfare system (U.S. Department of Health and Human Services, 1988). Minority children are more likely to be removed from families and tend to stay in foster care longer (McCullough, 1991). In California, the number of African American children in foster care is greater than the number of Caucasian children, even though less than 10% of the children in the state are African American (Besharov, 1990a). This reflects the lack of drug recovery, health, mental health, and social services within the minority communities that would serve to support the family and reduce the numbers of children removed from families. The Child Welfare League of America has challenged the child welfare system to respond to the bias inherent in reporting, investigating, and decision making when intervening with families of color (McCullough, 1991). In addition, there are not sufficient numbers of minority foster families to care for the children in out-of-home placements. This calls for proactive recruitment through minority churches, organizations, media, and creative arts.

Children of parents affected by substance abuse are entering the foster care system at younger ages than those previously in need of such care. The fastest growing population in the foster care system includes infants and young children (Wulczyn, 1991). Between 1986 and 1991, the need of out-of-home placement for very young children rose 110% (General Accounting Office, 1994). In some cities, almost 50% of children in out-of-home care are under age 5 (Herskowitz et al., 1989). These children tend to stay longer with more changes in placement within the system than the children who come from families not affected by substance abuse. In 1985, the national median for children remaining in foster care was 1.5 years. By 1990, children in foster care had been there for an average of 4.8 years (Office of the Inspector General, 1990). A study of New York City newborns discharged from the hospital to foster care found that 60% of the infants were still in out-of-home placement 3 years later (Besharov, 1990a).

Changes of placement within the system are so traumatizing to children that they should be avoided at all costs and considered to be system abuse when they occur. Re-placement always puts a child in crisis. Yet it is estimated that one third to one fourth of children in foster care have experienced re-placement (U.S. House of Representatives, 1989). One urban study tracked 97 infants over a 4-year period. During that time, 55 infants remained in foster care and some had been in as many as 15 different homes (Birth, 1990). Another study reported that 56% of infants who were exposed to drugs or alcohol and in out-of-home placements had been in two or more foster homes, 20% had been in three or more homes, and one child had been in eight placements (Besharov, 1990a).

A significant number of infants and young children entering the child welfare system have been identified to be at risk of physical, developmental, or emotional disorders as a result of medical conditions, environmental hazards, or biological vulnerabilities (Garfield, 1987). Included in this at-risk group are infants who carry the human immunodeficiency virus (HIV), have been prenatally exposed to drugs, were born with low birth weights, or were born to homeless women. A U.S. General Accounting Office study estimated that 62% of the very young children in foster care in 1991 were at risk for serious health problems (1994).

Some infants may have disabling conditions that qualify them and their foster families for early intervention services through PL 102-119, the Individuals with Disabilities Education Act Amendments of 1991, and for extra reimbursement in foster care payment. However, in most states the majority of infants at risk as a result of prenatal substance exposure will not qualify for early intervention services, but they may manifest neurodevelopmental immaturities that require sensitive parenting in order for them to thrive. Most foster parents are not trained and supported in their efforts to meet the emotional needs of a very vulnerable baby. Too often, qualified trained parents are given too many young children. The number should be restricted to two. Although parents may be able to offer a safe, stable home for more children, they will not be able to meet the special emotional needs of at-risk children. If more than two children under 5 years are part of a birth family needing placement, the children should be kept together. However, extra child care support should be offered to the foster family.

In many communities, the increased number of children and the decreased availability of foster families have resulted in the placement of children in the "first available spot." The provision of quality family foster care does not depend merely upon having sufficient numbers of family foster parents available. There must be an appropriate match between the receiving parent(s) and the child or children. Inappropriate matches result in the re-placement of children within the system.

A disproportionately high number of foster families are economically depressed. Financial stress affects the overall stability of the family and can lead to an overwhelming situation if an additional child requires financial or emotional resources beyond the foster family's capacity to cope. The child welfare system needs to provide enough financial, emotional, and service support to enable families to provide quality care for children until reunification with the birth family or relinquishment occurs. In addition, the system needs to find ways to encourage more middle class and upper-middle class families to provide foster care for America's children.

Congregate Care

Residential Treatment Homes   Residential treatment homes, with the 24-hour availability of medical and psychological professional care, have replaced larger state institutions in many parts of the United States. These community-based treatment models have been developed for children with mental, emotional, or physical disabilities that are considered severe enough to preclude them from being cared for in foster family homes.

Since the 1960s, there has been a trend toward the deinstitutionalization of all children, including those with special needs. Federal law mandates the least restrictive environment in the education of children with disabilities and disabling conditions. Child development specialists have emphasized the dangers that congregate care can present to the healthy development of individual children. In congregate care settings, a child's unique needs and strengths may be overlooked. Too often, compliance to group norms may be considered more important than the expression of individual needs (Provence, 1989). Because there is an overload of children in the system, congregate care is being used as an answer to the lack of foster families in the communities. However, even the most stringent critics of congregate care believe good residential care is preferable to multiple placements within the foster family system.

Emergency Shelters Emergency shelters that may serve from 6 to 50 infants and young children have proliferated. *Boarder babies* have become a phenomenon in many cities. Infants who are exposed to drugs account for a significant proportion of boarder babies who remain in the hospital. The increase in boarder babies parallels the rise of poverty among female-headed households and the lack of drug recovery services designed to meet the needs of mothers and newborns. The infants are often most fragile because the lack of adequate prenatal health care and nutrition adds to the effects of the prenatal exposure to drugs. These infants remain in the hospital or emergency shelter for extended periods of time beyond medical necessity because parents or relatives are unable to assume responsibility for their care and appropriate foster family settings are not available (Gittler & McPherson, 1990). This trend toward reinstitutionalization has raised great concern among child advocates.

Infants and toddlers in hospital-based or emergency shelter nurseries have ongoing contacts with the medical personnel and child development specialists. Licensing requirements focus on physical aspects of the environment and staff qualifications. However, currently there are no stated national standards of quality developmental care. Many hospital-based and emergency shelter nurseries do not assign a primary caregiver to the child. In the absence of a single consistent mothering figure and a stable family unit, these infants and young children are at risk for emotional harm. Emergency shelters, which were designed as temporary placements, too often become long term, resulting in another traumatizing loss for the child when another placement within the family foster care system is found.

Temporary infant and toddler shelter care programs have become a part of a comprehensive continuum of care. The Infant-Toddler Therapeutic Shelter Care Program at Children's Institute International in Los Angeles, California, has developed a model program to provide quality temporary child-centered care. Children's Institute International, through the model program, also provides the Los Angeles County Department of Children's Services (DCS) with the critical information needed to achieve one quality out-of-home placement experience for the child until reunification or a relinquishment decision is made. Children who are appropriate for temporary residential shelter placement include the following:

- Infants and young children for whom the Department of Children's Services does not have the sense of family history needed to make a placement decision
- Infants and young children who have experienced disruptive out-of-home placements
- Infants and young children who need multidisciplinary assessments and the development of a multi-agency integrated service coordination plan
- Infants and young children who need 24-hour nursing care
- Infants and young children within a family in which added time is needed to place them together in a foster family that is culturally and geographically responsive to the needs of the child and family
- Infants and young children targeted for immediate reunification with mother or father who is available for daily visits for which foster family care cannot accommodate
- Infants and young children who have experienced acute trauma and need one-to-one daily professional attention for stabilization

The quality of services at the Infant-Toddler Therapeutic Shelter Care Program is ensured by the following:

- The assignment of a primary caregiver to each child placed in residential shelter care
- The cultural background of the staff that represents the diversity of Los Angeles County
- The expertise of health, mental, child development, chemical dependency, foster care, and parent support service personnel, which can provide interdisciplinary child/family assessment and service, and assist DCS in the development and implementation of a comprehensive community-based family service plan
- The capability to keep siblings together until a single placement is found
- The capability of allowing daily supervised visits by parents
- The capability to assess parents and observe parent–child interaction, and the parent's capacity to follow through on parental and personal responsibilities
- The capability to assess and provide the birth families, foster families, and kinship families the support services needed to ensure quality and stability of care
- The development of an emotional care plan for each child that may include support, counseling, or psychotherapeutic recommendations for children and families

• Sensitive short-term preplacement plans for each child in transition to a new placement

   Small Group Homes   Small group homes also multiplied in urban communities. Although a model of small clusters of children with stable primary caregivers appears to be a child-focused solution, in many cases, poor caregiver pay results in high caregiver turnover. This leaves the child with unfulfilling attachments to parent-figures and at risk for later social and emotional difficulties.

   In some communities, foster care providers are trained to serve infants and toddlers who are at risk or have complex health care needs. Licensing regulations and child welfare placement policy often are the reasons older toddlers are removed from foster care providers once they are medically stabilized, allowing the foster care providers to work with infants and toddlers with greater needs. From a medical standpoint, the continuous availability of trained "baby moms" makes sense. However, the psychological harm from the separation of the older toddler from his or her mothering figure outweighs the benefit of available specialized care. Again, disrupted placements within the system should be avoided at all costs. Children should never be moved in order to "free up a slot."

System Obstacles to Quality Care

Obstacles to care within the welfare system management include high caseloads, multiple placements, and the lack of continuity and quality of care.

   A significant obstacle to quality care for children in out-of-home placement is the high caseloads carried by child service workers. The average caseload in some urban communities range from 60 to 90 cases per child care worker (National CASA Association, 1989). National standards of care as set by the Child Welfare League of America calls for 12–17 cases (McCullough, 1991). A small caseload allows the case worker to give adequate attention to the assessment of the child, birth family, and foster family regarding needed supports, and to the development of plans to promote quality care and family reunification. Small caseloads provide the time needed to monitor progress and modify the case management plan.

   Multiple placements with the accompanying inconsistency in the provision of nurturing care is felt by many to place a child at equal or greater risk than does prenatal substance exposure. The California Perinatal Substance Abuse Think Tank sponsored by the Governor's Child Development Programs Advisory Committee (Poulsen,

1992) recommended the following strategies to reduce the damage caused by multiple placements:

- Training must be made available to providers to enable them to cope effectively with the emotional, behavioral, and social complications that go along with the care of a child who has been separated from his or her family.
- Children who are at risk or have special needs and foster families should receive enough community support to maintain a stable placement until family reunification or adoption.
- Licensing that restricts foster parents to specific age groups can be detrimental to the child if it means another move within the system for that child. Licensing policies should be modified to ensure children are not moved because of age.
- Respite care for foster parents helps maintain stable placements.
- Foster care reimbursement rates and policies should be modified to ensure continuity and stability of placements. Under the current rate structure, a child must "remain qualified" to stay in a specialized foster home. This may result in rate reductions to foster care providers of recovering, stronger children. To maintain the original reimbursement rate, which they may depend on for the household income, they must demonstrate a continuing disability for the child.

Continuity of health and education care can be a challenge for the child who experiences multiple placements. Consistent health care and education placement for the child who is moved within the system can add stability and security to a child's life. In addition, continuity of care gives a needed historical perspective in the development and modification of service coordination plans.

Often, a child's history is forgotten in the mire of child welfare bureaucracy. Countless children do not have records of their health, developmental, and educational history. Significant health information that may influence future medical follow-up may be lost. Many states have developed *medical, developmental, and educational passports* to ensure good recordkeeping and the continuity of care for children in foster placements. Passports may include names and addresses of the child's pediatrician, dentist, and school personnel; birth, health and developmental history; and records of immunizations, medications, medical and mental health problems, developmental assessments, early intervention services, grade-level performance, and special education services. Passports should be reviewed and updated on a regular basis and kept by the foster parents.

In addition to the passports, which provide service coordination records, every child in foster care should have an *individualized transition plan* that includes preparing the child for a new home, preplacement contacts between child and receiving parents whenever possible, the opportunity for the child to say good-bye, and the opportunity for the child to express feelings of separation and loss.

Transition plans should be developed for each child at all points of entry into the system, changes within the system, and departures from the system. The transition plan should include these guidelines:

- Provide the child with the knowledge of what is happening, what will happen, and what will not happen in order to assuage imagined fears.
- Address immediate family loss and fears and anxieties about impending strange situations.
- Provide the child with reassurance that someone will be there to care and nurture.
- Ensure that information about the child's individual needs, tastes, choices, and fears will be communicated to the receiving family.
- Ensure that household rules, constraints, and privileges will be discussed explicitly with all parties concerned.

For infants and young children, transition plans should include favorite foods and toys and a record of bathing, sleeping, eating, dressing, and holiday rituals that can provide some familiarity and security to the child even though the caregiver is new. Caregivers should be encouraged to keep photograph albums, scrapbooks, treasured books, and toys so children can maintain their reservoir of childhood memories.

SPECIAL NEEDS OF CHILDREN IN FOSTER CARE

The challenge for the child welfare system is to develop foster families in each community that can meet the special familial, social-emotional, cultural, and educational needs of children when their families and relatives are unable to care for them.

Familial Needs

Federal law and traditional American values support the notion that birth families are the placement of choice for all children. The "reasonable efforts" of PL 96-272, the Adoption Assistance and Child Welfare Act of 1980, that apply to the prevention of family disruption also are mandated for family reunification once the child is removed from parental custody.

Child protective services are required to support the reunification of families through the provision of services in the community that would contribute to the family's capacity to provide a safe, secure home for its offspring.

Of equal importance is the need to facilitate the development or maintenance of parent–child relationships when children are in out-of-home placement. Infants removed from parental custody at birth are particularly vulnerable. Mother and infant reunite as strangers if the "reasonable efforts" to prepare for family reunification are not implemented. Programs need to be designed to facilitate mother–infant bonding when separation occurs at birth. Frequent visitations, mother–infant activities, videotapes, photographs, scrapbooks, and parent groups provide a climate that encourages quality interactions between mother and infant. Transportation and child care for the children who remain in custody are needed instrumental supports.

Children who are experiencing separation of parents need a *family contact plan* that will ensure predictable meaningful contacts that will occur over time. Birth parents may need assistance to cover transportation costs.

Daily visits are recommended unless medically contraindicated (National Council of Juvenile and Family Court Judges, 1991). However, many foster families are intimidated by birth parents who are substance abusers. A neutral site and monitored visits may have to be provided by child welfare workers.

Foster parent familial training should include the following:

- An understanding of issues of women in recovery
- An understanding of the treatment and intervention needs of families in recovery
- Strategies for assisting in the maintenance of mother–child ties
- Methods of maintaining safety and resolving conflict when interacting with families with a substance abuse history (Poulsen, 1992)

Foster parents need to understand the importance of birth family relationships for the child. They may need information about how to encourage birth parent–child communication and maintain relationships by mail, audiotape, videotape, telephone calls, and photographs.

Foster parents need training on how to discuss the birth family situation in truthful but positive ways that allow the child to better understand and accept the birth family. Foster parents need support to resolve their own feelings of fear, anger, or disgust about the birth parents that may be communicated to their foster child inadvertently.

In addition, too many children are separated from their siblings when in out-of-home placements. Siblings should only be separated when it is in the best interests of the child. Otherwise, every effort must be made for placement of a family of children as a whole. When siblings cannot be placed in the same home, a formalized plan for sibling contact should be developed that provides for ongoing and frequent contacts among siblings.

Social-Emotional Needs

All infants and children removed from their families are at emotional risk. Separation is always a traumatic event for the child, even if the child is placed in a safer, more stable, nurturing environment. The most significant effect of a child being separated from his or her mother and father is the disruption that may occur in the attachment process.

Attachment provides the child with the emotional fuel he or she needs to explore, discover, and learn. However, in order for healthy attachment to take place, there must be consistent nurturing, responsive interaction over time between a particular caregiver and child. Tenderness, empathy, and caring can develop only if a child is raised with tenderness received over time from a meaningful person. Healthy attachment is the basis for a child's later self-identity, self-esteem, and meaningful personal relationships. When a crucial bond between a mothering figure and a child is severed, the loss to the child is profound. The child mourns the loss of that person.

Although 6 months to 4 years are considered the most vulnerable ages for mother–child separations, it has been reported that separations can affect infants as young as 3 months of age (Yarrow & Goodwin, 1965). Behavioral disturbances result from the loss of an attachment figure and a loss of the predictability of the rituals of daily living and the sensory stimulation of a familiar environment.

Separation difficulties are reflected in a range of child behaviors. Typically, younger children regress in their adaptive skills. They may become more likely to cling and demand adult attention with dressing, bathing, and other activities of daily living. Children experiencing unresolved feelings of separation and loss may mask depression through nonadaptive aggressive behaviors or seemingly noncaring, indifferent attitudes. Conversely, reaction to separation can manifest in a child's desperate need for approval at the expense of self.

Distress goes beyond immediate discomfort; it affects long-term social-emotional development. Because of the role that healthy attachment has in supporting a child's development, losing a mothering figure and/or experiencing multiple placements can undermine a child's development. The greatest psychiatric damage occurs to children who come from families characterized by poorly attached relationships and to children who experience more than one separation (Rutter, 1979b). When there are multiple placements, only transient attachments can develop. These disturbed attachments result in the child learning not to commit to the attachment process. The child stops behavior that promotes attachment and becomes more centered on the self and material objects, resulting in an inability to control one's own behavior and the danger of not developing a healthy conscience.

The most frequently cited health problems of children in foster care are emotional disorders (Child Welfare League of America, 1988). Disruptions in placement can contribute to nonadaptive coping strategies, communication delays, and a chronic lack of willingness to form new relationships. Children are most often removed from their families because of difficult conditions at home. This negative emotional history combined with the acute trauma of separation from family makes a child vulnerable for emotional disorders. Infants and children who experience unresolved traumatic loss in the absence of supportive caregivers develop a sense of hopelessness that may result in psychiatric depression.

A foster parent's response to the child will have a critical effect on the child's capacity to resolve the loss emotionally. The challenge for the foster parent is to become the psychological parent and the haven of stability and nourishing security for the child. The foster parent can help the child recover a sense of security through the reestablishment of a bond between the child and a parenting figure. The child will only be able to resolve the crisis of separation and loss if subsequent relationships and sensitivity respond to his or her acute emotional needs (Rutter, 1979a; Yarrow & Goodwin, 1965). When foster parents spend extra quality time attending to a child's emotional needs, the child is better able to resolve feelings of separation and loss.

National standards of out-of-home care developed by the Child Welfare League of America (1988) stress that

> Caretakers should be provided with guidance on the trauma inherent in separation from parents and family, and how to anticipate and address these responses appropriately. Individual differences in children's and parents' responses to loss and separation should be included. Care-

takers should have the opportunity to discuss their own emotional responses to being temporary caretakers, and to the anticipated reactions of parents when their child is placed in out-of-home care. Because children cared for will be at different stages in their response to the separation from and loss of their families, training should be tailored for shelter home parents, foster home parents, and so forth. (p. 34)

A comprehensive mental health evaluation and emotional care plan, whether preventive or restorative, should be part of every foster child's health assessment and service coordination plan. According to the Child Welfare League of America standards for children in out-of-home care (1988):

> Caseworkers should expect and understand how to address the emotional distress experienced by children in care. This distress may be a normal response to being separated from their families; to their present situation; to being out-of-control; to the trauma of abuse or neglect; or it may reflect an inability to establish a comfortable relationship in a placement setting; or may be a manifestation of longstanding emotional problems. Caseworkers should be able to appraise the emotional status of a child, and to obtain a standardized screening test for those children with emotional problems. They should be prepared to help the newly placed child deal with the trauma that provoked placement, and with the difficulty of adjusting to a foster care placement. They should use their skills in this area to help select placements that are most appropriate for the child. Finally, they should be prepared and encouraged to seek the assistance of other professionals to address recognized or suspected emotional problems. (p. 36)

Cultural Needs

A child's self-identity depends in part on a sense of belonging to a larger group with whom he or she identifies. When a child is placed in a home that offers familiar racial, cultural, religious, and linguistic experiences, the trauma of separation can be lessened.

The disproportionate number of minority children in out-of-home placement has resulted in a situation in which many children are being placed in homes that represent a different racial, cultural, religious, or linguistic heritage.

Extra consideration needs to be given to these children. They need to have food, music, and toys that reflect their birth family experiences. They need opportunities to learn about their heritage and to value their heroes. Pictures, films, television programs, books, and rituals and rites need to be shared and discussed. Opportunities for relationships with peers and adults of similar heritage should be provided. Churches, mosques, and temples in the community are excellent resources for providing youngsters with opportunities for contact with their own culture.

Racial and cultural similarities and differences should be addressed, discussed, and appreciated in a familial context.

Educational Needs

Children in foster care tend to be students who are at risk. If a child is experiencing effects from prenatal alcohol or other drug exposure, he or she is at double risk for school failure.

The vulnerability of children in foster care is evidenced by the following statistics (Children's Research Institute of California, 1991):

- Approximately 80% of children in foster care have been retained by third grade.
- Approximately 75% of children in foster care are underachievers, working below grade level.
- Almost twice as many suspensions and enrollments in alternative education programs are for children in foster care than for children in general.

Lack of educational continuity because of changes in placement significantly contributes to school failure. Barriers to immediate appropriate enrollment in an educational setting include the lack of immunization records and a lack or loss of academic records. The lack of academic records can lead to inappropriate classroom assignment, a loss of high school credits, or a need for extensive educational assessments.

Changes in school placements often leave the foster children with feelings of isolation, alienation, fear, loneliness, and confusion. These children are not only educationally deprived but are also psychologically and emotionally deprived.

All schools should have a Foster Care Student Committee that follows these guidelines:

1. Develop a process to track records.
2. Assess academic needs and resources to identify and remediate learning gaps.
3. Support the child in dealing with experiences of a new placement, new school, new teacher, and new peers.
4. Monitor the child's progress from a preventive intervention standpoint.
5. Be a resource to teaching and administrative staff on needs and resources for children in out-of-home placement.
6. Help prepare the child for his or her next transition.
7. Be a referral resource for foster parents and birth parents who have been reunited with their child.
8. Send records to next school placement.

In addition, the high school Foster Care Student Committee should assist students in their emancipation plan to prepare them for departure from foster care at age 18. Such help may include life skills training, career counseling, vocational assessment, aptitude testing, and college counseling.

SUMMARY

The obstacles to quality care for children in out-of-home placement include the following:

1. Too many children are in out-of-home placement because of a lack of family preservation services in the community.
2. Caseloads of child protective services workers are too large to enable close monitoring of individual children and families.
3. Relative placements are not being adequately evaluated to determine appropriateness of placement and need for community support.
4. Foster families are not being provided the training and support needed to ensure one placement for each child until reunification or relinquishment takes place.
5. Children are being kept in hospitals and emergency shelters and small group homes because of a lack of foster families in the community.
6. Siblings are being separated by the child welfare system.
7. Children are being placed in homes of families with different cultural heritages.
8. Foster families are not trained to help children resolve the issues of separation and loss.
9. The child welfare system does not automatically provide a mental health plan as preventive intervention for every child in out-of-home placement.

To rectify these abuses within the welfare system, the 1991 National Commission on Family Foster Care (Child Welfare League of America, 1991) has identified the following child welfare practices as essential for the provision of quality foster care for infants and young children:

- Children should remain with their birth family whenever possible.
- Children should have one family foster care placement until reunification or relinquishment takes place.
- Children should be placed with their siblings.
- Children should be placed in geographical proximity to their birth family and in family foster care that is willing to promote birth family relationships.

- Children should be placed in family foster care that can provide for their special emotional, behavioral, developmental, and medical needs.
- Children should be placed in family foster care that is similar in ethnic and cultural identity.
- Children should be provided emotional support, counseling and/or psychotherapy for unresolved separation, loss, attachment, and abuse and neglect issues.

The California Think Tank Report, *Perinatal Substance Abuse: What's Best for the Children?* (Poulsen, 1992), recommended that foster family assessment protocols should be developed that address the following quality of care issues:

- Consistency of caregiving available
- Level of stress in the environment
- Cultural, linguistic, and religious similarity
- Ability to deal with special developmental, behavior, or familial problems associated with substance abuse
- Ability to accept all siblings
- Ability to promote a healthy attachment between the child and birth mother
- Ability to obtain health, mental health, and social services for the children
- Commitment of the family to keep children until relinquishment or reunification
- Proximity of out-of-home placement to birth parents

Appropriate family and educational placement decisions for children are critical for positive outcomes. Careful matching of children's needs with the receiving family's and the school's capacity to meet those needs must be of top priority.

REFERENCES

Adoption Assistance and Child Welfare Act of 1980, PL 96-272, (June 17, 1980). Title 42, U.S.C. 620 et seq and 670 et seq: *U.S. Statutes at Large, 94*, 500–535.

Besharov, D. (1990a). Crack children in foster care. *Children Today, 19*(4), 21–25.

Besharov, D. (1990b). Testimony before the U.S. Senate, Subcommittee on Children, Families, Drugs, & Alcoholism. Washington, DC.

Birth, I. (1990, January 14). In its way, this agency is a child abuser. *New York Newsday*.

Child Welfare League of America. (1988). *Standards for health care services for children in out-of-home care*. Washington, DC: Author.

Child Welfare League of America. (1991). *A blueprint for fostering infants, children and youth in the 1990s.* Washington, DC: Author.

Child Welfare League of America. (1992). *Children at the front.* (CWLA North American Commission on Chemical Dependency and Child Welfare Final Report). Washington, DC: Author.

Children's Research Institute of California. (1991). State capsule. In *Foster care services.* Sacramento, CA: Author.

Children's Research Institute of California. (1992). *The challenges and opportunities of kinship care.* Sacramento, CA: Author.

Curtis, P. (1992). *A research agenda for child abuse and neglect* [Testimony]. Washington, DC: National Research Council, Commission on Behavioral and Social Sciences and Education.

Digre, P. (1992). Testimony before the U.S. Senate Finance Committee. Washington, DC.

English, A. (1990). Prenatal drug exposure: Grounds for mandatory child abuse reports [Special issue] *Youth Law News, 11,* 3–8.

Gall, S. (1990). Testimony before the U.S. Senate, Subcommittee on Children, Families, Drugs and Alcoholism, Washington, DC.

Garfield, G. (1987). *Congregate care for babies: An alternative care arrangement or an old system of care?* New York: Community Service Society of New York.

General Accounting Office. (1994). *Foster care: Parental drug abuse has alarming impact on young children* (GAO/HEHS-94-89, Report to the Chairman, Subcommittee on Human Resources). Washington, DC: Committee on Ways and Means, U.S. House of Representatives.

Gittler, T., & McPherson, M. (1990). Prenatal substance abuse. *Children Today, 19*(4), 3–7.

Gross, J. (1989, April 9). Grandmothers bear a burden sired by drugs. *New York Times,* pp. 1, 26.

Hailey, J. (1990). *Tackling California's demand for foster care.* Sacramento: California Senate Office of Research.

Herskowitz, J., Seck, M., & Fogg, C. (1989). *Substance abuse and family violence: Identification of drug and alcohol usage during child abuse investigations.* Boston, MA: Department of Social Services.

Individuals with Disabilities Education Act Amendments of 1991, PL 102-119. (October 7, 1991). Title 20, U.S.C. 1400 et seq: *U.S. Statutes at Large, 105,* 587-609.

Klerman, L. (1991). *Alive & well? A research and policy review of health programs for poor young children.* New York: National Center for Children in Poverty.

Los Angeles County Department of Children's Services. (1988). *Assessment training program.* Los Angeles: Author.

McCullough, C. (1991). The child welfare response. *The Future of Children, 1*(1), 67–71.

National Council of Juvenile and Family Court Judges. (1991). *Protocol for making reasonable efforts in drug related dependency cases.* Reno, NV: Author.

National Court Appointed Special Advocates (CASA) Association. (1989). Born into addiction. *The Connection, 5,* 1–5.

Office of the Inspector General. (1990). *Crack babies.* Washington, DC: U.S. Department of Health & Human Services.

Poulsen, M.K. (1992). *Perinatal substance abuse: What's best for the children.* Sacramento: State of California, Child Development Program Advisory Committee.

Provence, S. (1989). Infants in institutions revisited. *Zero To Three, 3*, 1–3.

Rutter, M. (1979a). *Helping troubled children.* New York: Plenum.

Rutter, M. (1979b). Protective factors in children's responses to stress and disadvantage. In M.W. Kent & J.W. Rolf (Eds.), *Primary prevention of psychopathology: Social competence in children* (pp. 49–74). Hanover, NH: New England Press.

U.S. Department of Health & Human Services. (1988). [Provisional estimate of census data] Unpublished data.

U.S. House of Representatives, Select Committee on Children, Youth, and Families. (1989). *No place to call home: Discarded children in America.* Washington, DC: U.S. Government Printing Office.

Wulczyn, F. (1991). *A multi-state comparison of placement histories.* Data presented at the Child Welfare Symposium on Multi-State Foster Care, New York City.

Yarrow, L., & Goodwin, M. (1965). Some conceptual issues in the study of mother–infant interaction. *American Journal of Orthopsychiatry, 35*, 473–481.

8

Service Delivery Issues

G. Harold Smith

Children and families affected by drug and alcohol abuse and addiction have multiple needs. The local education agency plays a major role in developing and implementing comprehensive services to children with numerous needs and their families. The constraints and issues that interfere with the provision of needed services (particularly by multiple agencies) and the role of the school and school district in developing and supporting community-based services are discussed in this chapter.

CHILDREN AND FAMILY NEEDS

Student achievement is dependent on a great many variables over which a school district has no control. Substance abuse by a child's family has serious implications for a child's success at school (Smith, 1993). Clinical damages resulting from prenatal exposure to drugs and alcohol may be compounded by postnatal environmental issues arising from substance abuse by the child's caregiver (Chasnoff, 1992; Griffith, 1992; Schutter & Brinker, 1992). Children whose mothers abused drugs and alcohol during their pregnancy and/or who are growing up in a home in which these substances are abused share many risks for failure. However, because of the potentially damaging results of fetal exposure to teratogenic substances and the effect that substance abuse has on families, these children may have increased vulnerability for school failure.

There is a perception that substance abuse exists primarily in lower income minority communities; however, substance abuse is a reality in all schools. Although the drug(s) of choice may vary according to the socioeconomic levels of the community, the reality of potential damage resulting from prenatal exposure and issues presented to children's development by substance abuse in the home are also present in all schools. When the caregiver's choice of drugs is illicit substances, additional risks arise, including imprisonment, death, and exposure to violence, for the caregiver and family members. These risks have obvious implications for children's success in school.

The child who has been exposed to substance abuse prenatally and/or postnatally is affected by many factors, some of which operate in isolation, some of which are synergistic, and all of which potentially can have a major influence on developmental outcomes. Children from lower socioeconomic levels may be faced with basic survival needs in addition to the harmful effects of substance abuse on their families. Lack of adequate housing, inadequate nutrition, risk of exposure to community and family violence, loss of principal caregiver(s) because of imprisonment, abandonment, or death, and lack of access to community resources important for school readiness present a high risk for vulnerability for failure.

Children of higher income families are also at risk for failure because of the effect that drug abuse has on parenting, family lifestyles, and involvement of caregivers with the child, as well as the frequently observed emphasis on secrecy, lack of communication, and denial of emotional needs (Cashing, Amasses, Allusion, & Holcomb, 1992). These children typically do not confront inadequate housing, food, and other basic survival needs. They are affected by a greater emphasis on secrecy about substance abuse within the family and a risk of isolation from support networks of family and neighbors. Isolation may contribute to the child's perception that he or she is responsible for the family's dysfunction and drug and alcohol abuse, and that the family is alone in the problems arising from alcoholism or other forms of addiction.

The educational achievements of students are dependent on school and home environments. Because of low academic achievement of children from problematic social environments, local boards of education across the United States are beginning to address the extent to which schools are responsible for meeting the noneducational needs of children that influence school performance. This will require schools to be concerned about a much broader definition of the "whole child" than is traditionally anticipated in educational literature and practice, necessitating expanded comprehensive planning in cooperation with community agencies to meet educational and other needs of students and their families if these students are to be successful in school.

The needs of children and youth growing up in families that are affected by drugs and alcohol are beyond the resources of any single agency. The role of school districts in meeting the noneducational needs of children and their families continues to be a major issue in public education. To support student achievement, schools will need to develop collaborative working arrangements with health, social service, substance rehabilitation and treatment, and mental health service agencies for services to children and their families. Critical services needed in these collaborative efforts include providing information about organizations offering support for adults affected by substance abuse, mental health programs, drug rehabilitation and treatment, and after-school services for recreation, tutoring, and vocational training for students (Burgess & Streissguth, 1992; Cole, Jones, & Sadofsky, 1990; Coles et al., 1991).

Educational achievement is dependent on a child's physical and mental health status as well as the ability of the family to function successfully. Children who do not receive adequate parenting support will evidence needs in a broad range of development, especially socialization, communication, adaptive, and academic functioning. Schools traditionally have made the assumption that children receive adequate parenting and will arrive at school prepared for learning. Although classroom teachers and administrators will readily admit the fallacy of this assumption, the lack of resources committed by educational and other community agencies to support parenting and parenting training evidences a low to nonexistent priority in this regard.

SCHOOL ROLE FOR FAMILIES AND CHILDREN

For interventions to be effective, the child must be served as part of a family unit and the child's family must be made an integral part of the treatment team (Crittenden, 1992; Romijn, Plat, Schipper, & Schaap, 1992). Contrasted with the need for family-based services for vulnerable children is the fact that comprehensive family-based services are practically nonexistent (Salinas, O'Farrell, Jones, & Cutter, 1991). Service providers and advocates for vulnerable children and families affected by drugs and alcohol agree that services must be comprehensive and target the entire family if success is to be realized. At issue is a lack of comprehensive family-focused models of services that bring together all of a community's resources for social, mental health, physical health, addiction rehabilitation, vocational support, education, and family protection services. The goal is to provide an accessible vehicle for services from the community to be available to the school's community and its families. It is critical that the local board of education, through its policy decisions and practices, establish vehicles that link schools and other community agencies to provide services to children with multiple needs and their families.

Tommy

Last year the school's principal, Mr. Adams, contacted various public and private community agencies that serve the families in his school to determine their interest in developing a school-based child and family services team. Discussions among the various agencies resulted in the formation of a Community Services Team composed of representatives from the school and area physical health, mental health, and social services agencies. Mr. Adams agreed to serve as chair for the team this year. Beginning next year, each agency will assume responsibility to chair the team.

Tommy J. is a 9-year-old student in the third grade. Although his school performance has not been stellar, he has been promoted without any retentions. Tommy has been enrolled at his current school for 3 months. A review of his school records describes a number of moves among districts. He has moved to three different schools within his current district during this school year.

Tommy's performance at school has shown a marked deterioration in the past 3 months due to frequent absences, being late for school, and falling asleep in class. Tommy usually gets along very well with his classmates. Recently, however, he has been in several fights and on one occasion dissolved into tears following a confrontation with another classmate over a comment about his clothing being wrinkled.

Tommy lives with his mother. There are no other children. His father moved out of the home a year ago and provides very minimal financial and emotional support to his wife and son. Tommy's mother has been to the school three times, once for a regularly scheduled teacher conference, and twice as a result of disciplinary actions by the school. On all three of these occasions it was obvious that she had been drinking. Tommy has told his teacher that his mother drinks every night, and for the past several weeks he has had to find food for himself when he goes home.

Last year the school's social worker assisted the family in applying for health, housing, and food assistance and helped Tommy's mother to contact a community advocacy organization for legal advice. The latest concern has been the reported drinking by Tommy's mother that prompted a report to the child protective service (CPS) on the basis of possible neglect.

A Community Services Team meeting was requested by the school's social worker and principal. A plan of action was developed with the CPS caseworker who had assumed responsibility for service coordination with Tommy's mother. The caseworker met with Tommy and his mother. Tommy's mother decided that her major concerns were for assistance with housing and food. The caseworker made Tommy's mother aware that the CPS department will be monitoring the home situation and offered her a community parent training program.

After working directly with the family, the CPS caseworker has made the team aware that Tommy and his mother have a variety of problems that will have to be addressed by the cooperating agencies. Because the family obviously has a variety of needs, the decision was made by the school-based team that one of the priority considerations should be to address the abuse of alcohol by Tommy's mother and the effect this is having on her ability to provide adequate parenting to Tommy.

The CPS caseworker will continue to monitor the home situation and report regularly to the Community Services Team about the status of Tommy's care. The team has determined that if an emergency situation develops and Tommy must be removed from his home, the school will be responsible for facilitating transitions for Tommy to his new school. The school will work closely with the administrative staff of the district to attempt to keep Tommy in the current school with special transportation.

The CPS caseworker will provide support to Tommy's mother in an attempt to help her to agree to go to the area mental health center for assistance. The CPS caseworker will support this linkage and will communicate with the designated mental health staff member to facilitate the linkage for Tommy's mother. If inpatient treatment for depression or rehabilitation is necessary, a temporary foster care placement with his grandmother can be provided to Tommy.

The team agreed that if Tommy's performance at school could be improved this would provide a possible resource for continued support for him. A referral to the in-school educational support team was initiated for the purpose of determining appropriate strategies and interventions for Tommy to improve his educational achievements. The local school staff will continue to monitor Tommy's status at school. The guidance counselor will be responsible for meeting with Tommy on a daily basis to monitor his physical and emotional status and to build a sense of trust with him. The guidance counselor will be the contact for the school if Tommy is placed into foster care.

Poulsen (1992) and Swan and Morgan (1992) identify a number of issues influencing the development and delivery of family-based services for vulnerable children; included among these are the following:

1. Identification of families and children requiring services
2. Coordination of services and resources among health, social, and educational agencies
3. Establishment of systems to support transitions of families among agencies
4. Agreement on the authority of agencies for service coordination responsibilities
5. Level of funding and flexibility for how funds are used
6. Reliability of agencies as perceived by potential consumers

"Family infrastructure resources" (e.g., housing, food, clothing) are resources that a family needs for basic survival. When these are not available, the family cannot support their children adequately so that the children are successful in school. When these and other basic needs are met, the family can begin to address resources that improve quality of life and will support effective parenting, family cohesion, and empowerment.

Family Empowerment

It has been said that if you feed someone today, he will be hungry tomorrow. However, if you teach him how to grow his food, he will never go hungry again. Families and their children affected by drug and alcohol abuse may be in such desperate straits that their needs require immediate response for basic survival. The self-fulfilling prophecy of inadequate families results when a "crisis response" mode of operation becomes the norm for service agencies and the families they serve, versus a conscious and deliberate approach to help families become independent and achieve a higher quality of life through their own efforts. The task is one of helping the family learn how to meet its own needs.

Families with special needs may be overwhelmed with a resulting sense of helplessness in the face of poverty, substance abuse, and unemployment. These are the families who, even though they may have had at one time the potential capability of adequacy, will become lifelong clients of social service agencies with no hope of achieving independence and responsibility. This typically results because service providers fail to ascertain the strengths of the families and accept the need of the family to achieve self-advocacy and empowerment (Dunst, Trivette, & Deal, 1988).

The term *empowerment* is defined as a learned ability that permits and enables one to be responsible for personal needs and to meet the needs of those for whom one is the primary caregiver. Empowerment results from a conscious and systematic process of learning and practice that enables the family caregiver(s) to identify priority needs and potential sources to address these needs and to obtain appropriate support resources to enable the family to function at a more capable and independent level.

Societal changes have made and will continue to have significant effects on family structure and perceived responsibilities. For example, an increasing number of mothers are forced to seek employment in order to maintain an acceptable level of existence. This often results in young children being cared for in less than appropriate circumstances with a risk for developmental outcomes, child safety, nutrition, exposure to unsafe child care practices, and other detrimental issues.

Family empowerment begins with the family's initial contact with a community service agency. The process never ends, as families continue to need support and guidance in locating and obtaining appropriate services, learning problem-solving skills, making decisions, and developing skills to work within the administrative structure of agencies that offer potential resources to support the family. Service providers should be encouraged to plan systematic procedures in which the family caregiver is allowed to exercise authority and responsibility for determining the needs, priorities, networks for support, and resources. Families will vary in their ability to obtain community services. Some may require an extended period of support and guidance with gradual achievement of needed skills and a perception of worth and capability.

The terms "case management" and "service coordination" are sometimes used interchangeably to describe the process by which multidisciplinary resources are brought together to meet the needs of children and their families. "Case management" implies that an agency staff person is responsible for working with the family to ensure that identified services are obtained and used appropriately. This is a person outside of the family responsible for "managing" the family's needed resources.

"Service coordinator," however, emphasizes the responsibility of the family to coordinate and obtain needed services as a part of empowering the family to make decisions and be responsible for its well-being. It is important that families be helped to be responsible for identifying service and resource priorities, and appropriate community agencies, and to coordinate the delivery of services. When this occurs, the family will become increasingly independent and more capable of coping with its own requirements. Every family will not be capable of assuming this responsibility immediately. Issues of substance abuse, which may be coupled with mental health needs, may make this process frightening and unrealistic.

Families also will vary in the level of energy and stamina they have to pursue community services and possibly be involved with the care and development of their children. This is particularly true for families in which the caregiver is responsible for a number of children with special needs, has a lack of expertise or knowledge about social service systems, and may have acquired a sense of helplessness, constantly seeking someone else to make the decisions for the family and his or her children.

Primary service providers will require support and accountability in their relationships with families who have special needs. As the family unit is affected by multiple service agencies, it is critical that those workers who have the most direct contact with the primary caregiver be aware of a family's perceived needs, resources that may be available through extended family networks, and the level of knowledge and expertise of the primary caregiver in being able to locate and obtain required resources. This will require service providers to address intervention in a much broader way. Most service providers are accustomed to making decisions on behalf of the family—it is much easier, more expeditious, and services usually can be provided much faster than having the family deal with it personally. It may be very appropriate for this process to occur in critical need areas, particularly in terms of basic family infrastructure and child protection. However, once the major and primary needs of survival are met, it is the responsibility of the family and the agencies working with them to move the family to as high a level of independence of action as possible. A critical issue becomes not only "What services are required for this family?" but also "How can the family be supported in obtaining these services to support continued development and maximum independence for the family?" In this scenario, service providers go beyond a client–staff relationship and begin to work together in a nonthreatening partnership role for both parties.

SCHOOL ROLE FOR CHILDREN IN OUT-OF-HOME PLACEMENTS

Children whose families are affected by substance abuse are at higher risk for placement into foster care or other out-of-home settings. The number of children and youth being removed from their biological families is continuing to increase (Poulsen, 1992). A change in home placement will have potentially very negative outcomes for children's performance and behavior in school.

In most cases a change in home placement will require a change in school as well. This results in the child not only having to make an adjustment to a new home and new caregivers, but also to new teachers, new schools, and new peers. For a child already vulnerable for failure, the burden can be overwhelming—most adults would have difficulty dealing with all of this at one time. Schools have a role to play in developing collaborative agreements with area family and children's service and mental health agencies to ensure that these support services are in place.

Communication among child protective and foster care agencies and the school is critical. Consistent and predictable procedures to keep school personnel informed about pending or crisis interventions from social service agencies should be developed and agreed to at all levels. When a child service agency determines that a change in a child's home placement is necessary, agency personnel should be responsible for communicating this information to school staff immediately. Protocols developed by the cooperating agencies will determine the type of information to be relayed, the degree of confidentiality to be maintained, and the role of school staff in supporting children through this change.

When children cannot be maintained in their home district and a change in home placement is imminent, the role of the school staff in supporting the child's transition is important. State agency regulations may prevent a child service agency from revealing the issues and problems requiring a change in placement. However, there is no statutory reason that agencies cannot keep each other informed about pending and imminent changes. Some home and family situations may require an immediate response and the child must, for his or her own safety, be removed with little or no notice. Even in these cases, however, the school staff have an important role in supporting the child emotionally and physically.

School districts need to examine carefully their procedures and regulations and make every effort to maintain children in a consistent school setting. This may require a change in board policy and resources available to schools to support out-of-district placements. In some cases, this may not be feasible or even possible in light of state regulations, court orders, and other constraints over which the local board of education may have no control.

INTERAGENCY COLLABORATION

A significant issue for provision of needed services to families results from the manner in which resources are allocated to community agencies through state and community funding sources. Typically, legislation that authorizes funding targets specific agencies for specific services. As a result of this categorical funding, services for a family or its children may shift from one agency to another based on the age of the child, specific services required, eligibility criteria for agency services, and changes in legislative authority for programs.

During the past several years, a variety of vehicles and regulations have been established by federal and state child service systems to minimize interruption and lack of child and family service coordination. Part H of PL 102-119, the Individuals with Disabilities Education Act Amendments of 1991, deals specifically with required services and resources for preschool children. This component mandates that communities and states establish interagency coordinating councils (ICCs) to support effective coordination of services among agencies for children, including transition, parent and family support, assessment and evaluation, and developmental and therapeutic interventions.

The ICC model has shown varying degrees of implementation and success in bringing about collaborative service models. Key issues affecting interagency collaboration are 1) ownership of the process by cooperating agencies particularly at the local community level, 2) political issues that affect agencies, 3) the ability and willingness of both private and public agencies to make changes in service delivery priorities and strategies, and 4) the establishment of realistic goals for transagency collaboration at varying administrative staff levels (Swan & Morgan, 1992).

School-based transagency collaborative programs are receiving attention as a strategic resource for children with multiple needs and their families. Collaborative agreements among schools, social, health, mental health, and other community agencies support a range of services to students, parents, and other eligible family members. The decision may be made that direct services will be provided at the neighborhood school. In these school-based models, families are assisted in gaining access to food and nutrition programs, literacy programs, job training and placement programs, and other resources to improve the family's ability to function and affect the overall quality of life for the family (Edwards, Young, & Jones 1992; Elders, 1992; Larsen, 1990; Rist, 1992).

Jehl and Kirst (1992) identify a number of factors important to the success of school-based services including 1) the district's capability to support services within the facilities of the school(s), 2) the degree to which collaboration can be established with other agencies versus one agency attempting to dominate programs and services, 3) the implementation of comprehensive assessment of services that are required, 4) the commitment of agency resources that can be targeted to priority needs, and 5) the policy support at all levels for the proposed model of services.

Problems may arise because agency staffs from diverse disciplines are not familiar with one another's philosophy, resources, priorities, practices, or strategies. There may be critical differences of opinions on how children and families are best served as well as how agency resources should be utilized. This will require that agencies initiate cooperative planning and needs assessment activities to reach consensus on priorities, use of resources, and strategies. Interagency staff training will be critical to the success of collaborative programs to help personnel understand not only the roles and responsibilities but also the mechanisms of working with other disciplines in a variety of roles.

Two approaches to the development of school-based health and social services are emerging as the most important at this time.

1. *Models in which the school district develops school-based health and social services with their own resources or in cooperation with other agencies:* Some districts have determined that it is more expedient to employ personnel to offer selected services and to support

follow-up with other agencies. Others have developed collaborative agreements that bring resources from other agencies to the
school site.

2. *Models in which the district assumes a leadership role or a cooperative
   role with other agencies to establish family service centers in the community:* These centers may be located at. school sites or in other
   joint-use facilities. These represent a collaborative effort to make
   services geographically more accessible and to reduce fragmentation of services to families through a combination of resources
   from educational, health, social, and mental health programs or
   agencies. This model is often referred to as a *transagency* approach in contrast to an *interagency* model, which is perhaps
   more familiar.

Both of these models have benefits to children. The decision
to choose one over the other is usually dependent on the status of
communication and cooperation among the school district and other
agencies and funding sources. Barriers to these models include concerns about program control within various locations, the ability of
the family to gain access to locations of services easily, repetition of
referral and application procedures, and perceived reliability of services by consumers.

Regardless of which approach a district may determine best fits
the needs of its communities, interagency collaborative agreements
for follow-up and ongoing health and social services must be developed. Schools cannot do the job alone regardless of their commitment and intent.

SERVICE DELIVERY SYSTEMS

The ability of communities to deliver comprehensive health, mental
health, rehabilitation, education, and social services to children with
multiple needs and their families is facilitated or hampered by a variety of constraints. The degree to which staff from various disciplines
will be able to coordinate service delivery successfully will be influenced by political, statutory, and financial agency constraints that
may or may not be under the control and authority of an agency's
staff. If schools are to be successful as cooperating partners in community collaborative efforts and if the school is to be effective in a
leadership role while developing these models, it will be necessary
for leadership staff to be aware of and responsive to these inter- and
intra-agency issues.

Interagency collaboration mandates the breaking down of real,
perceived, and/or imagined barriers to communication among

agency staff at all levels from top to bottom. As the most important child service agency in any community, the school district has an obligation to initiate and sustain this process with other community agencies. Schools and their district leadership staffs should explore creative ways in which resources can be interfaced with other agencies to expand the range and scope of services to children and their families. This process may be hampered as much by the philosophy of leadership staff and boards as by actual and perceived regulatory barriers.

Financial Resources and Constraints

Understanding how an agency pays for its child and family service programs and the restrictions and mandated priorities for services is an important step in being effective in coordinating services and reaching consensus on agency roles and responsibilities in a collaborative effort. An agency will define its resources in a variety of ways.

Resources include funding, but in developing comprehensive child and family services a much broader definition is required. "Resources" include staff at all levels and how staff are used and assigned, facilities, transportation support, policies, and administrative procedures and practices. Funding from various sources may provide increased flexibility for how these dollars can be used to meet identified priorities that have been agreed upon by the cooperating agencies.

Agency funding sources and levels of funding will determine agency priorities, range and scope of services, flexibility in use of resources, and restrictions on how funds and other resources can be used. Most agencies have multiple sources of funding that come from local and state governments, federal agencies, foundations, individual donors, and sometimes fees for services from their clients. Many of these funds can be interfaced and possibly co-mingled, which can encourage agencies to develop a broader range of services while at the same time maintaining integrity for individual funding sources. However, funding of services from some sources may have very severe restrictions placed on how these are to be used with strict accountability for services actually provided.

All agencies have limited resources and typically do not have sufficient funding to do the jobs that are mandated. Just as the board of education must make decisions for priorities and use of available resources, other community agencies must make similar decisions to meet mandates for services and priorities that are critical from the agency's professional perspectives. These may not be the same priorities that are identified by other community agencies. Understanding how an agency pays for its child and family services programs and understanding restrictions and required priorities for use of these funds is an important first step for learning how to work effectively with other cooperating agencies.

Duplication of services, and failure to address community needs and priorities is a common charge brought against public agencies. Whether the accusation is true or not, when this complaint is leveled against any agency, it is an indication that the agency 1) has not used community input for developing its program of services, 2) is failing to communicate its mission and services effectively, and/or 3) is misdirecting resources as charged. These are critical issues that affect agency validity, real and perceived, and the ability of the agency to build a sense of trust with its targeted client populations.

As a result of mismanagement or administrative decision, an agency may not use all of the resources that are available or that could be used. When this occurs, oversight panels need to become knowledgeable of funding sources and demand accountability from agency staff for use of available resources. Agencies who have narrowly defined their mission or priorities may be very vulnerable to this issue. For these agencies the ability and willingness to link with other child–family service agencies should be a primary concern to maximize services and available resources.

The effective use of resources is dependent on a number of factors within and outside of agencies and their management systems. Communication with funding sources and other child–family service providers about community needs and issues is the most important step in targeting resources to critical services. The willingness of agencies to negotiate with other agencies and consumer representatives for the use of resources is an important measure of how well an agency can build a meaningful collaborative effort with their community. When resources are limited, this becomes a test of commitment.

An example of how resources can be used to expand programs and services occurred in a school in the metropolitan Atlanta area. The school serves a lower-income community that is racially and ethically diverse with evidence of widespread drug and alcohol abuse. To address the mental health needs of the school's students, a small amount of discretionary funds was allocated from the district to contract for mental health services from the community's mental health center. The school was given the authority to determine the needs of the school community (children, families, and staff) and how mental health services could be maximized to provide priority services to those in need.

As a result of direct discussion and negotiation between the school's leadership team and the mental health center staff, the number of available hours was expanded significantly. The involvement of mental health staff in the school provided a vehicle for communication and discussion with other agencies. This resulted in assignment of staff from community child protective services, social services, interpretation for non–English-speaking parents, and staff development resources for school staff, which were targeted to understanding the needs of children from the school's attendance district and supporting teachers working effectively with cooperating staff from the cooperating agencies.

Local schools are usually more attuned to the needs of their local communities than district leadership staff and members of the board of education. Individual members of the board may have an understanding of their communities, but the issue is to help all of the members understand the complexities and needs of the district and not just individual communities. To support the development of programs and services that will be effective in meeting the needs of vulnerable children and their families, administrative staff and boards of education should be encouraged to remove unnecessary restrictions on the use of funds and to encourage local schools to develop service delivery systems in cooperation with other agencies.

Statutory and Regulation Issues

Laws and regulations propounded by state legislatures or governmental boards can be extremely detrimental to the development of collaborative programs. Statutory regulations and restrictions typically focus on the question of "Who is eligible for these resources?" This results in more attention being paid to eligibility application procedures than in determining service needs and resource allocations. Regulatory procedures and processes are important to protect consumers deemed to be most in need of services. However, the creative challenge to local service providers, including schools and their districts, is to be accountable for services to targeted consumers and at the same time expand the potential effect of available resources to a broader community.

Increasing attention is being paid to the need for governmental agencies at local, state, and federal levels to waive regulations and restrictions on agency resources and how these are used. The obvious caveat to this trend is that schools and school districts must continue to be accountable for student achievement and responsive to legal restrictions that cannot be waived or amended.

Political Issues

Statutory and regulatory issues may interfere with the development of transagency services. For example, the ability and willingness of agencies to share confidential information on children and their families are beneficial to agencies and their clients. However, access to and release of certain confidential information between agencies is governed by very stringent federal regulations. For example, most states have very strict limitations on release of information concerning child abuse and neglect. Provisions are required that permit the district and other agencies to share information with client permission to reduce the redundancy of information that is collected and to support interagency planning and implementation of child and family services.

Governmental agencies too often approach the allocation of resources with an attitude of "We know what's best and we must protect the use of these resources to their intended purpose." This management style stifles local community initiatives and creativity.

Nothing strikes greater fear to an entrenched bureaucratic staff or individual than the issue of participatory management; that is, consumers and service providers together identify priorities, plan for commitment of resources, and evaluate program results. There is no other single factor that is as critical if agencies are to meet the needs of vulnerable communities.

Participatory management evolves from a perspective that communities represent a broad spectrum of service needs, consumers, and consumer representatives or advocates. Community and consumer representatives must be involved in meaningful and ongoing participation in the planning and delivery of agency services, including the establishment of priorities for use of funds and other agency resources.

There is nothing wrong with state and federal agencies identifying and supporting the allocation of resources for priorities if this process is based on legitimate data and meaningful community and client participation. Local communities and their governing agencies are responsible and accountable for how public funds are used. Both of these factors can be addressed through a comprehensive planning process involving all segments of the community's service delivery systems and its consumers.

Leadership

The superintendent of the local school district is responsible for sanctioning the efforts by community and/or district-level staff to plan and develop intra-agency program resources. The local board of education also may need to be involved depending on the extent to which district policies and administrative procedures may be affected by the multi-agency collaborative.

Leadership to develop a multi-agency collaborative model depends on a number of characteristics, the presence of which support effective communication and planning, the absence of which spells the potential for disaster. An individual may be appointed or may voluntarily assume the role of leader. However this individual assumes responsibility, the validation of his or her role by the agency's administration is most important. The agency's representative(s) must be perceived by other staff members as having the authority and the approval to proceed.

The person who is assuming responsibility for this task will require strong communication skills, the ability to establish effective relationships and linkages with key community agencies, and an understanding of the characteristics and needs of vulnerable children from a multidisciplinary perspective. Time must be allocated to get the job done.

The Multi-agency Planning Team

Obtaining a commitment to participate on a planning team in which agencies are seeking to influence one another, safeguard their own turf and resources, and communicate their philosophies and perspectives on families affected by substance abuse is the first task of whoever is appointed or volunteers to initiate this process. The willingness of top-level management in each agency must be supportive of this effort, and this must be communicated clearly and unequivocally to lower-level staff, particularly those who will be doing the actual work to develop the program service systems.

Each agency must be represented adequately. This can become a problem, particularly when large agencies with multiple program services need to have representatives from each of these components participate. This is very likely to happen in targeted services to this population with many needs. When an agency legitimately has multiple representatives, an agreement must be reached on who will actually represent that agency in decision making. Obviously consensus is the ideal way to proceed in developing any agreement. A vote always signals that someone lost.

Careful records should be kept of the committee's considerations and decisions not only to document the process the committee went through, but also to serve as a record of agreements, issues, and decisions for review by other nonparticipating staff and community. From the beginning, the committee must include representatives from the community who are not associated with an agency. This includes representatives (perhaps accompanied by an advocate) from the families to be served by the proposed planning process.

The team needs time to develop the cohesion and decision-making process that will allow it to function and to be successful. An early activity that can be very valuable in this process is to provide staff training by each participating agency for other committee members. In this way, each agency has the opportunity to highlight its key program and its perceived success and issues, and to help other participants begin to understand how decisions are made in that agency, restrictions or flexibility for services, terminology and "lingo," and how that agency identifies issues and needs from its professional perspective. This activity will help other participants to be able to communicate effectively with this agency using terminology that is meaningful to its staff. This can become particularly important if the committee appears to have reached an impasse and negotiation on priorities is resulting from a failure to communicate because of perspectives, understanding, and knowledge.

Joint Planning

The transagency planning committee should be established as early as possible to evidence joint ownership and responsibility for the success of the proposed program of services. This is a critical point in developing effective interagency service. Ownership of the process is critical and must be shared equally by all. Leadership of the joint planning process is optimally shared with all agency representatives having a meaningful and effective role. Propinquity is an important concept in developing a sense of "we-ness" among the cooperating agency personnel. At this point, the critical issue is helping staff members establish cohesion and communication among themselves. This speaks of the need for frequent meetings initially, opportunities to interact in a variety of settings, and developed respect for each other's perspective of needs and resources that can be brought to bear for children and their families.

Needs Assessments and Priorities

Most agencies are very willing to quickly tell anyone who is interested exactly what the needs and priorities are in a community. The agency's perception of needs and priorities may very well be true; however, planning committee participants also need to be aware that this also may represent a restrictive viewpoint, which may or may not be based on valid data. A decision about how planning data will be collected and analyzed will have to be made early in the planning process. Needs assessments usually are done by survey forms and sometimes by interview of professional staff. The missing element is an opportunity for meaningful input from actual or potential consumers of the collaborative services.

Rather than restricting this process to a prioritization of available services or a collection of data that is based on services, a more comprehensive approach to needs assessments is based on family perspectives of needs and issues of a much broader scope. Agencies usually will have the expertise to analyze these broad child–family issues and begin to identify services and resources that would be appropriate.

This is a key planning step in which needs are determined and prioritized, but it also presents a meaningful vehicle for consumers and consumer representatives to become involved in the process. A variety of data sources should be used, including census data, community surveys, interviews of potential consumers, interviews of service providers, and advocacy representatives. The determination of priority goals will require extensive discussions and, it is hoped, consensus building. If at all possible, voting on any issue should be avoided as this builds the potential for splitting the planning group along professional lines and personal philosophies.

After the agencies have developed this listing, a validation process is required. At this step, the actual consumers are asked to validate whether or not the proposed services will in fact address their concerns and what are the barriers that will prevent access to resources. For example, if health care for children is identified as a major need with transportation to health care centers being determined to be a feasible resource, the issue becomes 1) how do families gain access to transportation, and 2) is transportation alone going to solve the problem and permit all children access to needed medical services? The obvious caveat to planners is that although transportation may very well be a key resource, communicating this information to families, providing up-front funding by contract or other means to get the transportation to the families, and extending clinic hours to permit families to come after work hours will be an example of other concerns that must be considered by the collaborative planning task force. Typically no issue is going to be solved by one alternative and very few alternatives can stand alone as a solution. The linking and interfacing of contributing resources and issues is a critical planning task.

Identifying Resources

The identification of a community's resources usually will begin very slowly with only a handful of public and possibly private agencies being identified as having potential resources. The task of identifying the key decision makers and the role of the agency's governing board(s) will require a variety of resources and ongoing communication. Usually after the collaborating agencies are underway, additional community resources will begin to surface. A decision has to be made at that point whether or not to bring these agencies on board or to hold off until an effective vehicle for interagency communication has been established. There are positive points to both sides of the argument and the deciding point usually will rest on the determination of the importance and scope of services that can be provided by the identified agency and to what extent this agency can support the task of the collaborative efforts.

Agreements and Relationships

In order to make a collaborative model a reality, a number of important activities have to be undertaken.

1. The commitment of the board of education to the development of a collaborative model is paramount. This means that the board is willing to be involved in discussion with their peers in the cooperating agencies, participate in ongoing planning activities, and evidence a willingness to commit an appropriate share of resources to implement services. An ongoing vehicle for interagency communication must be established for the agency representatives.
2. Ownership of the process by a single agency or agency representative will doom the collaborative process before it even begins. All agencies and all participants must feel that they have an important role to play and that they will participate as meaningful decision makers with mutual responsibility for carrying out the decisions of the committees. Agencies may be unwilling to share authority and responsibility for programs, services, and other resources. The issue for the board of education is the extent to which it is willing to share its authority with other cooperating agencies to make decisions about programs, services, and resources. The local board of education is required to address the issue of how much it is willing to share decision making with other agencies on allocation of district funds and other resources. Initiating school-based or community family service cen-

ters requires a reallocation of resources by the collaborating agencies. School districts will be asked to contribute resources along with other cooperating agencies.

3. School districts must have meaningful and appropriate participation in any community planning task force. School districts often are ignored or forgotten when many community task forces are formulated. Usually this happens because these other agencies do not understand the role and responsibility of the educational agencies or the resources that a school district can bring to bear on children and family issues. For example, an attempt to form a community service system for children infected by the human immunodeficiency virus (HIV) was recently initiated in a major metropolitan area. The attempt to build a coalition of health, social, prevention, education, and advocacy agencies was not successful because of a perception that schools could not be trusted with confidential information and that the major need of families and children affected by acquired immunodeficiency syndrome (AIDS) was not education but rather service coordination, social services, and medical services. This completely overlooked the need for school personnel to be included as part of the community's comprehensive efforts to meet the needs of infected children and children whose caregivers were infected. Schools and school districts have an important stake in building effective collaborative models for health, social, rehabilitation, and educational services. A lack of these services will affect children's school performance and their ability to function successfully in our schools and communities.

Service Development

The role that each agency will play in actually implementing services will depend on that agency's mission such as providing available resources, professional expertise, and willingness to commit resources, officially and unofficially. This process typically requires a good deal of discussion and negotiation among the agency representatives. Responsibilities assigned and assumed by the agency include services that are nonnegotiable, professional expertise from the administrative and service staffs, and control of the level of flexibility for use of funding and other resources will determine how well an agency is able to collaborate with other community resources.

The expectation of the planning group should be spelled out carefully with specific strategies, timelines, and responsibility. This may be accomplished through a formal agreement or comprehensive planning. A formal agreement should be reviewed and ratified by the governing boards of each agency to ensure that the proposed services are concomitant with applicable regulations and policies.

Evaluation

Evaluation of service delivery should focus on the following areas:

1. Process evaluation that assesses the way services are actually developed and implemented. This area identifies agency responsibilities and how those responsibilities are met, priority service areas that are not addressed, number of individuals served, timelines, and so forth.
2. Impact evaluation reviews the outcome of services; that is, what actually happened to individuals as a result of the program's services being made available? Did more children receive more comprehensive services as a result of interagency collaboration? Were families better equipped to assume responsibility for their needs? Did children's educational achievements improve as a result of more comprehensive services being made available to them and their families?
3. Satisfaction evaluation addresses the perceived value and quality of service. Typically these data are collected from both consumers and service providers in order to present a comprehensive overview of services and use of resources.

Continued Planning

Effective community-based services require ongoing attention and support between community service providers and the individuals to whom services are directed. A vehicle is required to ensure that the process is ongoing and does not reach a stalemate simply because everyone assumes that services continue to be necessary and that they are being delivered effectively. Annual reports, dissemination activities, quarterly reports, and planning procedures are examples of how agencies and consumer representatives may ensure ongoing development of quality services.

SUMMARY

Service delivery to vulnerable children with multiple needs and their families is a process affected by a variety of factors. These factors may support the development of successful programs or they may interfere with the process resulting in an inefficient use of resources, duplication, and loss of children and families.

Schools have a responsibility and an important role in the development of community-based service systems for children and their families affected by drug and alcohol abuse because the school is the single, largest child-serving agency in any community. The extent to which a school district will be successful in providing leadership for community initiatives and how successful the district and individual schools will be in a collaborative model will depend on district leadership from the board of education and district administrative staff. An expectation and accountability for schools to develop and implement services will be crucial. Schools and school districts are only one player in the development of multidisciplinary and comprehensive services to children. However, their role is crucial to the success of any community's efforts.

Service delivery is a continuing process that involves agency representatives and consumer representatives throughout. Key elements of comprehensive planning include the following:

- Leadership
- Multi-agency planning team
- Joint planning
- Needs assessments and priorities
- Identification of resources
- Agreements and relationships
- Service development
- Evaluation
- Continued planning

REFERENCES

Burgess, D.M., & Streissguth, A.P. (1992). Fetal alcohol syndrome and fetal alcohol effects: Principles for educators. *Phi Delta Kappan, 74*(1), 24–29.

Chasnoff, I.J. (1992, June). Adoption of drug-exposed infants and children. *Perinatal Addiction Research and Education UPDATE* pp. 3, 5.

Cole, C.K., Jones, M., & Sadofsky, G. (1990). Working with children at risk due to prenatal substance exposure. *PRISE Reporter, 21*(5), 1–2.

Coles, C.D., Brown, R.T., Smith, I.E., Platzman, K.A., Erickson, S., & Falek, A. (1991). Effects of prenatal alcohol exposure at school age. I. Physical and cognitive development. *Neurotoxicology and Teratology, 13*, 357–367.

Crittenden, P.M. (1992). The social ecology of treatment: Case study of a service system for maltreated children. *American Journal of Orthopsychiatry, 62*(1), 22–34.

Dunst, C.J., Trivette, C.M., & Deal, A.G. (1988). *Enabling and empowering families: Principles and guidelines for practice.* Cambridge, MA: Brookline Books.

Edwards, P.A., Young, L., & Jones, S. (1992). Lower income and parents: Family, community, and school involvement. *Phi Delta Kappan, 74*(2), 72–81.

Elders, M.J. (1992). School-based clinics to the rescue. *The School Administrator, 8*(49), 16–21.

Griffith, D.R. (1992). Prenatal exposure to cocaine and other drugs: Developmental and educational prognoses. *Phi Delta Kappan, 74*(1), 30–34.

Individuals with Disabilities Education Act Amendments of 1991, PL 102-119. (October 7, 1991). Title 20, U.S.C. 1400 et seq: *U.S. Statutes at Large, 105,* 587–608.

Jehl, J., & Kirst, M. (1992). Spinning a family support web among agencies, schools. *The School Administrator, 8*(49), 8–15.

Larsen, J. (1990). *Drug exposed infants and their families: Coordinating responses of the legal, medical, and child protection systems: Executive summary.* Washington, DC: American Bar Association Center on Children and the Law.

Poulsen, M.K. (1992). *Perinatal substance abuse—What's best for the children?* Sacramento: Child Development Program Advisory Committee, State of California.

Rist, M.C. (1992, April). Putting services in one basket. *The Executive Educator,* pp. 18–24.

Romijn, C.M., Platt, J.J., Schipper, G.M., & Schaap, C.S. (1992). Family therapy for Dutch drug users: The relationship between family functioning and success. *The International Journal of the Addictions 27*(1), 1–4.

Salinas, R.C., O'Farrell, T.J., Jones, W.C., & Cutter, H.S.G. (1991). Services for families of alcoholics: A national survey of veterans affairs treatment programs. *Journal of Studies in Alcohol, 52*(6), 541–546.

Schutter, L.S., & Brinker, R.P. (1992). Conjuring a new category of disability from prenatal cocaine exposure: Are the infants unique biological or caretaking casualties? *TECSE, 11*(4), 84–111.

Smith, G.H. (1993). Intervention strategies for children vulnerable for school failure due to exposure to drugs and alcohol. *The International Journal of the Addictions 28*(13), 1435–1470.

Swan, W.W., & Morgan, J.L. (1992). *Collaborating for comprehensive services for young children and their families: The local interagency coordinating council.* Baltimore: Paul H. Brookes Publishing Co.

9

Model Programs

G. Harold Smith

A variety of issues typically are found in families affected by substance abuse. Substance addiction and rehabilitation, dual diagnosis of mental health problems and substance abuse, housing, employment, social services, inadequate parenting, lack of a consistent and predictable home environment, increased risk for exposure to violence, abuse, and abandonment are factors that do not contribute to the well-being and optimal development of the child (Bays, 1990; Jones & Houts, 1992; Jones & McCurdy, 1992). Some of these factors may act in isolation, while others, especially those resulting from the effects of drug abuse on parenting, will have cumulative and synergistic effects (Aylward, 1992). Programs and services targeted to vulnerable children and their families because of drug and alcohol abuse must address the diverse needs of children and their adult caregivers.

Educational, social services, physical health, mental health, and rehabilitation agencies, both public and private, are beginning to develop programs and services designed to overcome the deleterious effects of substance abuse on children. Although some of these are individual agency efforts, a greater emphasis is now being placed on developing comprehensive programs representing collaborative efforts between public and private agencies (Edwards & Jones, 1992; Elders, 1992; Hazel et al., 1988; Rist, 1992).

A variety of issues will affect how successful community programs will be in serving vulnerable children and their families effectively. The following requirements should guide the planning process by which models for services are developed and the actual delivery of these needed services:

1. Help vulnerable families understand the need for services.
2. Have appropriate vehicles in place to provide necessary support to caregivers to obtain access to the resources provided by community agencies.
3. Develop and support ongoing communication and cooperation between agencies and clients to facilitate access and delivery of services to clients.
4. Develop formal and informal agreements that result in a "seamless fabric" of services to families with special needs and their children.
5. Make available leadership in the community to support the development of vehicles that give agencies the opportunity to develop relationships and agreements for collaborative service systems.
6. Develop needed resources and service delivery systems with statutory and financial constraints that are flexible enough to meet individual family needs.
7. Overcome political barriers within and among agencies that may restrict interagency and intra-agency cooperation and service delivery.

Effective programs and service delivery systems reflect a belief that children should be served in the context of their total family. This is particularly important for children and their families who are vulnerable because of substance abuse. Addiction is a family issue affecting in some way every family member—adults and children. Within the family structure, individual children and adult members may require different services and resources. For example, the family member who abuses drugs or alcohol will require access to rehabilitation programs; children may require counseling services and modified education programs; other adults in the family may require assistance for family cohesion; the entire family may require social services that offer housing, food, and clothing.

Priscilla
Priscilla, age 23, is 4 months pregnant with her fourth child. During her last pregnancy she entered a substance rehabilitation program and has remained drug free for 15 months. Although her mother supported Priscilla through the births of her first three children, her mother has now refused to

provide any more support and has told Priscilla, "I am through with you."

Because of a previous report of child neglect, the community child protective service (CPS) is monitoring Priscilla and her three children. Recently, a "significant other," Danny, has moved into the home. Danny has a long arrest record, including assorted drug use and distribution charges, and is currently on supervised probation. The CPS worker reported that on the last home visit, Danny was extremely argumentative about the children's care and insisted that he is responsible for their discipline. The service coordinator noted that Danny appeared drunk.

A service coordination plan had been developed cooperatively by the CPS worker with Priscilla before Danny moved into the home. The goal of the plan is to support a successful outcome for her fourth pregnancy. She has not received any prenatal care to date. The service coordinator also has helped Priscilla to identify a variety of social and medical services that Priscilla can begin to receive for her three children.

With Priscilla's consent, the CPS service coordinator brought Priscilla and her family to the attention of the community's interagency team. This team is composed of community representatives from mental health, physical health, social services, and education agencies. The local law enforcement agencies and other private agencies have agreed to be involved on an "as-needed basis." Because of the potentially critical situation with Danny, his probation officer has been asked to participate in the team's planning.

The interagency team has identified the following critical issues for Priscilla and her children:

- Need for increased monitoring for child protection
- Concern that Priscilla may be unable to remain drug free
- Parenting training and support for Priscilla and Danny and especially for the two younger children
- Support from the family for the older child's success in school

The CPS worker will assume responsibility for service coordination with Priscilla. The following strategies were agreed upon by the team:.

1. The CPS worker will expand in-home monitoring to twice per week and will use this time to offer additional parenting training to Priscilla.

2. Staff from the child care and preschool programs for the two younger children will receive communication from the CPS worker and provide information to the team on the children's needs in this setting.

3. The CPS worker will communicate with the representative from the older child's school and help Priscilla identify ways that she can help him with his schoolwork.

4. Danny's probation officer will increase his visits to the home and require Danny to report weekly to his office. The probation officer will work with Danny to help him obtain regular employment or enter a job training program within 30 days. He also will discuss with Danny the importance of entering a drug and alcohol rehabilitation program.

The CPS caseworker met with Priscilla to review the interagency team's concerns. Priscilla asked for assistance in obtaining housing and food. Initially, she was overwhelmed by the seemingly endless list of things to do. Priscilla and the service coordinator identified the major priorities and developed a listing of weekly things to do for the next month.

Priorities for Priscilla include obtaining prenatal care, getting information about Medicaid eligibility and physical health screenings for the children, getting information about housing subsistence resources, and communicating by telephone at least twice per week in addition to the home visits with the CPS service coordinator. The CPS service coordinator will encourage Priscilla to join a rehabilitation support group to help her deal with personal issues and her relationship with Danny and his drug abuse.

The team noted their concern that Priscilla may not be able to complete all of the various activities successfully without assistance. Although the CPS service coordinator will be the primary service coordination manager, each agency has identified a back-up agency staff person who will step in and assist as either Priscilla or the CPS service coordinator requests.

ISSUES FOR PROGRAM DEVELOPMENT

The ability of a program's staff to meet the needs of its clients depends upon the relationship that develops between staff members and families. This relationship is built on mutual respect for the integrity of the family and will influence the extent to which families and service providers are able to work together. Because vulnerable families and their children are often receiving services from more than one agency at any one time, families may have an effective relationship with one agency and its staff and not have an effective relationship with another. Interagency planning can identify situations in which one agency may have a stronger relationship with a family. This agency may be able to support one agency taking the lead in the planning and implementation of services.

As a family is supported in obtaining multiple agency services, there is a risk that a child's caregivers may become overwhelmed with the complexity inherent in any bureaucratic agency. Services are better used by families when procedures can be minimized and duplication eliminated. As noted in Chapter 8, supporting the need for interagency and effective intra-agency service systems is much easier than bringing these to fruition.

Models of comprehensive services should be firmly grounded on available research rather than presumptions and perceptions. Myths arising from inaccurate reports in the news media as well as the bias in selecting research populations have had a major influence on community perceptions of the characteristics and needs of children and their families affected by drugs and alcohol (Newman & Buka, 1991; Poulsen, 1991; Smith, 1989).

DEVELOPMENTAL INTERVENTIONS

Children and families are unique and have varied needs and strengths. There is no typical profile for families and their children affected by drug and alcohol abuse. There is no single program model or service delivery system that will be universally successful. The key to any successful program is flexibility in how agencies organize and deliver a variety of medical, social, welfare, and other services to families and their children.

Model programs should evidence the ability to deliver a range of comprehensive services as well as a high degree of flexibility in how those services are organized and delivered. The comprehensive services should focus on family cohesion and economic stability, effect of substance abuse on the caregiver's lifestyle, and the ability of the family to be responsible for its own well-being.

- Prenatal interventions focus on services provided for the pregnant woman. The services include prenatal care, access to rehabilitation programs, adequate prenatal nutrition, and parenting training.

- Perinatal service coordination focuses on the critical period immediately prior to and after the birth of the child. Critical issues of concern include child and caregiver bonding, extended hospitalization, risk for abandonment, potential prosecution of the mother if she receives a positive drug screening, and medical issues for the child.
- Services to infants and preschool-age children focus on helping the child's caregiver(s) provide optimal environment and effective parenting with access to developmental interventions for the child.
- Programs for children of school age typically emphasize the developmental needs of the child with health, mental health, and social services responding to a complex array of issues and needs of the child and the family.
- Programs and services for adolescents should provide access to counseling resources and address the issues that may lead to intergenerational drug use by the youth.

Prenatal Interventions

Prenatal care and perinatal service coordination are critical for all pregnant women with an addiction, regardless of socioeconomic group or level (Coles & Platzman, 1990). Lack of prenatal care and inadequate prenatal nutrition place the developing fetus at risk for low birth weight and prematurity in addition to the potential negative effects of nonrestricted drug use on the woman and fetus (Finnegan, 1988; Griffith, 1991).

Prenatal care programs, because of their structure and assignment of resources, may present barriers to women who require services. The ability of staff to communicate effectively with women from different ethnic and socioeconomic groups, statutory requirements of the program to report substance misuse to authorities, reliability of services as perceived by the consumers, and the ability to communicate an understanding of constraints and priorities that may be different from the program staff all can be considered as potential resources or constraints on service delivery.

Project PREVENT, located at Grady Memorial Hospital in Atlanta, Georgia, utilizes a variety of strategies to build relationships with families with multiple needs and to provide ongoing prenatal and perinatal service coordination support for high-risk pregnant women who are drug dependent. Project PREVENT provides services to pregnant women who abuse drugs and alcohol at high risk for less than optimal outcomes for their pregnancy. Teams made up of social workers, peer addiction counselors, and child development specialists work with pregnant women who abuse drugs and alcohol during their pregnancy. Women may be referred to the project by family members or neighbors or by self-referral.

Following the birth of the baby, Project PREVENT staff continue to provide support for health care, housing, vocational training, parenting training, drug rehabilitation and treatment, and other resources that will provide a more positive long-term outcome for the child and family. The teams monitor continuing use of services through systematic review of clinic records, home visits, and interviews with the mother and possibly family members. A strong emphasis is placed on providing necessary follow-up to keep the mother and her child in the service delivery system for as long as is necessary. Services provided directly through Project PREVENT are without charge; clinic services are based on ability to pay (D.M. Carson, personal communication, July 29, 1992).

A key component in Project PREVENT is the use of peer addiction counselors who are women recovering from substance dependence who abused drugs and alcohol during their own pregnancies. These counselors assist their clients to obtain prenatal care, drug rehabilitation and treatment, housing, nutritional programs, and other social and medical services. Peer counselors make the initial contact with pregnant women at high risk in their homes. Because of the personal concern for each woman that is evidenced by the team, establishing a strong bond between the project counselors and each client results.

Anecdotal and follow-through data from the project emphasize the importance of the role of these counselors in the initial contact, support, and mentoring for clients. Their role is critical to the success of promoting healthier babies and improved quality of life for their mothers. Project PREVENT demonstrates that the personal relationships that are established between service providers and consumers is paramount for effective intervention models.

Issues and policies that need to be addressed in the development of effective prenatal care systems for pregnant women affected by substance abuse include the following:

1. What are the best ways to help pregnant women at high risk to be aware of the potential effect of continued substance use on the developing fetus?

2. How can information about pregnancy and drug abuse be made available in a meaningful and culturally sensitive manner to pregnant women addicted to drugs and alcohol?
3. How should resources be made available to support access to prenatal care, including transportation and child care?
4. How can mentoring and mutual support groups for parenting training and substance rehabilitation be developed?
5. How should ongoing support from the family be provided to encourage maximum participation in services after the birth of the child?

Neonatal Interventions

Support services for families with multiple needs who have very young babies are receiving a great deal of attention as a way to help caregivers learn how to meet the needs of their child to decrease infant mortality and improve child outcomes. Parenting training for child development, assisting the family in obtaining community-services, monitoring of the family's ability to care for the child, linking the family with appropriate mentoring networks, and providing required infrastructure resources (e.g., food, shelter, clothing, warmth) are all potentially required resources for the family to succeed.

The state of South Carolina has initiated a peer mentoring and parenting program that has been extremely successful in improving physical and developmental outcomes for babies born to women who abuse drugs or alcohol and who are from low socioeconomic, high-risk environments. The goal of the program is to reduce infant mortality using state-appointed "resource mothers." These are women who have children of their own and have shown success in childrearing practices. Under professional supervision, these women provide continued services following birth for assistance to families and children and support the family's access to health, social, literacy, and job training resources. Like Project PREVENT, these resource mothers come from socioeconomic backgrounds similar to those of the clients served by the program. Their ability to communicate about common concerns, the role model they present, and their common experiences and shared backgrounds give credence to their advice and guidance. Similar home-visit program services have been initiated in Hawaii (Cohen, 1991; Flax, 1992), Missouri (e.g., Parents as Teachers), and Tennessee.

Infant and Toddler Interventions

During the infant and toddler period (3 months–3 years), children prenatally and environmentally exposed to substance abuse are at risk for developmental delays resulting from inadequate parenting (Poulsen, 1991), exposure to abuse and trauma (Bays, 1990), removal from their natural family with placements into multiple foster care settings (Besharov, 1989, 1990), and continuing medical issues resulting from prenatal exposure, prematurity, low birth weight, and the potential deleterious results of medical interventions that may have been necessary at birth (Finnegan, 1988; Keith, Donald, Rosner, Mitchell, & Bianchi, 1986). Although research to date indicates that some of the neonatal behaviors observed in babies with confirmed prenatal exposure are not as apparent as the child grows older, delayed or dysfunctional language development, fine and gross motor skills, and social-emotional issues may continue to be evidenced into the child's later years (Chasnoff, Griffith, Frier, & Murray, 1992).

Key factors in determining positive outcomes are early intervention services for the child and support for caregivers in parenting and understanding the needs of their child. The earlier that children at risk for failure can be identified and appropriate services provided to them and their caregiver(s), the greater the potential for positive outcomes for the children (Cole, Jones, & Sadofsky, 1990; Newman & Buka, 1991). Children and families who are given early and consistent support have better outcomes than those who do not receive services.

Operation PAR (Parental Awareness and Responsibility) in St. Petersburg, Florida, is a combination center- and home-based program funded through a federal grant from the Office of Substance Abuse Prevention. The program serves infants and preschool-age children affected by maternal substance abuse and their families. The program has four major components: early intervention, screening and evaluation, referral, and follow-up using intensive service coordination, support groups for children and adults, educational services, and developmental child care (Davis, 1992).

Operation PAR has had major successes in positive developmental outcomes for children as a result of providing support resources to the child's primary caregiver. The program's goals target resources to the child's primary caregivers to achieve a higher level of competence in parenting and to pursue resources and skills for a higher quality of life through staff who provide access to social services, vocational training, literacy, and drug rehabilitation. Services are center-based with home services also provided to support parenting and access to community services. Staff include social service specialists, psychologists, and child development specialists who provide direct services to children and their families.

PROJECT INTERACT, located at Children's Institute International (CII), Los Angeles, California, was developed in collaboration with the Center for Child Development and Developmental Disorders, Childrens Hospital, Los Angeles. The program was designed to develop and enhance relationships between women affected by substance abuse who are in recovery and their infants. Women who are participating in the program may or may not continue to have custody or jurisdiction for their children.

The project is staffed by a team with expertise in parenting issues of women in recovery, development of mother–infant communication and relationships, infant and toddler development, and strategies for building resilience in infants with neurodevelopmental vulnerabilities or disabilities. There is not a prescribed curriculum. All topics are generated by the mothers, based on their immediate concerns, needs, and interests.

A group of mothers and babies meet on a weekly basis for 2-hour sessions. At the beginning of each session, mothers discuss the events and happenings of the week that related to them and their infants. Mother–infant activities are introduced, and the mothers predict how their babies will respond. Participants are led in a discussion to identify the differences in responses among the babies. Through these discussions, mothers learn to appreciate the individual, neurodevelopmental, and temperamental differences and learning styles of their infants. Thus, they begin to develop more realistic expectations of infant development and behavior. Sessions are videotaped and the parenting strengths for each mother are identified and discussed by the group. The final portion of each session focuses on parenting issues and family relationships—past, present, and future. Mothers are helped to see the connections between their childhood experience and their own parenting styles.

Preschool Interventions

A variety of intervention strategies and service delivery methods are being developed in programs for preschool-age children (3–5 years of age). These models provide support to the child's primary caregiver(s) for parenting training and teaching developmental activities to use with the child as well as medical-related services to children. Early intervention programs developed with federal, state, and local funds provide a continuum of direct services to children from birth to school age and their families as noted below.

Services recommended for children from birth to 3 years of age continue to be important for preschool-age children 3–5 years of age. Parenting training, support for the development of appropriate support networks for the family, increasing access to medical and social service resources, and educational interventions targeted to the child's developmental needs in the cognitive, language and communication, motor, and adaptive areas are all critical to meet the continuing developmental needs of the child.

Head Start Program The federally funded Head Start program initiated in the United States through PL 88-452, the Economic Opportunity Act of 1964, Title V, serves children from 3–5 years of age from lower socioeconomic families in all states. This program continues to receive increasing political and federal funding support as a result of its success with children at risk (Chafel, 1992).

At the federal and state levels, Head Start programs are addressing the issues of children exposed to substance abuse in their families through staff training rather than categorical program models. Head Start offers a range of services aimed toward developmental needs of children in cognitive, language, motor, behavior, and adaptive areas that are important for the child to be successful at school age. Family services provided by Head Start emphasize parenting training as well as supporting the family's access to community literacy and vocational training programs that will help to improve the family's functioning levels and quality of life. Collaboration between Head Start programs and local school districts offer the potential of strengthening transitions for children and their families at school age.

Project Relationship In November 1991, the Los Angeles Unified School District was awarded a model demonstration grant from the United States Department of Education, Office of Special Education and Rehabilitative Services (OSERS). This project came to be known as Project Relationship, reflecting the underlying premise that supportive relationships among service providers, families, and their children form the core of successful adjustments for children. The project has worked with children, families, and staff at nine publicly funded child care centers that are administered through the school district. These centers are located on elementary school campuses, serving approximately 120 children ranging in age from 2 to 12 years. Parents must be working or going to school and qualify as "impoverished" according to federal guidelines. Children are not enrolled or specially placed into the center; rather, the child care centers are selected by their family. Most of the children who do have disabilities are identified after they are enrolled.

The goal of the project is to provide support to children with special needs who are having difficulty coping with the demands of a child care setting. The model focuses on the utilization of a structured, relationship-based, problem-solving format for helping children, parents, and staff address issues and events that affect the functioning of the child and child care center staff. This goal is accomplished through the integration of special education personnel as members of the center's interdisciplinary team and as facilitators of the relationship-based process. The facilitator's role is to support the staff in developing solutions that draw on their experiences and match the style and demands of their setting.

Basic to the model is the belief that all behavior for children, staff, and families is based on communication. Children let us know how well they are coping with the demands of their environment through their behavior, which may be influenced by a wide variety of factors: general health, temperament, developmental and neurological competency, parent–child relationships, previous experiences, relationships with caregivers, and the level of stress and supports experienced by the family and community in which the child is a member. Behavior that is judged to be inappropriate may be a child's way of expressing feelings, needs, and wants. It is the child's way of coping with the expectations of the environment. Therefore, the child's behavior must be examined in terms of what it can indicate about the child. The task of a teacher or caregiver, according to the philosophy of Project Relationship, is to do the following:

1. Recognize and understand what the child is trying to communicate.
2. Modify adult expectations that are not developmentally or temperamentally appropriate.
3. Assist the child in learning more adaptive ways of expressing him- or herself.

Often, changing a child's behavior is a matter of first examining and changing adult behavior, expectations, and responses.

The underlying philosophy of Project Relationship in all staff development efforts is that the needs and wishes of the participants should determine the sequence and content of training activities. Staff development activities are conceptualized as team-building experiences.

Six important components of a relationship-based, problem-solving model have been identified as the following:

1. Gather information from all relevant parties.
2. Acknowledge opinions and feelings of staff, families, and children involved.
3. Discuss the situation and reach a consensus about a course of action.

4. Make a plan to carry out the agreed-upon actions.
5. Provide support to each other during the implementation.
6. Review how the plan is working and make necessary modifications.

School-Age Intervention

Children of school age, particularly those who have not received appropriate early intervention services before entering school, may demonstrate many of the same behaviors observed in youngsters exposed to drugs and alcohol. These behaviors may include hyperactivity, difficulty in self-regulation, and developmental delay in various areas. Additional issues for children affected by their family's use of drugs and alcohol include a potential for social-emotional problems resulting from a lack of attachment and bonding, physical or sexual abuse, or exposure to violence and trauma. Learning process and neurobehavioral difficulties may result from prenatal substance exposure or high-stress birth factors as well as environmental stress factors as noted earlier (Smith, 1989).

Adolescent Intervention

Adolescence is a critical developmental period in which the family environment plays a major role in the success or failure of the youth. At this point in the developmental process the adolescent is seeking to achieve independence in making decisions about a variety of issues including peer networks, deciding the importance of school and community activities, and his or her role in the family. Adolescence is a particularly sensitive developmental period for youth in families affected by substance abuse (Kumpfer, 1989).

The adolescent's typical developmental issues may counter the family's need for control and to maintain order and secrecy. This conflict may result in the adolescent being at high risk for abuse, exclusion, and experimentation with drugs and alcohol for self-medication (Emshoff, 1990).

Peer pressure and possibly the adolescent's seeking of self-medication to address depression and other psychological needs and social acceptance present a risk that the adolescent may perceive that an appropriate response to these issues is available through the use of drugs and alcohol. This decision-making process may be very similar to that used by the family and, thus, may present a risk for continued intergenerational substance abuse.

If support resources are available to youth at high risk in the school, alternative ways can be offered through value clarification activities, learning how to make appropriate choices, developing appropriate peer networks, and understanding the dynamics of the family that may affect his or her own behaviors and choices.

Effective counseling and support programs for children and youth exposed to substance abuse will help them begin to understand that they are not responsible for their families' substance use, they can make choices, and they can provide support to break the cycle of intergenerational use of drugs and alcohol (Robinson, 1990). In order for programs to be effective, schools may require assistance from community agencies, including organizations offering ongoing support for adults who are addicted to drugs and alcohol, mental health programs, drug rehabilitation and treatment, and after-school services for recreation, tutoring, and vocational training.

Student support groups similar to those sponsored by the Children of Alcoholics and Children of Drug Abuse movements are a valuable resource to schools. These peer support groups provide education on substance abuse, assistance in developing appropriate coping skills to address family issues, decision making, and peer relationships (Ackerman, 1983; Morehouse, 1989). These support groups may be organized to support liaisons with social service and health agencies for the student and family, help maintain close communication with foster care service providers who may be involved with the student, and encourage access to substance rehabilitation and treatment on behalf of these students.

Student Assistance Programs Student Assistance Programs (SAP) are a resource for teenagers who are either addicted to drugs and alcohol or are at high risk for substance abuse because of personal and/or family circumstances (Anderson, 1988; Carpenter, 1990). The SAP is a mutual assistance support group designed to support self-referral and identification by peers of students at high risk. These school-based programs use student peers recognized as leaders by other students. Peers act as leaders to the group and offer resources to understand personal needs, obtain access to community resources, and help to identify other youth who are at risk for substance abuse. Students may be referred to the SAP by other students or faculty, or the student may self-refer.

Within the support group, students may share information about their family that requires referral to child protective agencies. Students may require support in the decision to refer to community agencies and in the process continue to be assured of their own personal integrity and value. In the event the family takes issue with the reporting to another agency, the student is at high risk for retribution as well as exacerbation of relationships between the school and family. The priority concern of the school should be the student.

The physical safety, protection, and emotional well-being of the student may require close collaboration with other community agencies who may become involved with the family.

EDUCATION INTERVENTIONS

The techniques the school staff use to respond to the unique learning needs of students exposed to substance abuse will have a major effect on that child's self-esteem. If the school is successful in meeting individual needs, all children can be helped to understand that "I am important, special, and competent. I can be responsible for myself."

In order to meet the educational and other needs of children, the efforts of staff personnel at all levels within a school district are necessary. Of particular concern for local school planning is the issue of how the traditional roles and responsibilities of various staff positions provide resources for the needs of children and families affected by substance abuse.

Schools that are successful in their mission to educate all children reflect a belief that staff, children, and community share ownership in the school. Children are helped to understand that they have a rightful and meaningful place in their school. Staff feel they have a part in the decision making that guides the development of local school services within the framework of overall district priorities and resources. Communities look to the local school as a central point of reference for neighborhood development and cohesion.

The Board of Education

The district's board of education is potentially a valuable resource in meeting educational and other needs of all children, including those affected by substance abuse. The board of education is responsible for the establishment of policies, regulations, and sanctioned practices that direct the priorities of the district and the allocation of resources to meet the diverse needs of students.

It is the board's responsibility to assess the needs of the district and establish priorities for program development and allocation of resources. It is also responsible for monitoring the implementation of assigned priorities and determining the effect of allocated resources on the students and communities. Of particular concern for students exposed and vulnerable to alcohol and other drugs, the board of education is responsible for establishing a standard of accountability for student achievement.

The board of education should establish by policy and practice an expectation that all students will be provided an opportunity to receive an appropriate education that meets the current and long-term needs of its students to become participating and contributing citizens in their communities. This policy or mission statement should reflect a belief that all children can learn and, given appropriate learning opportunities, will achieve the goal of becoming contributing citizens in their communities. This mission and standard should be communicated clearly to the community at large and to each individual school community.

If the board is to meet its mission and goal of educating all students successfully, including those children who are vulnerable or at risk for failure, it will be necessary for the board to give direction and establish an expectation from the students and their families. In its role as a major child service agency in the community, it is reasonable for the board to give leadership to the development of networks among the district and other agencies to strengthen coordination of services to children and their families. A collaborative effort with physical health, mental health, social services, child protective services, and substance rehabilitation programs will be needed.

District Leadership Staff

Administrative and leadership staff are responsible for the identification of district-wide needs and to recommend priorities to support the decision-making process of the board of education. These staff members play a major role in keeping the board aware of instructional and community issues that will influence the board's priorities for action and allocation of resources.

It is the superintendent's responsibility to be aware of the issues of substance abuse, both prenatal and environmental, presented to the educational mission of the district. The superintendent must make decisions about recommendations to be made to the board for response strategies and required resources and ensure that action is taken to provide appropriate education programs for all students. It is the task of the superintendent and staff to collect data on student needs, assess these data to identify priorities, and develop appropriate recommendations to guide the development of policies and mission statements by the board of education. Providing a consistent and systematic process for assessing the needs of the district, providing for community participation in decision making, and helping to establish vehicles for interagency collaboration within the community as well as effective communication channels with legal enforcement agencies are critical in developing resources to meet the needs of students and their families affected by substance abuse.

School Leadership Staff

It is the responsibility of the school's instructional leaders to implement the priorities established by the district or at the local school level to meet the unique needs of that school community's students. School-level administrative staff must ensure that a process is in place to support the identification of students' instructional resource needs, assess the effectiveness of instructional programs in the school, encourage community collaborative efforts on behalf of the school's students, and participate in decision making at the district level in the identification of priorities and allocation of resources to meet these needs.

The organization of resources through *school-based management* is gaining increased attention as a way to support administrative and programmatic decision making as close to the school community as possible. School-based management is becoming a major tool in determining how best to meet individual community needs. School districts and individual school communities have used this concept of shared governance with varying degrees of success.

There are two critical elements to the success of school management and a philosophy of shared governance:

- The extent to which the administrative staff at the school level are accountable for student growth
- The extent to which classroom teachers are empowered to make educational decisions for children and are held accountable for student achievements

Classroom Teachers

The classroom teacher is the key resource for the district to be able to meet educational and other needs of children affected by substance abuse. All of the resources that are provided by a district will be of no use if teachers do not feel responsible for student achievement and are not willing or are unable to accept the critical role they play in implementing effective instructional strategies based on children's needs.

Within a given school faculty the teachers' level of training, years of experience, and differing philosophies on the mission of the school will vary. This awareness of a diversity of issues within the school community, which must be addressed, can be seen as a positive resource to the school's leadership staff. However, this diversity also can present tremendous challenges in reaching consensus on how students should be educated, how the resources of the school will be committed, and the extent to which teachers—rather than students or their families—can be held accountable for student growth.

Teachers will have to be selected carefully for assignment to programs for children exposed to substance abuse in their family environments. An issue to be addressed by training and support may be presented by staff who also have come from high-risk environments and may be dealing with some of the same issues and risk factors faced by those students (Garbarino, Dubrow, Kostelny, & Pardo, 1992). It may be necessary for staff members to be helped in addressing their own personal needs before they will be effective with vulnerable children. This may require a variety of supports for staff, including in-school support groups, linkages with community agencies, individual counseling by school staff, district-sponsored employee assistance programs, or other strategies designed to help the staff member deal effectively with personal needs.

Working with students with multiple needs is challenging and frustrating, particularly when teachers who are accustomed to consistent student growth are not able to assess growth of children who may be demonstrating achievements in very small increments and perhaps in less visible ways.

Burnout of teachers and administrative staff is a very real occurrence resulting from frustration, anger, a sense of helplessness, and a lack of personal confidence and satisfaction in meeting student needs. The personal as well as the professional needs of the staff will have to be addressed as part of the district and local school-based planning. Some examples of ways that teachers and other staff can be encouraged in their efforts include providing for support networking with peers within the school or possibly between neighboring schools, providing mental health support groups, developing recognition programs to help teachers perceive their importance and the achievements that are being made by their students, and recognizing each school's positive responses to community needs.

If teachers are accountable for student growth, they must be empowered to make necessary adaptations in classroom organization, curriculum, and use of available instructional resources to ensure appropriate achievement for students. Teacher empowerment is potentially a politically sensitive issue, particularly if this concept of shared governance is isolated from the multitude of supportive resources required for student growth.

Children from all socioeconomic levels bring problems to schools resulting from drug and alcohol abuse. However, the perception of most educators and other community agency staff members is that substance abuse is limited to lower-income minority communities.

This attitude may result in certain schools having a reputation of being "difficult" with low status being attached to assignments at these schools. Teacher turnover can be high in these schools contributing to a lack of consistency, unity of effort, and lowered expectations for student achievement. District- and school-level administrators have a responsibility to decrease turnover in all schools, but especially in those schools in which a significant number of students may come from dysfunctional families.

Restrictive transfer policies will place barriers to staff moving between schools that are perceived as having more status. A more positive and more successful approach will be to seek out ways in which school staff can be helped to feel ownership and pride in their students' and community's achievements. Positive recognition by the district of the efforts of all schools to meet student needs successfully—including but not limited to educational achievements—is an important component in maintaining school stability and consistency of staff.

As school staff develop a sense of ownership and pride in their accomplishments they are more likely to remain in the school. This places the burden squarely on the school administration and district staff to ensure that teachers and other staff members are supported in their role, receive adequate support, and are recognized for their efforts and achievements.

Teacher Training Teacher training is an important component for successful programs for children with special needs. Teachers require assistance to help understand the similarity of needs between children affected by substance abuse and children not exposed to drugs and alcohol. They also must understand the unique needs arising from potential neurological damage and/or environmental issues affecting behavior and learning resulting from family use of drugs and alcohol. As more information is available about the needs of children exposed to substance abuse, teachers can be helped to recognize that, typically, they already have a wide repertoire of teaching strategies and knowledge about students with special needs.

The Hillsborough County School District in Tampa, Florida, has initiated teacher training programs to help teachers recognize their ability to serve vulnerable children with their existing skills and knowledge. Training also is provided to develop a variety of new strategies and techniques that are helpful to all children but are especially important for students affected by substance abuse. Training modules provide examples of the physical environment of the classroom, daily schedules and routines, and transitions. Because of the high rate of success in working with teachers, this program has been made available for regional training conferences with the assistance of private foundation funding (Delapena, 1991).

Community Involvement

Most school faculties do not live in the community served by their school. This may present a barrier between school and community and a perception by the community that the school staff do not understand the issues of the community. Many states and individual school districts have mandated community involvement in decision making at the local school level. Although some administrators may view this as an unwarranted incursion into the operations of the school, the involvement of parents and community representatives in helping to devise strategies for students presents an opportunity for the school to evidence good faith to the community to meet the needs of children and their families.

School administrative staff and teachers have important roles and decisions to make within their purview as educators. However, because the needs of students are so diverse and often their families are also in such high need, without the involvement of parents and community representatives, it is difficult for school personnel to truly understand and be helped to accept responsibility for the development of services to address these issues.

Community and school–parent organizations are a valuable source for resources necessary to meet the needs of vulnerable students. With leadership and support, parent organizations present the opportunity for volunteers to work with students and to support teachers and provide a vehicle for meaningful participation in school planning for allocation of resources, activities, and strategies to work effectively with families and their children. This involvement results from a sense of ownership by the community in its schools that is essential if communities are to accept responsibilities for expanding resources to children and to bridge a potential gap between the school and its ability and willingness to respond to the needs of the community's children and youth.

Parent–teacher–student associations (PTSAs) can be a vital link between a school and its communities. These associations may include formal organizations chartered by national associations, school-based advisory committees, and other vehicles for school and community collaboration and participation in school-based planning activities.

School-Based Community Program Models Schools throughout the United States are beginning to develop a range of school-based and community-oriented resources addressing issues and needs of adolescents with families affected by substance abuse. Emshoff (1990) identifies several factors that support effective school-based interventions.

The school provides accessibility to a broad population of adolescents. Adolescents, particularly those with parents addicted to alcohol, have limited mobility for attending out-of-school programs. Initiating contact with an outside agency may be a potentially difficult or embarrassing act. The school setting gives recognition to the fact that parental alcoholism may have implications for academic performance and fits with the concept of the school as being concerned with the total functioning and development of children.

For interventions to be effective, the child must be treated as part of a family unit and the child's family must be made an integral part of the treatment team (Crittenden, 1992; Romijn, Platt, Schippers, & Schaap, 1992). A number of factors influence the development and delivery of early intervention family-based services for children vulnerable to failure: identification of families and children requiring services; coordination of services and resources among health, social, and educational agencies; systems to support transition of families among agencies; authority of agencies for service coordination responsibilities and funding; and reliability of agencies as perceived by potential consumers (Poulsen, 1991; Swan & Morgan, 1992).

The Fulton County School District in Atlanta, Georgia, has developed a collaborative program model in cooperation with county and state departments of health, mental health, and family and children service agencies. This agreement provides for cooperating agencies to assign staff to selected schools for direct services to children and families, including assistance for Medicaid applications, physical health screening, referral for services, counseling and support groups for staff and children, and parenting support groups. Funding for the program comes from state and federal (Medicaid) funding. No funding is required for any excess cost from the district.

The following three levels of leadership and staff involvement provide support for the program and facilitate interagency communication and cooperation:

1. An Executive Committee that is made up of the cooperating agency heads meets quarterly to address programmatic and administrative issues.
2. Department head–level staff from each agency meet monthly to

ensure compliance with agency regulations and protocols; address agency, school level, or school district concerns or issues; evaluate effectiveness of program services; and support continued planning for services.

3. Each school has formed a team composed of school personnel and staff assigned by each community agency. The school principal chairs these teams. Teams meet twice per month (or more often if needed) to address school-based program services, including referral of priority children and families, procedures, staff development, and evaluation of services. School team representatives meet regularly with the department heads committee to facilitate communication and problem solving.

CHILD–PARENT DRUG REHABILITATION ISSUES

When a child's caregiver is considering entering treatment and rehabilitation, the effect on the child or children must be given careful consideration. The following are some concerns relevant to the child and caregiver that need to be addressed prior to and during treatment:

1. Many states provide an opportunity for the child's immediate or extended family to accept responsibility for the child's care without penalizing welfare support payments. In these cases, the child's natural family member receives the same level of payment that would be paid to a nonfamily foster caregiver. Other states require the child's biological parent to give up custody to maintain foster care–level of payments without penalty. This presents special concerns to parents who must face a decision about loss of custody, perhaps on a permanent basis.

2. Many families affected by substance abuse are homeless and rely on public shelters for housing. Few drug rehabilitation programs offer a priority to homeless pregnant women seeking treatment.

3. When a parent enters treatment, the potential effect of the break in the relationship between the parent and children presents an emotional barrier to treatment as well as reconciliation for the family following rehabilitation.

4. In order to make a successful transition from treatment to an environment free of drugs and alcohol, parents face a number of issues including the need for vocational training and support, drug and alcohol counseling and support, child care for their children, educational placement for their children who need a highly stimulating developmentally appropriate environment,

reunification of the family, family counseling and support, and medical care, particularly if the caregiver is HIV infected.
5. Priorities for interventions for children should focus on developmental needs as well as address high vulnerability for intergenerational issues including abandonment, sexual abuse (including incest), and exposure to inadequate parenting strategies.

The Comprehensive Addiction Rehabilitation Program of Georgia, Inc. (CARP), located in Decatur, Georgia, offers a comprehensive array of services with priority placement for pregnant women addicted to drugs and alcohol and their children. This program addresses the major needs of women with children by supporting the woman in obtaining access to appropriate foster care services prior to admission; maintaining ongoing linkages between the mother and her children; providing child care services, counseling and support groups for the children, and providing joint residential programs for the woman and as many as 3 children below the age of 5 years within the treatment facility.

Services are maintained up to 2 months following delivery with supportive living resources available to the successfully released woman and her children. Follow-through services to the mother and children include assisted child care, coordination with child service agencies including Head Start and public school programs for children below school age, transportation support for the family to obtain services, and assistance with issues related to regaining custody if this has been necessary (R. Brown, personal communication, April 22, 1994).

Other Support Systems

The mechanism that permits the transmission of the virus that causes AIDS from the infected mother to her unborn child is well understood. Children who do not have HIV and whose mothers do experience issues different from children who are infected with the virus. For example, children whose mothers die of AIDS but who themselves remain healthy may be blamed for the death of the mother and be at high risk for abandonment and abuse. These children may require extensive counseling support to address potential guilt issues.

The child who is infected with the AIDS virus will require extensive physical health management. As the infected caregiver's physical and mental condition deteriorates, issues of foster care and child protective services should be addressed (McCarroll, 1988).

Adolescents are a particularly vulnerable age group for infection resulting from unsafe sex practices, substance abuse, and espe-

cially intravenous drug experimentation. Adolescents who are infected will face critical issues arising from peer acceptance, family
rejection, the need for comprehensive health care services, and qual-
ity-of-life issues. If the youth's status is complicated by substance addiction, sexual identity issues, and/or dual diagnosis of mental health
concerns, suicide may be a very critical concern to be addressed
through counseling support and coordination of services to the teenager and family.

Grady Health Systems, Grady Memorial Hospital in Atlanta,
Georgia, has initiated a variety of support systems for children and
youth infected with HIV and who have developed symptomatic issues with AIDS. Ongoing support systems for infected youth and
their families, careful monitoring of medical conditions, intensive
counseling and support resources for families, and service coordination have had a major effect on service delivery. One of the key
components of the program is the peer education and counseling
service in which youth with HIV infection and AIDS provide education to teenagers to prevent HIV infection. These support systems
are offered throughout the Atlanta area to schools and community-
based AIDS prevention education programs.

SUMMARY

Model programs for service delivery to children and their families will
reflect community standards of services to vulnerable families and the
leadership and support available to identify required program services linked with resources. It should be clear that programs are based
on sound research, rather than myths, regarding the needs of families
as well as a philosophy of empowerment of the child's family to become as independent as possible. As children grow older and families
become more capable, needs will change. Programs need the flexibility to meet these changing needs. Programs presented as having exemplary practices today will most likely appear to be outmoded in a
few years as knowledge about children and families with special needs
expands and experience teaches more effective ways for service providers to work effectively in teams.

REFERENCES

Ackerman, R.J. (1983). *Children of alcoholics: A guide for parents, educators and
therapists*. New York: Simon & Schuster.
Anderson, G.L. (1988). *The student assistance program model*. Greenfield, WI:
Community Recovery Press.
Aylward, G.P. (1992). The relationship between environment and develop-

mental outcomes. *Journal of Developmental Behavior for Pediatrics, 13*(3), 222–229.

Bays, J. (1990). Substance abuse and child abuse: Impact of addiction on the child. *Pediatric Clinics of North America, 37*(4), 881–904.

Besharov, D.J. (1989, Fall). The children of crack, will we protect them? *Public Welfare,* pp. 6–12.

Besharov, D.J. (1990). Crack children in foster care: Re-examining the balance between children's rights and parent's rights. *Children Today, 19*(4), 21–25.

Carpenter, M.R. (1990). *Making the right moves in student assistance programs.* Atlanta: Georgia Department of Human Resources and Georgia Department of Education.

Chafel, J.A. (1992). Funding Head Start: What are the issues? *American Journal of Orthopsychiatry, 62*(1), 9–21.

Chasnoff, I.J., Griffith, D.R., Frier, C., & Murray, J. (1992). Cocaine/polydrug use in pregnancy: Two-year follow-up. *Pediatrics, 98*(2), 284–289.

Cohen, D.L. (1991). Home visits seen as key strategy to combat a host of childhood woes. *Education Week, 11*(7), 1,24.

Cole, C.K., Jones, M., & Sadofsky, G. (1990). Working with children at risk due to prenatal substance exposure. *PRISE Reporter, 21*(5), 1–2.

Coles, C.D., & Platzman, K. (1990). Fetal alcohol effects in preschool children: Research, prevention and intervention. Prepared for the Office of Substance Abuse Prevention Conference on Drug-Exposed Children Ages 1–5: Identifying their needs and planning for early intervention, Washington, DC.

Crittenden, P.M. (1992). The social ecology of treatment: Case study of a service system for maltreated children. *American Journal of Orthopsychiatry, 62*(1), 22–34.

Davis, S. (1992). Prepared for *Educating young children prenatally exposed to drugs and at risk,* Washington, DC: Office of Educational Research and Improvement, U.S. Department of Education.

Delapena, L. (1991). *Strategies for teaching young children prenatally exposed to drugs.* Chicago, IL: National Association for Perinatal, Addiction, Research and Education UPDATE.

Economic Opportunity Act, PL 88-452. (August 20, 1964). Title 42, U.S.C. 2701 et seq: *U.S. Statutes at Large, 78,* 508–534.

Edwards, P.A., & Jones, L.S. (1992). Beyond parents: Family, community, and school involvement. *Phi Delta Kappan, 74*(2), 72–81.

Elders, M.J. (1992). School based clinics to the rescue. *The School Administrator, 8*(49), 16–21.

Emshoff, J.G. (1990). *A preventative intervention with children of alcoholics in protecting the children.* New York: Hawthorn Press.

Finnegan, L.P. (1988). Drug addiction and pregnancy: The newborn. In I.J. Chasnoff (Ed.), *Drugs, alcohol, pregnancy and parenting* (pp. 59–71). Boston: Kluwer Academic Publishers.

Flax, E. (1992). Reducing infant mortality becomes policy priority. *Education Weekly, 11*(28), 1, 16–17.

Garbarino, J., Dubrow, N., Kostelny, K., & Pardo, C. (1992). *Students in danger: Coping with the consequences of community violence.* San Francisco: Jossey-Bass.

Griffith, D.R. (1991). *Intervention needs of children prenatally exposed to drugs.* Congressional testimony before the House Select Committee on Special Education.

Hazel, R., Barber, P.A., Roberts, S., Behr, S.K., Helmstetter, E., & Guess, D. (1988). *A community approach to an integrated service system for children with special needs.* Baltimore: Paul H. Brookes Publishing Co.

Jones, D.C., & Houts, R. (1992). Parental drinking, parent–child communication and social skills in young adults. *Journal of Studies in Alcohol, 15*(1), 48–56.

Jones, E.D., & McCurdy, K. (1992). The links between types of maltreatment and demographic characteristics of children. *Child Abuse Neglect 16,* 201–215.

Keith, L., Donald, W., Rosner, M., Mitchell, M., & Bianchi, J. (1986). *Obstetric aspects of perinatal addiction in drug use in pregnancy: Mother and child.* Boston: MTP Press Limited.

Kumpfer, K.L. (1989, October). *Children, adolescents and substance abuse: Review of prevention strategies.* Paper presented to the American Academy of Child and Adolescent Psychiatry Institute on Substance Abuse, New York.

McCarroll, T. (1988). *Morning glory babies: A community effort to care for children with AIDS.* New York: Simon & Schuster.

Morehouse, E.R. (Ed.). (1989). *It's elementary.* South Laguna, CA: The National Association for Children of Alcoholics.

Newman, L.F., & Buka, S.L. (1991, Spring). Clipped wings. *American Educator, American Federation of Teachers,* pp. 27–42.

Poulsen, M.K. (1991). *Schools meet the challenge: Educational needs of children at risk due to prenatal substance exposure.* Sacramento, CA: Resources in Special Education.

Rist, M.C. (1992, April). Putting services in one basket. *The Executive Educator,* pp. 18–24.

Robinson, B.E. (1990, May). The teacher's role in working with children of alcoholic parents. *Young Child,* pp. 68–73.

Romijn, C.M., Platt, J.J., Schippers, G.M., & Schaap, C.S. (1992). Family therapy for Dutch drug users: The relationship between family functioning and success. *International Journal of the Addictions, 27*(1), 1–4.

Smith, G.H. (1989). *Children at risk due to prenatal exposure to drugs: An opportunity for the 90's.* Atlanta, GA: Fulton County Schools.

Swan, W.W., & Morgan, J.L. (1992). *Collaborating for comprehensive services for young children and their families: The local interagency coordinating council.* Baltimore: Paul H. Brookes Publishing Co.

Index